STRONG IN THE
BROKEN PLACES

STRONG IN THE BROKEN PLACES

A Theological Reverie on the Ministry of
George Everett Ross

LEONARD I. SWEET

THE UNIVERSITY OF AKRON PRESS
Akron, Ohio

© 1995 by
The University of Akron
Akron, OH 44325-1703
All rights reserved.

Manufactured in the United States of America
First Edition
99 98 97 96 95   5 4 3 2 1

LIBRARY OF CONGRESS CATALOGING IN PUBLICATION DATA
Sweet, Leonard I.
Strong in the broken places : a theological reverie on the
ministry of George Everett Ross / Leonard I. Sweet. — 1st ed.
p. cm.
Includes bibliographical references.
ISBN 1-884836-09-7. — ISBN 1-884836-10-0 (pbk.)
1. Ross, George Everett. 2. Episcopal Curch—Clergy—Biography.
3. Anglican Communion—United States—Clergy—Biography.
4. Sermons, American. 5. Episcopal Church—Sermons. 6. Anglican
Communion—United States—Sermons. I. Title
BX5995.R66.S94 1995
283'.092—dc20
[B] 95-31452
CIP

The paper used in this publication meets the minimum requirements of American National Standard for Information Sciences—Permanence of Paper for Printed Library Materials, ANSI Z 39.48-1984.
∞

CONTENTS

LIST OF BIBLE
TRANSLATIONS

ᕙᗯᕗ

NIV	New International Version
NKJV	New King James Version
NRSV	New Revised Standard Version
RSV	Revised Standard Version

GRACE

ᗰᗯᗱ

I break my bones before you.

—The ultimate Japanese genuflection
of respect and reverence

While I have broken more bones than I thought I had in respect
and reverence for the subject of this book, I also confess to having
broken fewer bones in writing this book than in any of the other
books I have written. Scholars are accustomed to massive accu-
mulations of debt during their research and writing. I wish I had
more people to thank in this "acknowledgments" section. There
are two reasons why I don't. First, virtually all of George Ross's
letters and manuscripts were destroyed either by himself, his family, or his friends. For someone who simply cannot resist opening
the study door or turning over the notebook cover of those I am
studying, this was especially frustrating. Marybeth Mersky of The
University of Akron Press was unfailingly helpful and good-spirit-
ed about assisting me with the few things that have been placed in
the George Ross Papers. But alas, this publication is not as strongly sourced as I would like. What follows is not by-guess-and-by-
God writing, but it is in no way historical "biography" either.

Second, of those who didn't refuse to talk to me or to return my
calls, most would discuss Ross only on the condition of anonymity. I was able to pick up a few crumbs of biographical ana and

anecdote here and there from discreet, loyal, and trusting persons. And some people, reluctant to provide much information, revealed more about Ross and about themselves than they seemed to realize. But generally I found my first serious foray into substantive oral history research filled with confusing and conflicting accounts. The journey became much more treacherous than I had ever imagined.

I want to thank especially the parishioners and officers of St. Paul's Episcopal Church who agreed to personal and phone interviews. My appreciation also goes to Ross's daughters, Mary and Anne, and to Ross's sister, Martha Jane Yutzey, for their cooperation and generosity. For them, the world is not necessarily a poorer place without George's unfinished sermons; most importantly, it's a poorer place without him.

By and large, this book emerges from what I have learned about Ross from reading his sermons, printed each week for private circulation, and from listening to worship services on tapes prepared each week for distribution to shut-ins. Although copies of these tapes and texts abound, they bring with them in-built problems from almost every angle. The historiographical difficulties, practical and methodological, are extreme. An historian trying to deal with this material is like a musician trying to comprehend the humming with which pianist Glenn Gould accompanied his magnificent playing.

I also have tried to listen to what Ross said about his preaching. Like so many creative people throughout history, Ross thought that the best of a preacher (or writer, artist, composer) is to be found not in his life, but in his works. Yet a preacher (or writer, artist, composer) is not best placed either to evaluate or understand his own preaching. W. H. Auden, who sniped at biography as "always superfluous [and] usually in bad taste," complained upon reading Van Gogh's letters: "Few painters read books, and fewer can express in words what they are up to." And again, "It is very good advice to believe only what an artist does, rather than what he says about his work."

Each sermon selected for this book was chosen, from among

the hundreds available, not because it was one of his most magnificent homiletic arias or because it was his favorite, but because I thought it revealed some aspect of Ross's preaching or of his zany and many parts. I wanted the reader to discover for himself or herself Ross's engaging combination of grandeur, monstrosity, generosity, self-irony, unsentimentality, and detached sensibility.

Lorna Sage talks about the "lightness writing has when it can levitate on other people's breath." Whatever lightness this quote-filled book has been able to achieve has not been without a heavy price. My research assistant, Betty O'Brien, brilliantly tracked down for me the breathings of many authors, when all she had to go on was a couple of gasps. If studies of the recently deceased are "the quick in pursuit of the dead," as Elizabeth Hardwick put it somewhat irreverently, Betty is the font of whatever quickness I might claim. My executive assistant, Thelma Monbarren, is involved in everything I do, but most often visible in nothing. Thelma may manage to keep out of sight, but she does not escape my gratitude or the appreciation of others in the know. Much of this book was written at "Aullwood," the homesite and gardens of Marie Aull. There I am aware most keenly that "peace" means for me the bringing into harmony and wholeness of what is scattered and broken in my life.

Those who were especially helpful in providing the critical perspectives from which I could maneuver include Dr. Joseph Goetz, Ross's childhood friend and my seminary colleague and friend. It was from some parking-lot conversations with Joe that I was able to see that the Superman myth, where the source of Superman's strength was the very thing that diminished him (kryptonite), was the key to understanding Ross's life. The first person I interviewed about this book, and the last to read the manuscript in its entirety, was Almus Thorpe, a former mentor and dean at Colgate-Rochester Divinity School/Bexley Hall/Crozer Theological Seminary. His reminder that simplicity need not always be comfort too quickly won has been a constant friend. The University of Akron is fortunate to have Elton Glaser as the director of its press. He is everything any author could dream of in an editor.

Paul Martin, someone quite off the chart of ordinary talent and wisdom, is the person most responsible for seeing this book to completion. Without his repeated "bucking up" at Bob Evans Restaurant and his phone encouragements, I would have abandoned this project many times. I owe him more than I can say. While this manuscript was in the final editorial stages, his wife of more than fifty years, Dorothy, died suddenly. It is in memory of Dorothy Garrett Martin that this book is offered.

FOREWORD

Not everyone will agree with M. Scott Peck's assessment that the founding of Alcoholics Anonymous in Akron, Ohio, on 10 June 1935 was "the greatest event of the twentieth century."[1] But everyone reading this book knows about AA, knows someone in AA, knows at least one of the Twelve Steps, and knows that AA has become one of the great social movements of the twentieth century.

This book is a retrospective on the ministry of a priest, George Everett Ross, who served as rector of the church where Alcoholics Anonymous was founded.[2] Ross struggled with alcohol addiction and died of AIDS in 1991. It is a book that keeps crossing the borders between biographical reportage, theological rumination, and homiletical reverie. But it does not fill in the many notable blanks in the curriculum vitae of George Ross. What is more, amidst a tabloid culture's demand that every notch and knobble be laid bare, every closet opened, this study's lack of the titillating tidbits is bound to disappoint. Complicating the book's genre even further, while I have tried to obtain imaginative entry into another preacher's preaching and push his words forward at every opportunity, there are many of my own words here too. Perhaps this book is best classified as a sequence of insights into matters spiritual, ministerial, theological, and biographical, and into the craft of preaching wherein they all are incarnate. Some say the subject of this study was the greatest preacher in the history of the Diocese of Ohio, a preacher who never ran out of creative puffs. In over thirty years of ministry, Ross never preached the same sermon twice, at least as far as I have been able to determine.

St. Paul's was more than one of the leading churches in the Akron community, where it was started in 1836 (and periodically re-started by generous gifts from the Firestone family). St. Paul's became at one time the largest congregation of the Episcopal Church in the state of Ohio. In the history of the Diocese of Ohio, there is written this terse remark: "In Akron, St. Paul's Episcopal Church has thriven, despite some discouragements. Often without a minister, they are not able to keep one long."[3] St. Paul's is a congregation where people expect great sermons, where they get great sermons or get rid of the reason why, and where they treasure great sermons. In my research for this book, I discovered lay people who collected Ross sermons the way some people collect stamps or butterflies. And they do not part with them.

Even those who liked to have roast pastor for Sunday lunch deemed Ross a great preacher: "You might or might not like George as a person, but, believe me, you wanted to hear his sermons." A statement like this from parishioners was not uncommon. At his touch, feelings fleshed into images, and thoughts became things. "He had a certain element of greatness to him," admitted one former warden who began the interview not by chipping away at the Ross pedestal but jackhammering it. Other parishioners loved Ross for the very things his critics said he lacked. They were constantly sending him effusive praise notes and thank-you tapes that fulfilled the biblical injunction to "be devoted to one another" (Romans 12:10 NIV) in ways that would have made even the Apostle Paul blush.

Ross may not have possessed the literary power of his Anglican predecessor John Henry Newman (though there are times, as you will shortly see, when he comes close), but he did share the same gospel of transfiguring grace. This book is the story of ministry at its best and most gifted, and ministry at its worst and most wounded. Søren Kierkegaard once described the philosopher as someone who builds a palace of truth yet lives in a hovel at the gate. This disconcerting picture applies to the preacher as well. Any celebration of one of the most eminently successful ministries in the history of St. Paul's Church must be held in check by the profoundly tragic, flawed nature of that ministry.

Every biographer thinks his or her subject is a supremely complex human being, and I am no exception. George Ross was as complex a figure as this historian has ever studied; his life makes Woody Allen's one of unclouded serenity by comparison. Not able to control his vast talents, he was a walking civil war, a tantrum of contrasting tempers full of spiritual warfare. Yet he created a rich, single-parent home environment for his children that was secure, loving, and stable. He was a doting son and dutiful brother. He was a beloved pastor and friend who performed in the Akron community innumerable unrecorded acts of goodness.

Graham Greene's book *The Power and the Glory* (1940) explores the mystery of grace: how can a priest who is frequently drunk and almost fatally flawed still convey and channel the grace of God? That same mystery of a warts-and-all kind of greatness was at work in George Ross, whose opportunity to serve God was half grasped and half wasted. How can one understand this? Voltaire said that we owe consideration to the living but only truth to the dead. What truths made George Ross's ministry a center for the minglings and meetings of the best and worst? Might it be that God can transform into the greatest sources of strength and blessing for others those places where we feel most cursed? Because of George Ross, generations of parishioners, townspeople, and strangers felt the nearness of God. Can anything better be said about a life?

Where architect Mies Van Der Rohe allegedly argued that "God is in the details," psychologist Carl Jung believed that God is in the diseases.[4] Jungians like James Hillman, Thomas Moore, and Robert Sardello are questioning the Western therapeutic model of psychotherapy, based on curative interventions and remedial repairs. Instead, they are looking on suffering and suffered experiences not so much as problems to be solved or eradicated, but as mysteries to be explored and transfigured. As Moore puts it in

Care of the Soul, "We cannot cure diseases; they cure us."[5] Or as a native American proverb expresses it with deadeye accuracy and deadpan seriousness: "Illnesses tell you who you are."

Alas, we are often remembered more for our faults than for our graces. The popular press loves to stick its forks in the crust of people's lives and test how easily morality can crumble. In the words of an old newsroom slogan, "If it bleeds, it leads." Almost six times more people read the guttersnipe press than read quality journalism. Our increasing willingness to settle for a tabloid view of the world makes the bleeding leads all the more messy.

At close quarters there is something wrong with all of us, and our disfigured features come to eclipse in people's minds our transfigured triumphs. A current theologian at the University of Chicago defines a saint as "a figure out of the Christian past whose life has been insufficiently researched." Even saints wear their halos clumsily.

The Wesleyan community has been grappling for some time with what to do with its founder, John Wesley. Wesley enjoyed perhaps the most powerful ministry in eighteenth-century England and in most areas of life seemingly had his act together. Yet Wesley was an absolute disaster when it came to relationships with the opposite sex. The African-American community has been contending with a seedy motel-room side to Martin Luther King, Jr., that conflicts with his sky-high reputation for justice and integrity. Most recently, the Reformed community is being forced to come to terms with a "killer Calvin," an "ugly," flesh-and-blood John Calvin who lied, deceived, and was bent on crusades—not just to bash or banish his enemies but literally to kill those who disagreed with him (like Jerome Bolsec and Michael Servetus).[6]

In one sense, this deeply crevassed, disfigured side to Calvin (or to Wesley or to King or to Ross) shouldn't surprise us: they were sinners, like all of us. Parts of their lives were totally out of sync with the teachings of the Lord they professed to serve. Preachers are like writers and artists—none are as good as their works.

In another sense, however, this dark side should shock us. Reviewers are attacking Paul Theroux's recent novel *Millroy the Magician* for its "suspiciously wholesome" portrayal of a preacher as innocent and faithful and true.[7] Surely these reviewers are ill-tempered cynics. There is an old cartoon of two men at a bar looking contemptuously at a minister who is knocking back the beer. One says to the other, "The thing I can't stand about him is his unholier than thou attitude." In spite of the fashionability of this "unholier than thou" spirit, religious leaders are called to lead exemplary lives. James the Apostle, while confessing that "all of us make many mistakes," nonetheless warned: "Not many of you should become teachers, my brothers and sisters, for you know that we who teach will be judged with greater strictness" (James 3:1 NRSV).

How does one bring these two sensibilities together? G. K. Chesterton said that God was once conceived "in a hole in the rocks."[8] Could that mean that God is conceived in those dark holes of our existence where suffering is most apprehended, suffering least comprehended, and suffering best transcended?

Is that how people like George Ross became "living stones," one of the strangest metaphors in all of Scripture (1 Peter 2:5)? Can it be the healing power of "the wounds of Christ" (1 Peter 2:21-25) that makes scars sacred places and wounds holy ground?

INTRODUCTION

Clinging to the Wreckage

JOHN MORTIMER, an English lawyer who became a playwright-novelist and created the "Rumpole" series for the British Broadcasting System, called his autobiography *Clinging to the Wreckage.* The title came to him one day when he was lunching with a gray-bearded sailor. He had asked the yachtsman if sailing on the English Channel was not a dangerous sport. "Not dangerous at all," said the man, "provided you don't learn to swim." Mortimer asked what he could mean by that. "When you're in a spot of trouble," he explained, "if you can swim, you try to strike out for the shore. You invariably drown. As I can't swim I cling to the wreckage and they send a helicopter out for me. That's my tip, if you ever find yourself in trouble, cling to the wreckage."[1]

BROKEN PIECES

If the truth be known, we are all clinging to the wreckage, holding on to the broken pieces of our lives with all we've got. In the biblical story of Paul's shipwreck, the shards of wreckage become the very lifejackets and lifelines of salvation: "Some on *broken pieces* of the ship" escaped safe to land (Acts 27:44 NKJV). It is not one of life's most pleasant experiences to look at, much less pick up, the shattered, sharp-edged fragments of our lives. Edith Wharton conveys the wretchedness of our wreckedness most powerfully in her novel *The Reef:*

When you've lived a little longer you'll see what complex blunderers we all are: how we're struck blind sometimes, and mad sometimes—and then, when our sight and our senses come back, how we have to set to work, and build up, little by little, bit by bit, the precious things we'd smashed to atoms without knowing it. Life's just a perpetual piecing together of broken bits.[2]

Life as a "perpetual piecing together" is no different for the clergy than for the laity. This book is a brief spiritual reverie on the ministry of one "pieced-together" Episcopal clergyman, George Everett Ross, who found in this metaphor of "brokenness" the essence of the Christian faith: the mercy of God in the brokenness of life, the "savage grace"[3] of God amid the suffering of life:

Christ accepts us—broken, limited, sinful and struggling long before we accept Him. Where we would put ourselves down, Christ bends to lift us up. Where we heap judgment and blame upon ourselves, He tenderly forgives and accepts us. Where we are filled with despair or overwhelming sorrow, Christ loves us with a love, which recreates us.[4]

In this metaphor of brokenness Ross also found a helpful way of dealing with the world around him, a world comprised of broken governments, broken economies, broken environments, broken sex, broken communities, broken relationships, even broken Christianity: "We could write a very long list of the broken things of this century that all the king's horses and all the king's men cannot put together ever again."[5]

Ross believed the Bible was about more than saving souls. To him, "personal salvation" was a modern, Western notion far from the heart of the Scriptures. For Ross, the Bible was about mending that which is broken, restoring that which is rent. The Bible revolves around pieces of creation, pieces of society, pieces of individuals' lives coming back together and being made whole.

A grandmother was sitting on her rocking chair mending

clothes, sewing a patch here, stitching a tear there. One of her grandchildren, who was playing at her feet, looked up at her and asked: "Grandma, what does God do all day?" Pausing for a moment to collect her thoughts, Grandma replied, "God spends all of his time fixing things that are broken."

No one gets through life unbroken or without needing to be "fixed"—including, and especially not, clergy. No one believed more highly in the exalted ideal of the priesthood, or more strongly insisted on it, than George Ross. Indeed, he was an early supporter and board member of Trinity Episcopal School for Ministry, the "protest seminary" founded in 1975 in Ambridge, Pennsylvania. Ross and others involved in the seminary protested declining qualifications for ordination and supported the resurgence of creedal Christianity and its apostolic standards for ministry.

But the problem of how to go on with life and ministry as a weak human being was present every single day of his existence. The very privilege of ministry may privilege ministers to disaster. British theologian Colin Morris argues that "those who handle sacred things are subject to special temptations. Far from close proximity to the Holy of Holies conferring a special exemption from sin upon us, we are in most peril just when we think we are safest."[6] That is why it may be time for us to tell the truth about ourselves, we the professionally holy.

TELLING THE TRUTH

Secrets are very damaging, as the fractured parish of St. Paul's can attest as it continues to heal from the hurt of not being told the whole truth. It may be the right moment to present ministry without its make-up on, to see ourselves as we really are, no matter how squeamish we may be around personal sickness, suffering, and truth-telling. Presbyterian cleric, essayist, and novelist Frederick Buechner advocates such openness in his book *Telling Secrets:*

It is important to tell at least from time to time the secret of who we truly and fully are—even if we tell it only to ourselves—because otherwise we run the risk of losing track of who we truly and fully are and little by little come to accept instead the highly edited version which we put forth in hope that the world will find it more acceptable than the real thing. It is important to tell our secrets too because it makes it easier that way to see where we have been in our lives and where we are going.[7]

What if we who are clergy told our secrets? Actually, ministers of the gospel have only one secret, that one special wound that doesn't heal. That one *big* secret secretes from every hiding place, even from the genealogy of Jesus, which according to Matthew's gospel included two prostitutes (Tamar and Rahab), one adulterer (Bath-sheba), and one woman who slept with her husband before they were married (Ruth).[8] Our secret has been discovered periodically throughout the history of the church but never more revealingly than by a sixteenth-century locksmith from Amsterdam. Tired of all the feudings between Protestants and Catholics over the ways Christ was present in the Eucharist, he asked, who but "a daft God would put himself in the hands of you priests?"[9]

There it is. That is the church's dirty little secret. It is, as they say on the TV show "Hard Copy," the story that won't go away but that too many don't want to look into because reality poses threats.

Every divine revelation has to navigate flawed character and damaged goods. God was daft enough to put the message of who God is not in superhuman hands but in human and even inhuman hands, hands that do all the strange and wonderful things that humans do, and then some. In this book you the reader are being invited not to look away from these hands, but to look *into* their cracks, their creases, their imperfections, and there perhaps confront your own unworthiness, there concede the broken dreams, butchered days, and battered hopes we share as members of the human family. Princeton sociologist Robert Wuthnow contends that "one of the serious ethical challenges facing Christians in the twenty-first century is having personal stories that tell them how to be caring and compassionate . . . heroes, public figures, role models at the collective level who can exemplify the nation's highest ethical ideals."[10] If he is right, then the "saints" of our future need to be seen and shown very differently than the "saints" of our past.

W. H. Auden once remarked that it is difficult to be a Christian if one is not a poet. The poet is everywhere present in the sermons of George Ross, either in the form of a quotation (William Wordsworth, Alfred Lord Tennyson, Matthew Arnold, Robert Frost, and Ogden Nash were some of his favorites) or in some other magnificent turn of phrase. Ross believed that poets can often help us look in the mirror better than anyone or anything else.

Ross's favorite Welsh poet (who also happens to be a priest), R. S. Thomas, defines Homo sapiens as "that cracked mirror": "that cracked mirror, / mending himself again and again like a pool? / Who threw the stone?"[11]

TREASURES IN EARTHEN VESSELS

This imagery of brokenness is straight from the Scriptures. Psalm 31:12 (NRSV) reads: "I am like a broken vessel." Elsewhere the Apostle Paul confesses: "We hold these treasures in earthen vessels" (2 Corinthians 4:7 NKJV). All of us have feet of clay. We are all cracked pots or, as John Calvin put it, "cracked cathedrals." Whether one is talking about "pillars of the church" or "pillars of the community," there are only clay-based pillars. Even a "pillar of modern civilization" like economist and political philosopher George F. Kennan begins his autobiography with a declaration that serves as his first chapter title: "Man, the Cracked Vessel."[12]

Broken into a number of pieces, we can't be put back together again, even by all the Humpty-Dumpty healers in the world. We are a heap of bits jumbled together with ineradicable traces left by childhood hardships and adolescent mishaps. In the words of Henry Fielding in *Tom Jones:* "The finest Composition of human Nature, as well as the finest China, may have a Flaw in it; and this, I am afraid, in either Case, is equally incurable; though, nevertheless, the Pattern may remain of the highest Value."[13] Benjamin Franklin, in a 1764 letter to his daughter Sarah, used a different metaphor but drove the point home about clergy even harder than

Fielding: "I do not mean you should despise sermons, even of the preachers you dislike, for the discourse is often much better than the man, as sweet and clear waters come through very dirty earth."[14]

Good is always streaked with evil. One of Ross's favorite Anglican theologians, sixteenth-century Richard Hooker, boggled at the ways in which "the best things we do have somewhat in them to be pardoned."[15] Evil is never unmixed with good. Nobody is "*all* bad." Nobody is "good through and through." There are no unambiguous goodies and baddies. There are no pure motives. There are no unmixed motives. Motives are constructed out of semantic and subjective, not rational material.[16] Once again, in the words of poet W. H. Auden: "And motives like stowaways / Are found too late."[17] On the shoreless seas of postmodern life, motives don't "de-lurk" until long after actions.

In *The Gulag Archipelago*, Aleksandr Solzhenitsyn tells about his friendship with an army officer during World War II. This friend was almost identical to Solzhenitsyn: they had the same aspirations, prejudices, loves, and values. But after the war, their paths diverged. Solzhenitsyn became an imprisoned, then exiled artist. His friend became a brutal interrogator for the Soviet gulag. What made the difference?

If only there were evil people . . . committing evil deeds, and it were necessary only to separate them from the rest of us and destroy them. But the line dividing good and evil cuts through the heart of every human being. And who is willing to destroy a piece of his own heart?

During the life of any heart this line keeps changing place; sometimes it is squeezed one way by exuberant evil and sometimes it shifts to allow enough space for good to flourish. One and the same human being is, at various stages, under various circumstances, a totally different human being. At times he is close to being a devil, at times to sainthood. But his name doesn't change, and to that name we ascribe the whole lot, good and evil.[18]

All human motives are mixed into the heady cocktail of undiscovered desire.

In one cartoon Charlie Brown holds up his hands before his

friend Lucy and says: "These are the hands which may someday accomplish great things. . . . These are the hands which may someday do marvelous works! They may build mighty bridges, or heal the sick, or hit home runs, or write soul-stirring novels! These are hands which may someday change the course of destiny!" To which Lucy replies: "They've got jelly on them." This book celebrates the irrepressibility of the human spirit with jelly on its hands. Carl Jung is alleged to have remarked in a speech that the evil that surfaces in us, and resides deep within us, is of such a monstrous nature that for theologians to talk of original sin and to trace it back to a relatively innocent marital slip-up is almost a euphemism. The case is far greater and is grossly understated. Holocaust historian Philip Paul Hallie, in the PBS special with Bill Moyers entitled *Facing Evil,* confessed his discovery that "there is a force, a dark flowing force, that goes right through our minds and bodies, that carries us toward evil."[19]

George Ross liked to quote Somerset Maugham's biography of Cervantes, where he wrote of the moral struggles Cervantes faced in his life: "I do not believe that there is any man who if the full truth were known of him would not seem a monster of depravity; and also I believe that there are very few who have not at the same time virtue, goodness and beauty."[20] There is no one of us who does not come out of life a bit flawed. Our goodness and our badness merge together in unpredictable ways. Those who do right things do not do everything right. To give but one sharp example, William Holman Hunt, whom God used powerfully in the nineteenth century through such paintings as *Light of the World,* was a brothel-visitor, wife-beater, child-abuser.[21]

THE CONFLICT WITHIN

The very best in George Ross was but a page-turn away from the very worst in George Ross. Ross testified to what he called "the conflict within us of divergent impulses":

Recently . . . I found myself in a telephone booth in London. In this booth there was a sticker, which read: "If you are tired of sin, read John

3:16," beneath which some wayward evangelist of another persuasion had written: "If you are not tired of sin, call 721-5511." We laugh, but let us be honest: the longer we live the more we realize that in the human heart, in every human heart, in yours and mine, contradictory impulses are at war.[22]

Ross acknowledged the divine and the diabolical within himself, quoting Mark Twain: "Every one is a moon, and has a dark side which he never shows to anybody."[23] How Ross produced such exceptional sermons or pastored so deftly such a difficult parish, in the midst of his own inner turmoil, marital strains, and incalculable obstacles, while fighting alcoholism and wrestling with inner demons, is the story of this book.

The broken conditions of our humanity elicited Christ's redemptive touch. It is for this reason that Christians have a cross with which to contend. To be sure, the cross itself has become problematic. We have turned away from images of the cross and brokenness to more sanitized metaphors because the cross offends contemporary aesthetic sensibilities; or because some feminists deem it applausive of oppression; or because theologians prefer the resurrection over the crucifixion.[24] As Kierkegaard once complained about the church of Denmark, the church has often "taken the strong wine of the gospel and made it lemonade."[25]

Yet the cross is more than a speed-bump on the road to resurrection; Good Friday is more than an ugliness blotted out by Easter morning; the Christian symbol of the cross is more than a giant plus sign that stands for a positive way of successful living. As one systematic theologian has written, "Failing to keep the cross at the center of salvation and the death of Jesus at the center of the cross, Christians and the Christian point will continue to pass each other in the night."[26]

Jesus' words "Pick up your cross and follow me" (Matthew 16:24) are not the same thing as "Pick up your room and come to dinner" or "Pick up your wallet and make a donation (Give to the United Way)" or "Pick up the house and furnish your mind with positive thoughts" or "Pick up the yard and discover God in creation" or even "Pick up your life and grow a healthy self-image."

"Pick up your cross and follow me" is an invitation to sacrifice, suffering, and pain, an invitation we can accept only because in the cross the suffering and pain of the world have been taken up into heaven, where God embraces and becomes part of the world's suffering and pain.

The cross bridges eternity and earth. It is both connecting tissue and dividing line. In 1825 John Bowring put it in a way that has become very familiar: "In the Cross of Christ I glory, / Towering o'er the wrecks of time; / All the light of sacred story / Gathers round its head sublime."[27] Only in the cross can we "glory" because it is only the cross that has the power to make divided people whole people again.

Cornel West, arguably the leading African-American philosopher in the world today, insists that "the heart of our Christian faith is concerned with trying to understand the cross. What is the meaning of the blood that flowed from that cross?" West confesses that, for an African-American male like himself, "it is a formidable challenge . . . to remain part of the Christian tradition. . . . There is only one way to do so with integrity: I must scrutinize all of history through the eyes of the cross."[28]

The cross confronts all human explanations of evil and confounds all human attempts to come to terms with it. The Eucharist was the place where the confronting and the confounding came together in a way that moved Ross from death to life. To celebrate Mass is, in a sense, to undergo surgery oneself and to perform surgery on the world. For Ross, it was only in kneeling around the table and altar that any of us can become, in Hemingway's words, "strong in the broken places." Ernest Hemingway liked to talk and write about the "broken places" of society. But my favorite quote from all his writings is this one: "The world breaks every one and afterward many are strong at the broken places."[29]

It is not just "the ordained" who are unworthy of representing God. Every one of us is unworthy to stand and confess to being a disciple. Every one of us loves and lives this reality of brokenness. But the good news is this:

God uses broken things.

Jesus makes it clear in John 12:24 that unless a seed is buried and broken open by soil and rain, it cannot grow. It is as simple as that. No brokenness, no growth. That is why we must not push the pain away. That is why we must not paste over our cracks. The popular American preacher Vance Havner proclaims that "God uses broken things: broken soil and broken clouds to produce grain; broken grain to produce bread; broken bread to feed our bodies."[30]

We are now at the heart of the "mystery" of the gospel, "mystery" which is best defined not as unclarity but as infinite clarity. And what is this infinitely clear mystery? None other than this: by his stripes we are healed. This was the precise text for Dietrich Bonhoeffer's last sermon before he was executed at the death camp of Flossenburg: "He was wounded for our transgressions, he was bruised for our iniquities, . . . and with his stripes we are healed (Isaiah 53:5 RSV)."[31]

Life lived in this mystery is what the church needs in its ministers above all else, Ross believed: "This much we know: we will not follow a hireling. We will not listen to a preacher about whom we must ask: 'Has he never been in love?' 'Has he never suffered?' 'Has he never lost a friend or had his heart broken?' 'Or fallen in failure to be raised again by grace?' The hireling we will not hear—because he lays not down his life."[32]

THE WOUNDS OF CHRIST

The infinitely clear mystery of the gospel draws us—no, drives us—to the wounds of Christ. Down through the ages, poets and hymnists have pointed our attention to these sacred injuries.[33] C. S. Lewis wrote of Christ's wounds in "Love's as Warm as Tears":

> Love's as hard as nails,
> Love is nails:
> Blunt, thick, hammered through
> The medial nerves of One
> Who, having made us, knew
> The thing He had done,

Seeing (with all that is)
Our cross, and His.[34]

Thomas Parnell, a poet and hymnist who died at thiry-nine in
1718, wrote the poem "On Divine Love by Meditation on the
Wounds of Christ." It includes these discomfiting lines:

Holy Jesus! God of Love!
Look with pity from above,
Shed the precious purple tide
From thine hand, thy feet, thy side,
Let thy streams of comfort roll,
Let them please and fill my soul.
Let me thus for ever be
Full of gladness, full of thee.[35]

In a postmodern age that is more enamored of pierced ears than
pierced hands (Salvador Dali's corpse on the cross has no wound
prints), our attention is also being drawn to the wounds of Jesus
by physicians and the medical community. In the words of one
brain surgeon turned poet and essayist, "Both writing and surgery
are concerned with wounds."[36] So too is classical Christian theology, where health, wholeness, holiness have the same root.[37]
An important expression of mystical spirituality was devotion
to the wounds of Christ. "The church dwells . . . in the wounds of
Christ," wrote Bernard of Clairvaux, "and must remain there in
perpetual meditation."[38] The medieval veneration of and participation in the wounds, as typified in the poem beginning "Your
wounds shall be my dwelling place," achieved virtual cult status
in the baroque period. The daily contemplation of medieval Christians, which included invocations of the "most holy *Life-Energy-
Blood* of Jesus hanging and bleeding on the Cross," fall strangely
on contemporary ears.[39] Very few religious communities today
can even remotely identify with the belief of the eighteenth-century German pietist community (Herrenhut) that "Nothing will
satisfy us any more but wounds and wounds and wounds and
wounds."[40] Yet the neglect of the symbolic meaning of the
wounds has had distorting consequences on the community of
faith. Indeed, theologian J. S. Whale is not far wrong in his presen-

tation of one reason why contemporary theology isn't more alive and kicking: "The trouble so often is that we sit around the fire with a pipe in the mouth and feet on the mantelpiece and discuss theories of the Atonement instead of bowing down before the wounds of Christ."[41]

What were these wounds? There is general agreement, as the Wesley hymn intimates, that there were five wounds.[42] First were the whip wounds, where the flesh on his back was broken. Second were the thorn wounds, where the flesh on his head was broken. Third were the spear wounds, where the flesh on his side was broken. Fourth were the nail wounds, where the flesh on his hands and feet was broken. Almost always the nail wounds were split into two wounds (hands and feet) to comprise the five wounds Christ bore on the cross. But since they were caused by one instrument, they seem to me symbolic more of one wound than two. If this alternative counting is allowed, what was the fifth wound of Christ?

To understand the nature of the fifth wound, perhaps we need to reexamine crucifixions. Although the precise origins of crucifixion are lost, crucifixion in ancient Palestine enjoyed a long history. Introduced into Palestine during Persian times, crucifixion was the art of public torture, the pursuit of cruelty through judicial execution. Finally abolished in the West by Constantine in the fourth century, the science of death may never have seen a more cruel ritual of torture than crucifixion.[43]

There were two main types of crosses used for crucifixion. The *crux commissa* or the low cross (*crux humilis*) was shaped like a T, with no upright extending beyond the crossbeam. The high cross (*crux sublimis*) or *crux immissa* was shaped like a traditional cross, with the upright extending above the crossbeam. The upright of the cross was left in permanent position at the crucifixion site. The crossbeam, which weighed about one hundred pounds, was carried by the condemned across the nape of his neck as part of the processional to the place of execution. Arriving at the place of execution, the victim was laid on the ground with arms outstretched on the crossbeam. The wrists were nailed to the cross-

beam with five- to seven-inch long spikes. The condemned was
then lifted up, and the crossbeam attached to the upright.

While there are records of literally thousands of crucifixions in
the ancient Near East, archaeological evidence exists for only one
person. It comes from ossuary evidence found in a burial cave.
(Ossuaries were small stone boxes in which skeletal remains were
deposited.) In 1968 at Giv'at ha-Mivtar just northeast of
Jerusalem, Israeli archaeologists discovered the remains of a
young man between the ages of twenty-four and twenty-eight.
Known as "John" (Jehohanan), he was crucified sometime in the
first half of the first century A.D. This spectacular discovery of the
remains of someone who had actually been crucified, although
misrepresented in the original publications of the findings,[44] settles many uncertainties about how crucifixions took place and
confirms key aspects of the gospel accounts.

Osteologists tell us that John's right and left heel bones were
most likely nailed laterally to the cross. At first it was thought
they were fastened together and nailed through the metatarsus to
the olive wood cross by one massive spike. But the extant 11.5
centimeter iron spike, the head of which had fragments of a
block of either acacia or pistachio wood attached to it at both
ends, is simply not long enough to secure both feet by a single
nail. Although many crucifixions were done with the arms of the
condemned *tied* rather than nailed to the cross (as the two thieves
next to Jesus are often portrayed in Christian art), in Jesus' case it
is most likely that the iron nails were drilled into the crossbeam
through his arms just above the wrist of the forearm bone between the carpal bones (the radius and the ulna). Although there
was only moderate loss of blood in the hammering of these spikes
(no major artery was ruptured), the trunk of the median nerve was
severed, thus inflicting great pain. A small wooden crossbar or
seat known as a *sedile* or *sedicula* was placed under the buttocks
to support the body, thus prolonging death and increasing the
agony.[45]

Today we would call a crucifixion a media event. Everything
was done to prolong the pain and make the spectacle and the cal-

culated display of agony last for days. It is important to remember the psychological embarrassment and humiliation as well as the physical pain. Those who were crucified were customarily nailed to the cross naked. There is some evidence that, because of Jewish sensibilities, the Romans sometimes permitted the victim to wear a loincloth. Whether or not Jesus was naked, his bodily functions were obvious through the loincloth, and his lack of control humiliating. Nothing rendered a human being more powerless or vulnerable than crucifixion.

Although the actual cause of death varied from one crucifixion victim to another, the two main causes were exhaustion (traumatic shock) and exhaustion-induced asphyxiation (suffocation).[46] The exhaustion became so severe that the upper body would slump forward, contracting the lungs and cutting off the air (asphyxia) in death. But this death came slowly, often extending the agony for several days.

One of the major mysteries of the cross was why Jesus died so quickly—only six to seven hours after being nailed to the crossbeam. John Wilkinson, medical missionary and theologian, summarizes four main theories about why Jesus died so quickly: embolism (as theorized by Vincent Taylor), asphyxia (as suggested by Pierre Barbet), acute dilation of the stomach (as proposed by John Cameron), and rupture of the heart (as first advanced by William Stroud).[47] Commenting on the crucifixion from a medical standpoint, Ernest F. Scott has observed that Jesus

died long before the time which was usual in crucifixion, and perhaps his death was not wholly due to the effects of the torture following the terrible strain of the preceding days. The loud cry with which he died seems to betoken a sudden spasm, and the fourth evangelist tells us that when a spear was thrust into his side after death there issued what appeared to be mingled blood and water.[48]

It is for this reason that Scott joins Stroud and others in conjecturing that the immediate cause of Jesus' death was a rupture of the heart.

If this is true, the fifth wound of Christ was the spirit wound of a broken heart. The flesh in his physical heart was broken by the wounds to his spirit. Jesus died "broken-hearted": despised and rejected, weeping over Jerusalem, his spirit torn to shreds by a sinful world dying itself of heart disease—hardness of heart. Medical researchers are finding out with every new experiment just how connected to the spirit and to each other the mind and body really are. Stress and grief carry with them physiological consequences. Psychology and physiology are one and the same. In short, Jesus died of a broken heart.

The Native American poet Simon Ortiz, when he first saw the Grand Tetons, said "This is how it looks when God's heart breaks."[49] For the Christian, the cross is how it looks when God's heart breaks. The death of Jesus is unashamedly the "Heartbreak on Calvary." The broken heart is, in fact, a physical symbol for the spiritual reality of salvation, which is why the recurring biblical image of heartbreak is so powerful, as in Psalm 34:18 (NKJV: "The Lord is close to the broken hearted"). In the words of the poet Chad Walsh, "The cross is a heart-breaker; the empty tomb is a mind-breaker."[50] It is for this reason that the Passion of Christ, who brought heaven to earth in his body and blood, has brought meaning and life to human brokenness and death.

Samuel Shoemaker, who gave his life to the poor and disenfranchised in New York City, was once asked by a friend, "Why don't you just run away from it all before you are broken by this inhuman burden that you have placed upon yourself?" Although he was in poor health and especially discouraged, Shoemaker is supposed to have replied, "I would like to run away from it all, but a strange man on the cross won't let me."

The place Shoemaker refused to run from in 1926, Calvary Chapel, was the very place that inspired Bill Wilson to write something known as the Twelve Steps of Alcoholics Anonymous and to found something known as Alcoholics Anonymous. Bruce Bairnsfather, the creator of the famous "Old Bill" cartoons during World War I, drew for Shoemaker a bowery resident leaning against a wall, the cross peeking from around the corner. The caption reads: "There's a place near by, where a Carpenter still mends broken men."[51]

THE MENDING

More than anything else, it was this kind of a community that George Everett Ross wanted to form in the church where AA started. Sunday after Sunday, Ross told his people exactly what the Christian tradition does and does not offer a suffering world. They could never experience any brokenness that Christ has not already known. The only protection they could expect against evil is a God who takes on evil, a God who would not abandon them to their suffering, and a God who works within that suffering to bring forth hope and healing. It was the cross of Christ, Ross confessed to his congregation, that diffracted "rainbows" from the "rain" of his own brokenness, enabling a creature named George to live abundantly under God's blue skies. In fact, every brokenness imaginable has already been experienced and healed by Christ. As Eugene O'Neill wrote in one of his plays: "This is Daddy's bedtime secret for today: Man is born broken. He lives by the mending. The grace of God is the glue."[52]

"God's love does not protect us *against* suffering," the German theologian Hans Küng insists. "But it protects us *in* all suffering."[53] God doesn't sweep away evil—to do that would be to sabotage the Creator's totally free creation; to do that would be to banish the risk of unbounded love that made God's own suffering inevitable. Nor does God make evil "meaningful" or "purposeful"; to do that would be to make evil not evil.

Hand surgeon Paul Brand was neither the first, nor will he be the last, to make this observation about the hands of the resurrected Christ:

One of the things I find most astounding is that, though we think of the future life as something perfected, when Christ appeared to his disciples He said, 'Come look at my hands,' and He invited Thomas to put his finger into the print of the nail. Why did He want to keep the wounds of His humanity? Wasn't it because He wanted to carry back with Him an eternal reminder of the sufferings of those on earth? He carried the marks of suffering so He could continue to understand the needs of those suffering. He wanted to be forever one with us.[54]

God is not an absentee Creator who started the machinery in motion and then left it alone to operate by itself. Paul says in his address at Athens: "God is not far from each of us, for in him we live and move and have our being" (Acts 17:27–28 NRSV). George Ross built his ministry on the conviction that, through Jesus Christ, God is emotionally involved, eternally invested in the human enterprise.

We have a God, Ross said, who "does not stand *above* us," who "does not stand *aside* us," but who "always stands *beside* us." As Ross and others like him have observed in the midst of their pain and suffering, the unique thing about the gospel of Jesus Christ in the history of religions is this: "No other god has wounds."

We come, all of us, to Christ in our loneliness and need; and we find that He is lonely, too. We show Him our scars; He shows us His. We show Him our crown of thorns; He tells us the story of His. We thirst and so does He. It is upon the basis of our common humanity that God comes to us. As we share our sorrows and pains with Jesus, He shares God's love and grace with us.[55]

Advent, the four weeks leading up to Christmas, was Ross's favorite time of year. Perhaps it was his love of traditions, like the Advent wreath that always became the centerpiece for the special Christmas meals he cooked for his family, or his love of denouncing a church culture that rushed through Advent to get to Christmas, or the anticipation of singing his favorite Christmas carol ("Away in the Manger") on (and not until) Christmas Eve, or the ritual of putting up a tree on the same date, the 21st of December, which also helped to celebrate daughter Mary Eugenia's birthday. Or perhaps it was his love of walking in the cold night air, or driving in the snow through Sand Run Parkway taking daughter Anne Elizabeth to school while they listened together to classical music on WKSU. His last Christmas spent on earth, when he alone knew how terribly sick he was, he proclaimed to his people: "Whatever life has done to us, whatever limits we have, whatever sorrows we must bear, the way of God is the way of love. Those who walk that way will have a wonderful Christmas, no matter whatever else is true in their lives."[56]

In these words Ross brings us to the heart of the Christian gospel—an upside-down theology, a topsy-turvy spirituality where the full is carried in the empty, the strong in the weak, the unlimited in the bounded, the blessing in the cursing. We admit our weakness, that we may receive God's strength. For George Ross, this meant that if we glory, we glory in the cross. He himself put it like this: we can be "greatest at our weakest" when we allow God to "touch our weakness with His strength."[57]

In fact, Ross traced his decision to enter ministry partly to an English class at Ohio Wesleyan where he was introduced to Maxwell Anderson's play *Winterset:* "God spoke to me when I read that play." In the final scene a young man tracks down the gangsters who killed his father, only to discover that they are the brothers of the girl he loves. He decides not to strike back and is ultimately killed by them—and the girl with him. As the curtain falls, the girl's father, an elderly Jew, is shocked into a sudden awareness of the tragic and heroic meaning of their story. To his son, the murderer, the father says:

They are wiser than you and I. To die when you are young and untouched—that's beggary to a miser of years, but the devils shake and are daunted when men set their lives at hazard for the heart's love. I wish I had so died years ago. Before you are old, you will wish that you had died as they have died. On this star man can stand up and look out blind and say: "In all these turning lights I find no clue and in my blood no certain answer; yet is my mind my own, yet in my heart is a cry toward something dim in the distance which is higher than I am and makes me emperor of the endless dark, even in the seeking.". . . What odds and ends we live otherwise![58]

Like the elevator girl in the motion picture *The Apartment,* who carried a broken mirror in her purse because "It makes me look the way I feel," Ross summoned the courage to enter ministry when he realized that God didn't put God's treasure in scratch-free mirrors or bullet-proof boxes but in frail, earthenware vessels like you and me. The love that shines out of brokenness and pain is the love that brings "an eternal freshness, a newness of life."[59]

In A. N. Wilson's splendid biography of C. S. Lewis, there is a discussion of why Lewis's autobiography *Surprised by Joy* covered up so much about Lewis's own personal wreckage. Wilson believes it was because Lewis never did come to realize "that God's grace works by the *means* [italics mine] of human weakness, not by side-stepping it."[60] George Ross did not know of "side-stepping" grace. He trusted the truth of that old saying, that in heaven God isn't going to look us over for our medals, but for our scars.

In the last year of his ministry, Ross asked his congregation one Sunday morning: "When I'm finished, when my life is over, will anyone have attained a better image of God because of who I was and what I did?"[61] In the five chapters that follow, I try to answer that question by looking at Ross's ministry in light of the wounds of Christ. My intent is not to map the fault lines along which Ross's life slipped, fractured, and reformed: divorce, alcoholism, surely one of the worst closures ever in the history of the Diocese of Ohio. Rather, my intent is to probe how brokenness can become a source of soul force and an avenue of creative energy.

My hope is also to connect our wounds to the five wounds of Christ: his broken hands and feet, symbolic of broken pieces of body—our physical wounds; his broken side, symbolic of broken relationships—our communal wounds; his broken head, symbolic of broken thoughts—our mental wounds; his broken back, symbolic of broken promises—our actional wounds; and his broken heart, symbolic of broken faith—our spiritual wounds. In his wounds was the world's wellness. In our wounds is our wellness.

CHAPTER ONE

WOUNDED HANDS
AND FEET

ꙅꙮꙅ

Broken Pieces of Body

O wounded hands of Jesus, build
In us thy new creation;
Our pride is dust; our vaunt is stilled;
We wait thy revelation:
O love that triumphs over loss,
We bring our hearts before thy cross,
To finish thy salvation.

—Walter Russell Bowie[1]

ESTIMATES VARY, but for certain we can say that 10 percent of the population, or 25 million people, have some kind of physical disability. The United Way argues that the figure is much higher: their statistics reveal that more than 37 million US-Americans over fifteen years of age suffer functional physical limitation. If truth be told, 100 percent would be a more accurate accounting. To be "disabled" is to not be able to do things other people can do. That is true for every one of us. We are all "Jerry's Kids."

Disability is the theme of one of George Ross's favorite passages of Scripture, the Twenty-third Psalm. Martin Buber called it the "Nightingale Psalm," and poet/priest J. Barrie Shepherd calls it "the most memorized, the most cherished piece of literature in all of faith."[2] One of Ross's most lasting memories was hearing a young Indian preacher in a Baptist church in India sing the Twenty-third Psalm in the Telegu language.[3] The best known and most beloved of all the Psalms, it rings with phrases ("green pastures," "still waters," "cup running over," "valley of the shadow") that strike a whole keyboard of emotions. Although these six longest-short verses in the Bible are popularly known as the "Shepherd Psalm" or "Shepherd Song," the psalm more properly should be called the "Sheep Song," since it is written from the perspective of sheep.

Tending sheep provided the training ground for many prophetic leaders—Moses, Elijah, Amos (some say), and David. Clovis Chappell, in his classic sermon on the sheep psalm, argues that the words "I shall not want" are the "most logical ever uttered." They follow logically from the first premise: "The Lord is My Shepherd."[4] *If* the Lord is our Shepherd, *then* logically we shall not want.

To get from one pasture to another, David, as a boy, walked his father's sheep through what was known back then as "The Glen of Gloom." With a sling in his pocket, a rod on his back, and a staff in his hand, David traversed the Judaean highlands that were ripped through with deep ravines, one of which was known as "the valley of the shadow of death." This was a frightening place to walk. Single file along rocky pitfalls, the sheep passed through a narrow path on either side of which lurked wild dogs, wolves, hyenas, and robbers hidden in caves. As King, when David became another kind of shepherd, he no doubt remembered these walks through the "valley of the shadow" and how he got through them.

I

The two key words that make Psalm 23 "The Disabled's Psalm" are *though* and *through*: "though I walk through the valley of the shadow of death, I will fear no evil."[5] The valley of the shadow of disability and death is not a question of "if," but "though." Not "if" we go through the valley but "though" we go through the valley.

All of us have valleys we've been given at birth. The second part of Peter Barnes's trilogy *The Spirit of Man* is called "From Sleep and Shadow." In it, Israel Yates says that "as long as a man sees himself above other men he has limits and God cannot pour His holiness into him—for God is without limits. But I'm not proud, standing five foot ten in what's left of my stockings, curing carbuncles and hemorrhoids and capering up and down in the gutters of the world. And so God pours His glory into me."[6]

Standing tall at six feet two but hobbling all his life from eye problems, depression, allergies, and alcoholism, George Ross was a vessel into which God poured divine glory. Ross boasted about never needing to see a doctor, and until his death-dealing bouts with pneumonia and other AIDS-related illnesses, he was seldom outwardly sick or frail. Ross's braggadocio about never being ill notwithstanding, his pendulous mood swings caused some around him to suspect he was manic-depressive. His hyperactivity in hospital calling, his refusal to admit that he ever offered enough worship services, the exceedingly high standards he set for himself and his ministry, the desperate lostness of his spirit after resigning from St. Paul's, and his inability to stop hanging out at the church—all suggest that he preached out of a frantic inner necessity. Whether this "disability" was physiological or psychological is of less consequence than that it was always with him, not to mention his lifelong fight with alcoholism, itself a daily walk through the valley of the shadow.

Scholars are only now discovering the extent to which these birth-valleys were as true for biblical figures as for us. Judith Z. Abrams has examined the Isaac story in Genesis, and she concludes that Isaac from birth had some form of serious disability. (See her translation of Genesis 21:6—"God has made me a laughing stock. Everyone who hears of this will laugh at me.") Yet Isaac's physical and/or mental disability did not prevent God from choosing him as a central link in Jewish salvation history.[7]

The key word is "though" because all of us make our own valleys. Or as a psalmist put it elsewhere, "He made a pit and dug it
out, and has fallen into the ditch which he made" (Psalm 7:15,
NKJV). I shall never forget a Mother's Day sermon I heard some
years back. With a sanctuary packed with flower-festooned mothers, the preacher announced: "I know, I know this is Mother's
Day. But the Christian tradition would prefer we talked about
Christian families today. So that's what I'm going to do." The
preacher then went on to tell about how the story of families in
the Bible is not the story of one perfect family after another but
the story of one problem family after another. "You think *you've*
got a dysfunctional family? You think you know about what life is
like in a family with all sorts of disabilities? You haven't seen anything like the disabled, dysfunctional families of the Bible." The
preacher based the sermon on history's First Family—Adam, Eve,
Cain, Abel.

"Between the mountains lie the valleys," Ross wrote, "the valleys of the shadow of struggle and doubt and tragedy and sorrow—
the valleys of trouble. . . ."[8] All of us have valleys to go through,
valleys of despair, of aging, of suffering, and of death. But
"though" we must needs go through these valleys—though we
sin, though we fail, though we hurt, though we are broken,
though we die—yet we need "fear no evil." The psalmist does not
say, "I will never be afraid of anything." Ross constantly instructed his parishioners in their need to fear and tutored them in what
they should fear. There is a lot to fear.

But in the same way Jesus taught us to pray, "Deliver us from
evil," so the psalmist says, "I will fear no evil." Yes, there will be
evil; yes, there will be suffering; yes, there will be disabilities of
the body, mind, and spirit; yes, there will be pain; yes, there will
be injustices. It is not only the radiant halos of the mountains, or
the rainbow-hued spheres of the blue skies, in which the divine
lives and moves and has its being. But in the slough and "though"
of the valley, God is with us.

Life isn't all loaded tables and overflowing cups. Sometimes the
cup life presents us isn't even poured sparingly, much less half-full

or brimming. Sometimes our head isn't anointed with oil but grimed with grease. But whether green pastures or blue Mondays, whether the valley of the shadow or the seaside of still waters, the *God-with-us* bears all the blues and grime of the world.

Ross had a pet hate that he stroked more firmly the older he got: "cry-babies." Few things sapped a person's mental and physical health more than facing a complainer. Ross could not imagine a job he would rather do less than spend each day handling people's complaints. For this reason he felt a special compassion for Moses, who knew the valley of complaint perhaps better than anyone in history (see Numbers 11:4–6). Ross could rise to almost every pastoral occasion except when it came to people who complained, whined, and sought to establish a positive identity based on being victimized.[9] Which means Ross became increasingly cranky.

"Victim chic" calls for everyone to see oneself as a victim. All of us can find in our past reasons to claim to be victims—hurts, penalties, disabling contradictions. Will we choose to remember the vitality of our past or these wrongs? After a multi-ethnic mix of doctoral students went to see the movie *Schindler's List*, a talk-back session was scheduled with a local rabbi. It quickly deteriorated into a shouting match as each ethnic group competed for "victimhood" status and argued over who was the chief "victim" among them. Philip Gourevitch, editor of the Jewish weekly *Forward*, laments our pervasive victimology as "a common idiocy of our age, hardly unique to Jews: to seek one's value in one's devaluation by others. We are hated, so we must be great enough to warrant hatred, the thinking goes, we are a cause, and easy righteousness is on our side."[10] Ross would have no part of victimhood and admonished his people to stop playing the part of the helpless "I've-been-hurt-by-you" victim and giving in to the victim's sense of self-righteousness.

The victim mentality translates into a growing cynicism and suspicion about everything and everyone—about motives, about reliability, about trust. People expect to be ripped off, lied to, betrayed, abused. One young buster, when his parents turned into the "Yum-Yum Tree" restaurant for lunch, cried out "Not here. Any restaurant that calls itself 'yum-yum' can't be good."

Of course, if one is a victim, then violence, not to mention judgment and hatred, can be justified, or at least excused. Ross preached long and hard about supplanting a society that distinguished right from wrong with a society that embraced every excuse and was "understanding" to the point that individuals were not to be held accountable for their personal behavior. Ross's beloved George Will has written that

In premodern, superstitious ages, people who behaved badly said, "The Devil made me do it." In this age of reason, a fired Northwestern professor says his disability made him do it: for six years after his mother died he deposited almost $40,000 of her Social Security checks. He blamed "extreme procrastination behavior" caused by depressions. A Penn State student complained to police about a breach of contract: a student she had hired to take an exam for her flunked it.[11]

Under the category of "The Abuse Excuse," too much sugar made the killer of a San Francisco mayor and supervisor "do it"; the frenzy of the moment made the rioters "do it" to trucker Reginald Denny; persistent patterns of abuse made the Menendez brothers and Lorena Bobbitt "do it" to their families; an adolescence run amok was responsible for Katherine Power, a.k.a. Alice Metzinger, "losing her way" and taking part in a 1970 robbery in which an accomplice decided to "do it" in the back to a father-of-nine bank guard.

For Ross, life was neither a "trap" nor a "treasure trove" but a "trust":

In the *Wilson Quarterly* recently I read about a little water spider, found in ponds and ditches, which lives beneath the water's surface in a kind of diver's bell. This is how he copes with life: he makes a thimble shaped case of silk, which he anchors by fine threads to the weeds at the bottom of the pond. The spider goes up to the surface and, by means of hooked hairs which cover the lower part of this body, he entangles a little bubble of air which he carries down and releases inside his little home. The air rises to the top of the silk bell and displaces a certain amount of water. Then he goes up again and again and again for more air and liberates it in the same way. Up and down he goes until finally the bell is filled and he can rest. For a while he lives beneath the surface in what he has brought down from the world.

Now silk bell spiders may live that way and this is fine; but, sad to say, that is the way many human beings are also living. To be sure, most of us are not that withdrawn, fearful and secretive. I suppose that most of us find that our pessimism and optimism, or affirmation and negative feelings alternate in our lives. . . .

This morning we come here for the express purpose of celebrating the Christian approach to life in this world. As Christians we affirm that the world is neither a trap nor a treasure trove just for us. Rather, it is a trust from God. Because of the resurrection of Christ, death holds no final fear for us as Christians; and because God has made it, the natural world is not our enemy, but our dear friend. Life is not something to be anxiously hoarded and carefully preserved as if it could not continue without our help. Rather, life is a gift from God to be celebrated with joy. . . . We live out our faith in the joyful, hopeful, loving way in which we embrace life and death here on earth as gifts from a loving Father.[12]

Ross believed one's mettle was tested when walking through the valley more than during any other time of life. As James Michener, one of Ross's favorite summer authors, put it: "Character consists of what you do on the third and fourth tries."[13] Or as Jack London advised fellow writers: "You can't wait for inspiration. You have to go after it with a club." There was an element of stoicism to Ross that made him impatient with those who complained about the hand life had dealt them, or who refused to try to do something significant with that hand, no matter how poor or weak it seemed to be.

The Apostle Paul had a valley: but in the midst of his prison he could write, "rejoice in the Lord always, and again I will say rejoice" (Philippians 4:4 RSV). St. Augustine had a valley: but in the midst of the barbarians storming the gates, he saw a vision of the City of God and preached it to the housetops. Martin Luther had a valley: but while the medieval world collapsed all around him, he announced where he was standing and he nailed his stand to the wall. John Wesley had a valley: but when the Anglican church closed its doors in his face, and people threw tomatoes at him, he preached in the fields and highways to the outcasts and outsiders, and he started a spiritual and social revolution that saved England.

II

The second word in understanding the appeal of Psalm 23 for Ross was this word *through*. The valley of the shadow is something one goes *through*. It is not a resting place, or wallowing spot, but a passageway. Poet Melvin Dixon, who lives with AIDS, testifies to *through* power in the following fashion: "I come to you bearing witness to a broken heart. I come to you bearing witness to a broken body. I come to you bearing witness to an unbroken spirit."[14] Valleys are not where we settle down but where we camp; they are not where we set up housekeeping but where we hang out for a while. Christians make life's valleys their passageways, not their resting places.

If all of us are damaged in some form or limited in some fashion, the question becomes whether we allow our disabilities to lock us up in life or to open us into fuller dimensions of living. Do we accept God's choosing of us, as damaged as we are, or are we disabled from choosing what God would have us be because of our physical handicaps and shortcomings? We can walk *through* our problems, walk *through* our sorrows, walk *through* our failures, because we know the Lord will walk *through* with us.

Joni Eareckson Tada and Harold Wilke have done more to open the church to the physically challenged than anyone else. Indeed, God is using these two people powerfully, as God used Isaac: their ministries are two of the most significant in the church today. Harold Wilke was born with no arms. With his feet, this cleric writes, drives, cooks, and makes love. When it came time for President George Bush to sign the 1989 Disabilities Act, it was Harold Wilke he asked to cosign the legislation with him.

Ross was deeply moved by the story of Joni Eareckson Tada, a beautiful young woman athlete who was diving into some shallow water and broke her spine. A quadriplegic, she draws and writes from her wheelchair by placing instruments in her teeth. She spoke these words after her marriage, words that Ross often quoted: "God's grace can overflow from a half-broken cup."[15]

Kenneth Caraway, a United Methodist pastor with a motorcycle ministry, puts the *through* promise of the gospel like this:

There is no box
made by God nor us
but that the top can be blown off
and the sides flattened out
to make a dance floor
on which to celebrate life.[16]

The dance of life, Ross believed, was made possible by what he called the Easter effect of the Easter event:

No, we don't know what lies on the other side of the great door, but we do know that the Master is there. No, we don't suppose that in this life we shall always be free of pain or sorrow; it sometimes happens in this life that we walk with crutches. Maybe so, but *if* so, then as Christians we need never be defeated because inside us there is an invincible joy, an irrepressible laughter, an Easter song. *"Christ is risen"*—that is the *event*. Alleluia! Death has no more dominion over us! This is the *effect*. Alleluia![17]

The *through* side of the Twenty-third Psalm Ross demonstrated in a variety of ways throughout his life. His impaired eyesight and intense headaches, which he attributed to chronic sinusitis, for example, did not prevent Ross from devouring reading material. Ross read everything he could get his hands on. He subscribed to the *New York Times*, the *Wall Street Journal*, the *New Yorker*, as well as the standard religious periodicals of oldline Protestantism (*Christian Century, Christianity and Crisis*, and so forth). He read biographies for personal enjoyment as well as for sermon illustrations, and his ability to recite poems and write with immense poetic energy betrayed a deep familiarity with poetry. After his death, booksellers, who usually have to be dragged to look at a priest's collection, fought over his huge library (part of which he had already given to Trinity Episcopal School).

One year (1984) he kept track of the books he had read word for word, cover to cover, either from his antique ball-and-claw footed reading chair or his beach chair. These books were above and beyond those he consulted to keep abreast in ministry or opened for sermon material. They were the books he read for personal enjoyment: Eco's *The Name of the Rose* (1983); Michener's *Poland* (1983); Martin Cruz Smith's *Gorky Park* (1981); Francis Bacon's

Essays; Russell Baker's *Growing Up* (1982); Mary Renault's *The Nature of Alexander* (1983); Stringfellow Barr's *The Will of Zeus: A History of Greece from the Origins of Hellenic Culture to the Death of Alexander* (1961); Gore Vidal's *Creation* (1981); George A. Buttrick's *The Parables of Jesus* (1928); Mary Renault's *The Praise Singer* (1978); W. W. Tarn's *Alexander the Great* (1948); Barbara Tuchman's *March of Folly* (1984); Alistair Cook's *Mencken* (1955); *The Book of English Villages* [that is, John Burke's *English Villages*] (1975).

Fourteen books in a year may not seem like much. But with Ross's eye and headache problems he found reading much more straining and tiring than most of us. David Mix, a Marine lieutenant who in 1967 lost his left leg below the knee to a Bouncing Betty in Vietnam, confessed to the son of a paraplegic that "there comes a time in the life of an amputee when he realizes that everything takes three times as long."[18] Every disability carries with it at least a three-times-as-long factor.

Ross read more than books. Books, even books about his beloved England, were no substitute for a trip to England or a walk through a country garden. Traveling was perhaps the greatest stimulant of his life. His reading eye and listening ear encompassed art, music, cinema, travel, and, always and everywhere, people—all of which never left him the way they found him. Ross boasted he never returned from a trip the same person he was when he set out:

In New York the other day I came across a little old lady in a wheel chair selling pencils on the street. You've seen such people in New York if you've been there. Her hair was thinning. Her teeth were gone for the most part. Her legs were all gone. On her face there was simply nothing to read. I watched her there for a moment, and, as I did so, along came a young man in the bloom and blush and promise of life, literally leaping down the street. As he passed her, he leaned down and kissed her on the head. I'll never forget his words, "Hi, ya, beautiful! How ya doin'?" It was evident that this was a ritual, probably something that happened every day, because she looked up at him with recognition and a light came back into her eyes. A broad toothless grin broke across her face. She raised a gnarled hand to wave and also, I think, to salute. She answered, "Just great, Jimmie, just great. And gee you're lookin' swell yourself!"[20]

If things had been different in his life, and the *thoughs* turned out differently, Ross probably would have been a seminary professor. When asked to describe their priest, more than one parishioner has said "He was a born teacher." One of his theology professors called him the "brightest and best student I ever had."[20] Ethicist Joseph Fletcher similarly regarded Ross as his most brilliant student. Actually, Fletcher hoped that Ross would succeed him at Episcopal Divinity School at Cambridge, Massachusetts, at his retirement.[21] As it was, from his parish base, Ross taught homiletics at Bexley Hall for a few years, as well as a speech course at Kenyon College.

Ross played *through* the hand life dealt him. His family situation, as well as physical struggles with addiction, worked against his obtaining an advanced degree. Yale historian Roland Bainton paid this tribute to his father, a parish priest who also had to learn to live within and *through* limits not of his choosing:

[His] congregations never numbered more than two hundred. He was an inconspicuous minister. He was a contented minister. Early he realized that he would never play a conspicuous role in the life of the church. Had he been invited to a renowned pulpit he could not have accepted by reason of the infirmities of the flesh. He suffered from glandular tuberculosis in college, and though this was surmounted he continued to be sickly. . . . One thus hampered could not have carried a major assignment. Herbert Bainton knew it and was not cankered by jealousy, tormented by ambition or racked by frustration. Within the framework of frailty, he aimed at excellence, reminding himself that . . . "the wayside pool reflects the fleeting clouds as exactly as does the mighty ocean."[22]

If he could not become a seminary professor or dean, Ross would make his church into a seminary. His multiple classes and weekly lectures on biblical themes, which were famous far beyond St. Paul's parish limits for moving believers beyond a rote, rudimentary Christianity that only knows the gurglings of faith, became the sites of his own displaced yearnings.

He never complained about the academic road not taken and was impatient with people who used their physical circumstances as excuses for settling into a bookkeeping existence or as escapes from living:

We are like the lepers. Like them, we experience suffering, pain, rejection and despair. Like them at the village gate, we beg for help and healing; and like them, we receive the healing and abundant mercy of God in the face of Jesus Christ. Ah, but that is not the whole story. Having received grace upon grace, what then? Shall we then go with the nine who went their way, helped, but not whole—or shall we again and again return to give thanks and praise to God, not only with our lips, but in our lives, and so be made wonderfully well?[23]

In whatever the circumstance, Ross found a stance for praise. He was never content with mere crumbs of comfort. He kept sentiments of self-pity under firm control. His teacher in how to deal with disabilities was a woman who had lost her leg in a traffic accident. It was his very first pastoral call.

She was the most depressed person I had ever met up to that time. I had just graduated from seminary; and no sooner had I arrived at my first church than the rector decided that it was high time for him to take a snooze in Bermuda. As he left, in his breezy way, he gave me my preaching assignments and told me to visit this woman in her house. Perhaps only curates will appreciate the fond thoughts with which I waved this dreadful man off at the airport. So began for me a series of long afternoon visits with the woman who changed my life. My first visit was predictably disastrous. She was as angry as I was nervous. Other visits followed and we talked and we talked and we talked about the accident and the tragedy of it and the sadness of it all. Her life would never be the same. How could she believe in a good God in a bad world like this? "Why me, and why now, in the prime of my life?" And so on and on. I made a good decision. I decided not to try to cheer her up or to answer any questions about God. Instead, I simply let her talk and sometimes shout it out. Always when I left, we prayed, and more accurately, I prayed; she sulked. Then about six months later the great change began. The dirty dishes disappeared from the sink. The *New York Times*, which generally covered the carpet two inches thick, was stacked in the corner. I found her sitting like a queen, presiding over a Spode tea service which she had somehow managed to extricate from the attic where it had been since her mother had died. "What in the world happened to you?" I asked. "Oh nothing," she answered. "I just decided last night that if I am going to live a one-legged life, I am going to live the best, damned one-legged life in Columbus, Ohio!"[24]

More troublesome than his walk *through* the valley of weak eyesight and chronic headaches was his walk *through* addiction to alcohol. Some people have rogue periods of an entire life. Others have rogue periods of a day or week. During Ross's rogue periods, he drank anything and everything—wine, whiskey, gin, vodka. Sodden with alcohol, he would get into the shower at 3 A.M. on Sunday mornings and, in a drink-muzzled voice, sing "A Mighty Fortress Is Our God" to wake him up and focus his energies on preparing the morning sermon. No matter how soaked in alcohol his evening had been, the Sunday sermon remained dry and sober. The bread Ross offered on Sunday morning was always fresh from the oven.

Amazingly, his sermons never betrayed these rogue periods. In every sermon, there is the rare pleasure of a word placed to perfection, a thought exactly and elegantly stated, a story exquisitely told. Who can understand the psychology of "inspiration"? The muses bestow the greatest of gifts in the most mercurial of ways.

Ross frequently drank himself into stupors, which became so severe even his vulpine resourcefulness began to falter. In 1978, when his double life threatened to jeopardize his pastoral duties and preaching, he checked himself into a drug addiction rehabilitation center in Cleveland. When he emerged from de-tox, he threw himself into ministries for those with drug addictions.

While he never stood in the pulpit and proclaimed "I am an alcoholic," he never denied it, did not hide it, and was not secretive about his problem. He reactivated the AA chapter that operated out of St. Paul's and became a faithful member of it for a number of years. He awakened the Diocese of Ohio to issues of addiction and at St. Paul's sponsored annual workshops for clergy that raised their consciousness and strategies for treatment. Well into the 1980s, St. Paul's lived out of its AA genes, and the church made available to the diocesan and local community some of the best resources in the country—people like Vernon Johnson, whose book *I'll Quit Tomorrow* (1973) has become a classic of the AA movement.

As was Ross's pattern, he was very focused for a while on problems of addiction, but his attention gradually became diverted by other issues (in this case homelessness and loneliness). Ross stopped regular attendance at AA, though he claimed until the day he died never to have taken another drop except what he received by intinction from the common cup. Ross remained sensitive to those who needed help with their drug problems, especially those who could not afford it, as this excerpt from a 1990 sermon makes clear:

One out of three addicted poor people in this country is turned away from treatment centers. We can afford, apparently, to send battle ships to Colombia; but we cannot, seemingly, afford treatment centers in our inner cities! In the city of New York, 10,000 addicted people are lined up for treatment which they will probably never receive because there is no room for them. We face a spiritual, not a military, problem this morning, and unless the church is bolder in its witness to the dignity of human life and to the love of God and to the saving sovereignty of Jesus Christ, who alone gives meaning and dignity to human life, we can expect to see the social fabric of this country continue to deteriorate.[25]

Disabilities can form either a millstone or a mantle. In the former, broken pieces of body retain a repressive significance in human life. In the latter, brokenness obtains an expressive significance in human life. We decide. We can organize our life on the principle of despair. On that side, we will dwell in hostility, anxiety, resentment, disease, and loneliness. Or we can organize our life on the principle of trust. On that side, we will find community, compassion, forgiveness, creativity, and hints of heavens yet unknown.

George Ross told the stories of two young boys, both paraplegics, to illustrate how broken pieces of body can either bless or curse ourselves and others. The first paraplegic was Kenneth Wright, a high school football star, hunter, and wrestler. An ill-fated wrestling match in 1979 left Kenneth with a broken neck and subsequent paralysis from the chest down. Unable to accept or adjust to his disability, Kenneth asked two of his friends to take him in his wheelchair to the woods one afternoon. He brought with him a 12-gauge shotgun, and there, at age twenty-four, took his life.

The second paraplegic was James A. McGowan. At the age of nineteen, Jim was stabbed in a street fight and paralyzed from the waist down. He is confined most but not all of the time to a wheelchair. NBC featured him on "Morning News" because he made a successful parachute jump, landing on his target in the middle of Lake Wallenpaupack in the Poconos. It appears that Jim lives alone, cooks his own meals, washes his own clothes, keeps his own house. He drives in a specially equipped Jeep. He has written four books and was the photographer for the first book on the history of wheelchair sports. A few years ago he tried to swim the English Channel.[26]

More important than the hardware of biology is the software of spirituality, the ways in which we cope and change because of our hard-wired limitations of hot leads and dead ends. What mars human beings can also be what makes them. In one of the sermons in this collection, Ross recalled that his "first experience with English literature" was "Pat-a-cake, pat-a-cake, baker's man, / Bake me a cake as fast as you can." He called this "deathless poem" a "good introduction for any child to the twentieth century where *everything* must be done as fast as we can."[27] Ross's "second major work of English literature" was:

> Pussy-cat, pussy-cat,
> Where have you been?
> I've been to London
> to look at the queen.
>
> Pussy cat, pussy cat,
> What did you there?
> I frightened a little mouse
> Under her chair.[28]

That poem was as instructive for modern children as the first, Ross insisted, for "if frantic exertion is one mark of the 20th century, meaningless endeavor is another. . . . The supreme tragedy for anyone is not ill health or failed ambition or personal collapse under the crucifying cruelties of this world. The supreme tragedy for anyone, when the angel of the evening rings the curfew bell, is to have 'had the experience but missed the meaning.' "[29]

Physical suffering and deformities can become the grains of sand around which the richness and resonance of life grow most meaningfully. Our broken bits and pieces of body can lead us to retreat, revenge, or rebirth. Ross's favorite way of illustrating this was to tell the story of ten minutes he spent on the Hoh River of western Washington State, ten minutes that lasted his lifetime:

Out of the morning mist a magnificent bald eagle swept down and in one smooth movement caught his salmon fresh from the sea and was gone again. It was a sight I shall remember 'til I die. That magnificent bird had once emerged from its fragile shell, as helpless as we are at birth. But it survived, because of the nest. Then the feathers grew. The eyes brightened. The talons strengthened. One day the bird stood poised upon the nest and all the future of its life lay before it, the vista vast, the glorious rivers and forests and fountains of the earth. To take possession of it, however, he had to stretch his wings, take the daring leap, trust the air, have faith in whatever great eagle gods there are and go! The instinct to fly and the instinct to nest met in that moment. There comes a point in everyone's spiritual life when that issue is joined and must be faced.

Will we dare to fly, to test our wings, to see the great wide world in all its manifold wonder, or will we nestle down were we are, complacent, conservative, content to patch and tidy and rearrange the mud and wattles of our existing ideas and schools and churches and businesses and nations?[30]

Ross believed that what often prompts us to "take the daring leap" is our very infirmities. "Scripture tells us that Job was saved by suffering. No sooner had he nested down, than the Lord afflicted him. It was through suffering that Job's complacency was shattered and his spirit tested. If there is no other way for the Lord to get us out of our nests, there is always the tried and true way of suffering."[31]

There is no escape from living in the clutches of infirmity and mortality. And there is no final answer this side of eternity to the questions: Why me? Why now? Why this? In a fall of 1989 sermon entitled "Living with the Unsolved," a sermon that revealed more of Ross's spiritual struggle with the AIDS virus than he ever intended or realized, he exegeted for his congregation the Lukan passage where the apostle asks "Lord, increase our faith" (Luke 17:5–10). Like the disciples, he argued, "most of us are living with unsolved problems." And in their cry "O Lord, increase our faith!" we can hear and feel "the heartache of unsolved problems in their lives."

We hear the murmur, not only of their prayers, but of countless prayers. "O God, if you are good, why did my child die?" "Why do the homeless wander helpless on these streets?" "Why do the wicked prosper while the righteous man is full of sores?" . . . "Lord, why, just as I am beginning to feel some wisdom, some joyful insight into the meaning of my life, why, just now, as I am getting the hang of it, does the doctor say, 'Put your affairs in order; it won't be long?'"[32]

Ross confessed to finding "as much inspiration from those who live with the unsolved" as he did from "the successful who seem to have found solutions." One of those who inspired him was Edward Livingstone Trudeau:

He lived with an unsolved problem in his life. He was the victim of tuberculosis and spent most of his life encouraging other people with tuberculosis, most of them from the slums. Late in his life he made a speech to the Medical Society of Harvard College, in which he said: "My sympathy wasn't always, but nowadays is, naturally with the vanquished. The world applauds and bows before success and achievement. It has little thought for those who fall by the wayside, sword in hand; and yet it takes more courage to fight a losing fight."[33]

To fight the losing fight of life with dignity, grace, and courage and without bitterness, resentment, and self-pity—Ross's reading of the Bible made this way of living "the way we walk toward God." In the words of his beloved poet e. e. cummings, the goal of life is not to succeed but to proceed:

The Church is not an infallible society with irrefutable answers to life's great questions. The church is not a platform for the infallibly certain; it is rather a community of broken, frail human beings who are committed to living cheerfully together amidst the uncertainties of life with such faith and love as God gives.[34]

In this sermon Ross said he found new meaning in the John

Henry Cardinal Newman hymn "Lead, Kindly Light, amid the en-circling gloom." "I cannot read [it] without being deeply affected," he confessed. The sermon ended with this prayer:

O God, we do not ask for visionary eyes to see the distant scene. We pray for just enough of your grace to take the next step faithfully on our way today with those we love. You have set us, Lord, in the midst of many perplexities that test and try us. Here and now we see through a glass dimly. Dear Lord, give us a faith that knows that one day we shall under-stand even as we have been understood; through Jesus Christ our Lord. Amen.[35]

On 9 June 1991, George Everett Ross, after having received the Eucharist from an associate, entered this promise, "And God who gives beginning gives the end, / . . . / A rest for broken things too broke to mend."[36] Ross had finally found the psalmist's God who "restoreth my soul," words that can also be translated as "I come to life again" or "He gives me new life."

SERMONS

ꙮ

"Knock and It Will Be Opened"

Text: Luke 11:1–13

About a hundred years ago the Salvation Army was founded in Great Britain. Not long after the Salvation Army had been established, there appeared in England a very remarkable, religious personality. He claimed to be Jesus Christ returned to earth. He claimed to heal the lame, to restore sight to the blind and hearing to the deaf. He claimed that he could perform miracles. He was so possessed of great oratorical ability that in spite of what seemed to be ridiculous and absurd claims, he managed to gather together a following. One evening in a great lecture hall in London, as he was speaking, there could be heard in the distance the sound of music. As the music came closer and grew louder, it was evident to anyone who had ever heard a Salvation Army band that such an organization was approaching the hall. As indeed it did. And playing as mightily as they could, they walked down the center aisle of that lecture hall to the complete astonishment of everyone. When they reached the platform, the Salvation Army captain mounted the stairs, confronted the speaker, and asked him this

Sermon preached at St. Paul's Episcopal Church, Akron, Ohio, on the Eighth Sunday after Pentecost, 24 July 1977. George Ross Papers, The University of Akron Archives.

question, "Are you really the Christ? Tell us plainly." The speaker replied, "Yes, I am the Christ returned to earth." Looking steadily at him, the Salvation Army captain said, "Very well, then show us your hands." And he did. Without saying further, the captain went back to join the band. They struck up an old gospel hymn, and as they marched out of the hall, they sang again and again the old refrain: "I shall know him, I shall know him, by the print of the nails in his hand!"[1]

That gentleman a hundred years ago in England was not the first nor will he be the last to come among us as a pretending savior to offer us miracles and cheap and easy grace. But Christianity is tested and the Savior is proved only if he bears in his own body the nail prints of our human sin and the spear wound of our human suffering.

In the Second Lesson this morning Jesus Christ offers us two images which may not please us much for they are images about our sinfulness. "Imagine a neighbor at midnight," he said, "who goes to a friend for help and knocks upon his door, and that friend calls down, 'This house is shut; that door is locked, and I will not help you'" (cf. Luke 11:5–8).

Well, you say, that is an exaggeration. There may be some like that, but as an indication of our humanity, is not that too severe? I ask you, before you dismiss it altogether, to pause for a moment to reflect with me. I wonder who it may be knocking at your door today. It may be a child in Africa who will be dead before midnight from malnutrition. Or it may be someone not so far away, even at the other side of the city, who, in humble beseeching asks, "Why these rats? Why this slum?" While you eat your supper this evening, before you have concluded your meal, sixteen brothers and sisters will have died of starvation. I hear a voice, frail and weak: "Day by day I lie on this bed in this nursing home room and stare at that door, and no one ever comes." I seem to hear a voice that is hoarse and trembling: "Day by day I sit in this prison cell and look at that iron grating and hope and pray that someone has not forgotten me and might come to see me." But no one does.

I believe that our Lord Jesus Christ is here speaking to us across the centuries about our vast capacity for indifference. Our guilt cries out for someone to speak a word of forgiveness. Our needs cry out for someone to understand. Our deep despair, which we may not even name in our own prayers, cries out for someone to open even a small door of hope. We knock! We knock!

Jesus is talking about our inhumanity to one another, and he does not overdramatize. He could have. He could have given us truly horrendous stories of atrocity, murder, rape, and torture. God knows his world was as full of such illustrations as ours is. But no. With that wonderful restraint, which characterized all his teaching, he told just this simple story about a man who needed a little bread in the middle of the night and a neighbor who called down: "Go away; I will not help you." It is through the small window we might see the vast indifference of man to man.

The more I ponder the mystery of my own sinfulness and of yours, the more I begin to see what Jesus means. I have come to see that sin is finally not for many of us, probably not for any of us here, doing something dramatically evil. Sin, finally, for the most of us, is indifference, not caring, not responding in love—when human need knocks at our doors, and only after that disposition becomes chronic by habit and that character hardens, does it eventually bring forth all kinds of active evil. It is from passive indifference that active sin proceeds.

Then he asked this question, "Which of you, as a father, would give your son a snake when he asks for a fish, or a scorpion when he asks for an egg?"

You throw up your hands; again you say, "Further exaggeration. No parent would act that way, surely I would not." But, before you dismiss this out of hand, ponder it with me for a moment. A child comes to you asking the meaning of life—"Why am I here? Where did I come from? Where do I go?" Children may not ask those questions in just that way, but they have their way of asking, and they do ask those questions. You turn on your television set and for two or three hours in the evening you invite into your living room every form of human violence, depravity, and absurdity and sit down with your children to watch it. Dr. Gallup in-

forms us that our children on the average watch about 25 hours of
television each week. I do not know how many hours the parents
of this congregation spend with their children in the study of the
scripture or in prayers at home or in religious teachings, but I do
know this on the basis of some research: that the average child in
this parish this past school year spent about 12 minutes per week
in our church school. Twenty-five hours of trivia interspersed
with violence versus 12 minutes in the church school because
some parents did not care enough to bring their children. "Which
of you with a child will give him a scorpion when he begs for an
egg?"

Jesus could have exaggerated; he could have talked about the
terrible things that happen in family life: the hatred, violence, and
massive cruelties which human beings inflict upon one another
behind the shuttered windows of their private homes. Instead,
characteristically, he uses a question that is almost ridiculous in
its language, but do we not see his point, painful as it is? The Lord
is speaking about our sin and he is telling us what we already
know—that sin infects all our human relationships—not only
with our neighbors next door, but with our children and our parents and our wives and our husbands at home. It is an inward cor-
ruption that touches all our behavior.

Now, if I were to stop this sermon right now, I would go from
this room as discouraged and down hearted as you may now be
feeling about yourself, for when a preacher speaks of sin, it is a
mirror to every honest man and woman in a church. I know that.
But the sermon does not stop here, and, far from being discouraged by this passage from St. Luke, I find it one of the most wonderful and encouraging passages in the whole scripture. These
harsh images are found in the context of gracious words. "Teach
us to pray," the disciples besought him, and he gave them the
words of his own prayer: "Abba, my Father, holy in heaven." It is
in the context of that prayer and of those gracious words that he
then tells about men and women and their need to pray, about the
indifferent neighbor and the foolish parent.

By this I believe that he wants us to see that our prayers rise to

God from our sin and not from our virtue, from our need and not from our righteousness. It is as the publican standing with head down and heart broken, not as the priest in self righteousness, that we must pray to God. It is only on our knees that we are bold to say "Our Father" for he is the one who comes to save sinners, not the righteous, the sick, not the well, to save and to be the shepherd of the lost and the hope of the depressed. To them he says, "Knock, and it will be opened, though it be the darkest midnight of your life."

I want you to notice that he does not promise that your troubles at that time will end, or your sickness be taken away, or your success in life assured—none of that, not in this passage. On the contrary said he, "Here on this earth you will suffer." What Jesus offers is the open door to eternity so that we may walk *through* our troubles as through a doorway into larger life. If any savior would come to you offering another way, ask to see his hands.

I have found a parable of this great Gospel that I want to share with you. It is a passage from Helen Keller's autobiography. Many of you know it. If ever there was one closed in by suffering, it was that little girl who could not hear and could not see and could not speak. Then there came to her one day from the Lord a woman named Annie Sullivan Macy. After months of suffering and frustration and anger, she finally found a way to communicate with Helen by tapping messages on her hand and so began to unlock and open up a whole world. One day Helen asked her, "What is love?" Annie tried to explain. This is how Helen Keller remembered it in her diary:

She drew me closer to her and said, "It is here," pointing to my heart. . . . Her words puzzled me very much because I did not understand anything unless I touched it. I smelt the violets in her hand and asked . . . "Is love the sweetness of flowers?" "No," said my teacher. Again I thought. The warm sun was shining on us. "Is this not love?" I asked, pointing in the direction from which the heat came. . . . It seemed to me that there could be nothing more beautiful than the sun, whose warmth makes all things grow. But Miss Sullivan shook her head, and I was greatly puzzled and disappointed.

Finally, she tried one again:

"Love is something like the clouds that were in the sky before the sun came out. . . . You cannot touch the clouds, you know; but you feel the rain and know how glad the flowers and the thirsty earth are to have it after a hot day. You cannot touch love either; but you feel the sweetness that it pours into everything. Without love you would not be happy or want to play."

Then, writes Helen Keller, "the beautiful truth burst upon my mind—I felt that there were invisible lines stretched between my spirit and the spirits of others."[2]

She was still blind when she wrote those words. She was still deaf and remained deaf until she died. That was not taken away. But a door to larger life within her suffering had been opened.

That is what Jesus Christ can do for us, no matter how lost in suffering, no matter how deep in sin, no matter how feebly and shamefully we knock upon the door of grace. "Knock and it will be opened!" As Helen Keller put it, a beautiful truth will burst upon you and you will know that there are invisible lines stretching between your spirit and the spirit of all the other people of the earth and the spirit of God himself.[3] Knock and it will be opened, and the hands that will reach out to embrace you will be hands that are pierced and so hands that can save.

LET US PRAY:

Almighty God in Heaven, we bring our lives before you with penitence for our indifference to human need and with deep sorrow for our sins; we praise you, dear Lord Jesus, for all your goodness, but most of all for your compassion for us when we deserve it least. Our hearts are full of joy for the open door to larger life which you offer us even when our knocking is faint and feeble. Holy and Blessed Spirit of God lead us from this hour of worship with new hope, new freedom, new power for the work you have set before us and new courage for the earthly journey we must yet travel. For Thine is the kingdom and the power and the glory for ever. *Amen.*

Temptation and Suffering

After the baptism of Jesus, the Holy Spirit led the Lord into the wilderness, and there for forty days he was tempted by the devil.

Text: Luke 4:1–13

Lent begins in the wilderness and it concludes on the cross. Lent has two themes: temptation and suffering. I want to talk about them both this morning.

TEMPTATION

First, I ask you to think with me about sin and temptation. All our sins, plural, spring from one sin, singular. You cannot understand either the Garden of Eden story or the wilderness temptations of our Lord if you do not have some insight into the truth. The nineteenth-century French poet, Charles Pierre Baudelaire, wrote a book which he entitled *Les Fleurs du Mal* (*The Flowers of Evil*, 1857). The Scripture sage said: "Of the writing of books there is no end"; and certainly there is no end to the writing of books about human wickedness. Yet all our sins *plural* spring from one sin *singular.*

Aristotle said that the tragic hero is the man with many virtues, but with one tragic flaw that brings him down. Sophocles,

Sermon preached at St. Paul's Episcopal Church, Akron, Ohio, on the First Sunday in Lent, 16 February 1986. George Ross Papers, The University of Akron Archives.

45

Aeschylus, Shakespeare, and a host of others have given passionate incarnation to that insight. It is the little flaw that brings us down. Do you remember the doggerel from the nursery?

> For want of a nail, the shoe was lost,
> For want of a shoe, the horse was lost;
> For want of a horse, the cause was lost;
> For want of a cause, the kingdom was lost,
> And all for the want of a horseshoe nail.[4]

A rich young ruler came to the Lord, and Jesus loved him. Jesus loved the young man's virtues, his youthful earnestness and seriousness; but Jesus said, "Young man, one thing you lack." At the end of the story, what do we read? "The young man went away *sorrowing*" (cf. Luke 18:18–38). His tragedy was the one thing missing. No matter the number of our virtues—one single flaw in character can bring us down. Alcoholism has done it to some of the brightest and best of this generation. A roving eye can do it. Vanity will do it. A little leak under great pressure defeated the brightest scientists and the bravest astronauts and the vast wealth of the country and made us weep. A little thing. In Colorado a three hundred year old tree lay smashed on the stones. For three hundred years that tree had withstood freezing cold and hurricane winds; its tough roots had clawed into the adamantine cliff. And yet it fell. Why? The park ranger said, "Notice that tree. It is the victim of an infestation of Mexican beetles, which have nearly wiped out all our big old trees." The wind, the cold, the inhospitable environment could not bring the tree down; but a little bug, which you could not see except with a magnifying glass, had brought it down. I remember reading about seven whales which beached and died on the coast of Maine. A Woods Hole Laboratory biologist stated that those whales died because a virus had attacked the hairs in their inner ears. The greatest creature we know was destroyed by one of the tiniest things in the world.

Before the Lord entered upon his ministry, he went into the wilderness and was tempted of the devil. The devil said to him,

"Use your great powers to make a better world, to reform the church and to put things right. You can do it. All these kingdoms, all their glory, I give to you. They can be yours. Jesus, you were a brilliant boy. In the Temple all the elders recognized, even in your youth, your intellectual genius. And now you have been baptized. You have received the Holy Ghost. To your undoubted natural gifts has been added a wonderful spiritual endowment. You are not only a born leader, but a great man. I want you to go out and do a great job in the world."—Thus spake Satan. Do not think that the devil spends all of his time trying to get the boys to look at the girls and vice versa. (As a matter of fact, God likes to do that himself!) And do not think that the devil gets into little boys and girls and makes them do nasty things with the window shades and so on. All these recent movies about the devil are entirely beside the point. Nobody is going to be even slightly tempted by such a ridiculous nuisance. The devil, as Shakespeare said, "hath power t' assume a pleasing shape."[5] It is the devil's work to make us so to dwell upon our strengths that we overlook the little virus, the little insect thing, the tragic flaw, the missing nail, the little leaking weak point which, left alone, will bring us down. Jesus won a victory in that wilderness that would radiate throughout the rest of his life and which shines on into eternity. He identified and overcame the flaw, the one thing which can bring the strongest person down. The hidden flaw, the inner fault is the sin of pride, of self-sufficiency; and until you win a victory over it, your defeat in the end is guaranteed. We can win all the prizes. We can go to the head of the class and climb to the top of the corporate ladder. There are not a few gifted people in this room this morning; but if you have never won a victory over yourself, in the end you will go away sorrowing—and you can count on it. All the temptations are the same temptation, and all the sins are the same sin finally. "Use your own strength, Jesus; you can do it by yourself," says the devil. But the Lord says, "Get behind me, Satan. Man shall not live by bread alone; but you shall worship the Lord your God and him only shall you serve."

St. Matthew reports that after Jesus had so spoken, angels came and ministered to him (Matthew 4:11). Do you see the wonderful meaning of that? Herein is the discovery which all the church's songs celebrate: that when you experience victory over yourself, vast powers become available to you! In all the temptations,the devil urges Jesus to go it alone, to do it himself. Richard II in Shakespeare's play is a man totally under the spell of the devil when he soliloquizes: "I am myself alone."[6] That is the voice of a doomed soul. Milton puts Satan at the bottom of Hell, completely encased in a block of ice. Every word from the devil has but one message: "Go ahead and do it yourself. You can do it." If Lent has no other message for us than this, we will be blessed: "*You can not do it by yourself.*"

Jesus went out of the wilderness in the power of the Spirit to gather a church. He refused to save the world without his friends. We not only need God; we need one another. We are members of one another. It was frustrating for Jesus to gather a group such as he gathered around himself, to make himself vulnerable to their ignorance and their folly and their misunderstanding and their disloyalty. But in his humility, born in that wilderness victory over himself, he resolved to gather a church so that we might learn how utterly important the church is. A pot luck supper does not sound like much to me; sometimes it is not much. A house church, a study group, a prayer meeting, a vestry conference, public worship on Sunday morning and the coffee hour afterward— what does it all mean if not this: that it is all in accordance with the pattern of Christ. The Christian life is a life which is lived by faith in God and also in friendship, in community with others.

After Jesus had won victory over himself, he was ministered to by angels; and, in the power of that experience, he gathered his church around him.

SUFFERING

The second focus of Lent is suffering. Jesus won a victory over self in the wilderness at the beginning, and that is why at the end he was able to win a victory through suffering on the cross. In the

Temple the elders admired a young boy's brilliance (Luke 2:46-47); but admiration is not salvation. We can admire Jesus as they did. We can write all the creeds about him we want to. We can build churches in which he is always being complimented. We can say all manner of adulatory things about him, but adulation is not salvation. By study, we may attain to brilliance. We may memorize the entire Bible; some have. By diligence, we may achieve success. But *it is only through suffering that we come to greatness* in the spiritual life. In the Temple they said, "Well done"; the old grey beards said, "Good for you. Smart boy!" But at the foot of the cross a grizzled Roman soldier, sunk in sin and lost in ignorance, looked up and saw in the instant the glory of Jesus *because of the way he suffered.* "Truly this was the Son of God" (Matthew 27:54). Consider chapter five in the Epistle to the Hebrews: "In the days of his flesh, Jesus offered up prayers and supplications, with loud cries and tears, to him who was able to save him from death, and he was heard for his godly fear. Although he was a Son, he learned obedience through what he suffered; and being made perfect he became the source of eternal salvation to all who obey him, being designated by God a great high priest" (Hebrews 5:7–9 RSV). And then the writer says something that hits home: "About this we have much to say which is hard to explain since you have become dull of hearing. For though by this time you ought to be teachers, you need some one to teach you again the first principles of God's word" (5:11–12 RSV).

He learned by what he suffered. What did he learn? He learned that until you win a victory over yourself, you cannot help anyone else. He learned that sin is persistent. Unlike the mailman, the devil does not ring just twice. He comes again and again. Time and time again Jesus was tempted. Our lesson tells us that in the wilderness he was with the wild beasts for forty days. He learned that a man can survive that experience if he stays faithful to God through it. There are times when we are surrounded by wild beasts, when we discover that life is far more difficult than ever we thought it would be. There is danger on the right hand and on the left; and, if we relied on our own strength, the wild beasts would take us in a minute. Jesus learned that with God you can get through that experience. You can survive it, not by holding on tight and not by summoning your great might, but by holding on to God. "Did we in our own strength confide / Our striving would be losing."[7] Jesus learned that help comes to those who, *in suffering*, keep the faith. The angels came and ministered to him. He learned that if you want to live *for* others, you must learn to live *with* others; and so he gathered a church.

Jesus is not a tragic hero who shows us how to overcome our tragic flaw. He is a loving friend who shares with us the life of God and invites us into it. Lent is the season wherein we may go below the shallow season of our lives into the somber and yet glorious depths where flows the everlasting stream. In Lent we contemplate the grand design of God for human life—its possibilities, its peace, its glorious purpose; and this vision challenges the weak and foolish way we have been living. The conquest of self, the humble love which submits its outcome to a church, the triumphant victory through suffering that calls from the worst the best—these are the magnificent themes of Lent—I pray that your Lent may bring you to the most joyful and most refreshing Easter that you have ever had. Let us pray for one another, that together we may learn the way that leads to life eternal through the saving grace of Jesus Christ our Lord. *Amen.*

Our Questions and God's

Pontius Pilate asked Jesus Christ, "What have you done? Are you a king? Are you the King of the Jews? What is the truth?"

Text: John 18:33–37

No doubt my memory plays me tricks, but I seem to recall that my first experience with English literature was: "Pat-a-cake, pat-a-cake, baker's man, / Bake me a cake as fast as you can."[8] That deathless poem is, doubtless, a good introduction for any child to the twentieth century where *everything* must be done as fast as we can. My second major work of English literature was:

> "Pussy-cat, pussy-cat,
> Where have you been?"
> "I've been to London
> to look at the queen."
>
> "Pussy-cat, pussy-cat,
> What did you there?"
> "I frightened a little mouse
> under her chair."[9]

And that, too, is instructive for modern children; for, if frantic exertion is one mark of the twentieth century, meaningless endeavor is another.

Sermon preached at St. Paul's Episcopal Church, Akron, Ohio, on the Last Sunday after Pentecost, 24 November 1985. George Ross Papers, The University of Akron Archives.

T. S. Eliot said of a certain unsuccessful painter that he had the experience, but missed the meaning. So it was for the feline visitor to the Court of St. James, and so it is for countless men and women in the world today.

One day Napoleon gathered a demoralized and mutinous army under the shadow of the great pyramids. *"Mes soldats,"* he cried, "thirty centuries look down upon you." For a surly moment they were all silent as they digested the meaning of that. Then, with one voice and as a single man, they rose in thunderous cheers. It is a magnificent thing when anyone can rouse the human heart to the glory of the hour; and few, too few, have had such an experience.

Far, far more than thirty centuries looked down on that secluded room in the castle where Pontius Pilate and Jesus Christ stood face to face in momentous encounter before the Crucifixion. It was one of those tidal moments in the history of the world, as Shakespeare said, "which taken at the flood" might lead a man to glory.[10] Pilate, the insignificant, the obscure, frightened, timid, worried bureaucrat might, in that moment, have become Pilate, the magnificent. But now all time looks down upon him with regret—merely one among the numberless who have had the experience, but missed the meaning.

The supreme tragedy for anyone is not ill health or failed ambition or personal collapse under the crucifying cruelties of this world. The supreme tragedy for anyone, when the angel of the evening rings the curfew bell, is to have had the experience but missed the meaning.

Pontius Pilate typifies a frequent error in religion. He supposed that the religious enterprise consists in *asking* questions, whereas it consists almost entirely in *answering* them. "Who is God?" we ask. "Where is He?" "Are you a king?" "What have you done?" "What is the truth?" On and on to endless volumes the endless questions run. But true religion is born, not when man's question is answered, but when at last God's question is heard. "Adam, where art thou?" (Genesis 3:10), "Elijah, why are you here?" (1 Kings 19:9), "Isaiah, whom shall I send and who will go for me?" (Isaiah 6:8), "James and John, my brothers, what do you want me to do for you?" (Mark 10:36), "Bartimaeus, do you really want to see?" (Mark 10:51), "Peter, do you love me?" (John 20:21). Saul, breathing threats, came to Damascus; and suddenly there was a light from heaven and a voice asked, "Saul, Saul, why do you persecute me?" (Acts 9:4).

When such questions trouble one's mind and shape one's soul and break one's heart, a man or woman moves personally onto the great stage of biblical religion; and they will never be the same again.

Jesus and Pilate met in a castle chamber long ago, but always and everywhere we are face to face with Jesus Christ. He is the unavoidable One. An old rabbinic story tells how a student was accosted one day by an unbelieving fruit vendor. Holding out the most beautiful apple in the barrel, the fruit vendor said, "Young man, I will give you this apple if you will show me where God is." The young man stopped and gazed at the beautiful apple and thought for a moment and answered, "I will give you two apples, I will give you ten, if you will show me where God is not."

So it is always and everywhere, under all circumstances, you and I are face to face with God. And yet there are certain moments in life when the experience of encounter is especially intense, and one of those moments is the holiday season which we now enter—Thanksgiving, Advent, Christmas.

Tonight at eight o'clock the Choral Society of this church will begin the holiday season with the music of Johann Sebastian Bach. As I sat in my study yesterday afternoon pondering this sermon, the music of the master came floating down the corridor like a voice from God. I never listen to the music of Bach without the profound conviction that here indeed was a man for whom the experience of living and the meaning of life were wonderfully combined in love for God. To hear his music is to hear the Spirit of the living God speaking through the spirit of a lively man. "Bake me a cake / As fast as you can." No doubt we will hear that, and some of us will hear it once or twice too often in the holidays that are coming. But God forbid that we should fail to hear as well the "Magnificat" of Bach and the voice of God.

In the mail in a few days you will be receiving from me a letter and in it I will speak to you about the poor and the suffering among us here in Akron and about their tragic needs. I know that it will be possible to read the letter and to question it and to wash your hands. Some will. Or it is possible to listen to the question which this letter brings: seeing that God has wonderfully blessed us and that the poor suffer as they do, what exactly for Christ's sake are we going to do about it?

A story came out of Rumania years ago—about a village church that planned to witness to the poor. The poor were staying away from the church for some reason. And so Bibles were bought. Tracts were written and printed. The preacher prepared an inspiring sermon for an evangelistic rally. Conspicuously absent that day was one of the farmers of the area. As everyone was musing darkly over his absence and his lack of Christian fervor, one of the farmer's sons arrived at the church. He began unloading sacks of wheat from his wagon. These he set at the church door and said, "*This* is my father's witness."

It is not very hard to ask religious questions. Pilate, in the space of just a few moments, asked Jesus four questions; but Jesus asks us only one though we live with him for a lifetime: "*Do you love me?*" We answer tonight with the music of Bach and this morning with the beauty of holiness in the service of worship. Nevertheless, he asks the question again" "*Do you love me?*" And we answer, "Yea, Lord, you know we love you." He replies, not only to all of us as a church, but to each one of us privately and personally: "Do you really love me? Feed my lambs; feed my sheep."

"What did you there?" "I baked some cakes as fast as I could." "I frightened some little mice under some chairs." Such, alas, will be the full report upon their domestic lives and public behavior, which some will give when the evening angel asks.

To have the experience of living, but to miss the meaning of life is the only final tragedy here below. But when faith in God combines with love for one another through the influence of Jesus Christ, all our questions about God are mysteriously answered, not because he has answered *us,* but because we have answered *him.*

"Do you love me? Feed my lambs."

LET US PRAY:

Lord God, may our holidays be blessed because blessed by Thee. Open Thou our hearts and our lips to give Thee praise, in the beauty of holiness in the worship of the Church with our friends and families; and because this would please Thee most, open also our hands in generous compassion towards those for whom this holiday brings pain and suffering. This grace we ask in the name of the One who came to us in poverty that we might always find him and love him among the poor, Jesus Christ our Lord. *Amen.*

The Human Face of Jesus
(Jesus Heals the Centurion's Servant)

A certain centurion had a slave whom he loved, and this slave was at the point of death. When the centurion heard of the works which Jesus did, he sent his servants to Jesus and begged Christ to come and help. As Jesus was approaching the soldier's house, messengers came from the centurion saying, "Lord, you need not come all the way. Speak the word only and our servant will be healed." When he heard this, Jesus marveled and said, "I have not found faith like this, no, not in all Israel."

Text: Luke 7:1–9

G. K. Chesterton, in a book about Charles Dickens, observed that good biographers tell us not so much what a man owned as what he admired.[11] Tell me what you admire, and I can tell you fairy accurately who you really are. We see the tragic side of that daily. J. R. R. Tolkien's fantasy, *The Lord of the Rings*, tells about the nine great kings, the Ringwraithes, who possess the rings of

Sermon preached at St. Paul's Episcopal Church, Akron, Ohio, on the Second Sunday of Pentecost, 1 June 1986. George Ross Papers, The University of Akron Archives.

power. Over the years the Ringwraithes are gradually devoured by the powers they possess until finally they lose material substance altogether and must borrow the physical bodies of other beings in order to move around.[12] I read recently of a Bulgarian chess player whose mania for the game literally cost him his life. He became so obsessed with chess that he gave up all other interests, became a recluse and finally starved to death. When the police came, they found him slumped over the chess board, a victim of the powers he possessed. That is an extreme case, but it is also a parable. We have all known people whose artistic talent or business interests or athletic prowess ruined their families and destroyed their own spiritual, mental and physical health. As the insane arms race escalates, we are fearfully aware that the powers we possess may be the powers that devour us. So the general rule holds: what we admire may ennoble us, but it also may destroy us.

In the New Testament we are given tantalizingly little information about the personality of Jesus Christ. We cling to every scrap and fragment of it. Is not it odd that we know more about the domestic life of Augustus Caesar than we know about Jesus of Nazareth? Recently a book was published in Germany with the title *The Human Face of Jesus,* the latest contribution to the quest for the historical Jesus, which has preoccupied New Testament scholars for nearly a century.[13] Albert Schweitzer, an earlier participant in the debate, said that Jesus "comes to us as one unknown, without a name, as of old by the lakeside [in Galilee]."[14] Each generation must discover for itself, in the struggles of its faith, who Jesus is. Perhaps. But I believe and submit, without entering here into the complexities of the debate, that we may know much about Jesus as a man. We may know much, provided we ask the right questions of the New Testament. One of the right questions, surely is this: Whom did Christ admire; whom did he praise? If we know that, perhaps we may meet again the vibrant personality behind the ancient books.

The Gospel lesson for today from Luke gives us a precious clue. On his way to heal a slave, Jesus stopped in mid stride to marvel at, to admire an officer and a gentleman of the Roman Empire. As

I survey the life of the Lord, I am increasingly struck by the simi-
larity of the various people whom he admired. He admired this
Roman soldier who loved a dying slave, and He admired a Samaritan business man who saw a naked victim on the road and
stopped to help (Luke 10:33–37). He admired an elderly and much
abused father who ran to welcome home a wayward son (Luke
15:11–32). He admired a depressed, discouraged sinner in the
Temple who stood afar off by himself and prayed (Luke 18:13). He
admired a desperate woman in a crowded street who dared to
reach out to touch the hem of his garment (Matthew 9:20). He
loved a thief who even at the hour of death was kind to a fellow
prisoner (Luke 23:41–42). He loved Zacchaeus, who climbed a tree
and made a fool of himself for Christ, so desperate was his need
for God (Luke 19:1–10).

These are some of the people Jesus Christ admired. Put their
names on one side of the roster; then list on the other side the people whom Jesus Christ did not admire. He did not admire the professional, who told him to heal the sick only during office hours
(Luke 6:6–11). He did not admire the all-American boy who loved
fairness more than mercy and would not come in to celebrate a
degenerate's resurrection from the dead (Luke 15:28). He did not
admire the lawyers who know what was legally right, but not
what was morally good (Luke 11:45–52). He did not admire the
rich investor whose narcissistic selfishness made him as spiritually poor as he was materially affluent (Luke 12:13–21). He did not
admire the pious, church-bound clergy who walked by on the other side of secular human need (Luke 10:31). He did not admire the
narrow-minded church folk who like to congregate on the Sabbath, but whose week-day gossip piled derision on the social out-
cast and the morally suspect (Luke 20:45–47).

Always our character is measured by the things that we admire,
balanced by the things that we deplore. I feel very close to the human nature of Christ this morning as I listen to him praising a
Gentile soldier who was so very unlike himself. The human face
of Jesus is that of a village carpenter and a poor man, a Jew, an itin-
erant preacher without benefit of ordination, a marked man head-

ed for an ignominious death. The centurion was a wealthy man, a Roman commander, an aristocrat of the Empire, a successful man of the world. How different they were! We imagine them standing there in Palestine so long ago, each one a mysterious stranger to the other, and yet looking at one another with profound esteem and admiration. I feel close to the human nature of Jesus when I think of it, and I am deeply moved. I feel the passionate depth of his love and the Catholic breadth of his mind, unhindered by prejudice of any kind, unguardedly open to the humanity of other people, spiritually unconstricted by the little theology of the little church, compassionate toward human beings in their suffering, wherever and however he found them. The soldier was an alien in the land, but so in many ways was Jesus. Perhaps that shared experience drew them together. They both served kings beyond the immediate situation in which they found themselves.

Jesus admired the soldier because the man had somehow found grace to transcend limits which otherwise would have confined and narrowed him. He had crossed the ancient class barrier by loving a slave. He had crossed the age-old religious and racial barriers by building a synagogue for people of a faith other than his own. Throwing away all worldly sophistication and prudence, he had humbly turned for help to Jesus Christ in the hour of need. Unconverted, unbaptized, unconfirmed, his manner of life was morally ambiguous at best; but Jesus saw in this man something wonderfully admirable. He saw compassion joined with faith in profound humility. "That," said Christ, "is the kind of personhood I admire." The Centurion had wealth, station, prestige, all the things a successful, middle class man in Galilee, or in Akron, is supposed to have. But he laid it all aside for the love of a suffering slave and humbly turned to God in prayer. When Jesus saw that, he said, "Here is a person after my own heart. I walk this way too."

I feel very close to the human nature of Christ when I stand beside him on Sunday mornings to hear week after week how he admires the benevolent centurion, the forgiving father, the praying publican, the compassionate Samaritan, the penitent thief. When

I listen attentively to the stories of the people whom Christ admired, I feel his living personality very near to me; and as I do, I feel myself growing in the Spirit. We thank God that we may love Jesus, not only as our Divine Lord and Savior, but also as our human friend who now and then bids us pause to admire things—to admire the lilies of the field, how they grow; and the children, how they play; and the people, how they hunger and thirst; and the company of the suffering faithful, how brave they are; and God's many-splendored world beneath the many-splendored stars, how wonderful, how admirable it is.

And as we come to admire with Christ what he admires, we feel something strange but splendid happening inside us. We feel ourselves sometimes growing larger than ourselves—or could it be that in such moments with him we find ourselves as beautiful, as wise, as faithful, as loving as we really are?

LET US PRAY:

Heavenly Father, we thank you for all your goodness and mercy upon us from the beginning of our lives until this moment; give us the eyes of the Spirit to see your creative hand behind all created things, your loving purpose in all our sorrows, and your image in every human soul. Grant that by what we learn to admire with Christ we may more and more become admirable ourselves. To God, to Christ and to the Holy Spirit be all honor, praise and glory, now and ever. *Amen.*

CHAPTER TWO

WOUNDED SIDE

ꙅⱯꙅ

Broken Relationships

I N THE CARTOON "MARVIN," Marvin's mother looks down at little Marvin who has just taken his hammer and broken his toys into a thousand pieces.

"Why must you always break your toys, Marvin?"

Thinking to himself, Marvin smiles, "I'm just practicing for when I grow up. I'm going to be a broker."

Most of us don't want to spend life being "a broker." We want to be builders, fixer-uppers, healers. But we all spend a good portion of our lives being "brokers." It is *homo duplex,* the battle between good and evil. Evil is the ultimate breaker of the world.

Being "brokers" was the theme of many a George Ross sermon. It was also the thrust of one of the most unusual sermons in all of history. It takes place near the middle of the Herman Melville epic *Moby-Dick.* The preacher is the eldest member of the crew of that Nantucket whaling vessel, the *Pequod.* The congregation is comprised, Melville says, of thousands and thousands of sharks, swarming around the mammoth carcass of the first whale these fisherman have killed on their voyage.

The context of the sermon is a kind of victory meal by the harpooner who killed the whale, a man called Stubb: whale steak cooked to his preference by that senior member of the crew who is to become the preacher. Stubb is annoyed by the slapping of the sharks' tails against the hull of the *Pequod,* as well as by the incessant sounds of the tearing, ripping, and devouring of whale flesh by this congregation of sharks. So he orders the old man to preach to them or urge them to do their sharkish business with more civility and dignity.

The old cook, dropping a lantern "low over the sea, so as to get a good view of his congregation," solemnly flourishes his cooking tongs and begins to preach.

"Fellow critters, I'se been ordered here to say dat you must stop dat dam noise."

"Cook," Stubb interrupts, "you mustn't swear that way when you're preaching. That's no way to convert sinners."

So the old man starts again, this time addressing the sharks as "Belubed, fellow-critters." Soon enough, slipping up once more on his preaching style, and needing another reminder from Stubb to "talk to 'em gentlemanly," he tries it a third time. He tells the sharks that he cannot blame them for their voraciousness. That is nature, he says, and it cannot be helped. But to govern that wicked nature, he goes on, that is the point of life. You are sharks certain, he says, but if you govern the shark in you, then you will be angels. For all an angel is, is nothing more than a shark well governed.

"Well done, old Fleece!" cries Stubb. "That's Christianity."

In a characteristic turn of theological reflection, Melville observes that if you were to turn the whole affair upside down, putting the sharks aboard the ship and the whalers in the water, "it would still be pretty much the same thing, that is to say, a shocking, sharkish business enough for all parties."[1]

We are all sundered and tossed, divided between that which is sharkish in us and that which is "angelish." This tension between the flesh-tearing, eye-tearing side of our lives, and the winged side of hope and trust in God's deliverance, bisects every one of us.

To talk about "sides," even one's "side" of things, is to raise the issue of relatedness.[2] Ever since God split Adam's side and created male and female, it has been our "sides" and "sidedness" that has cut us off from one another, from nature, and from God. The French psychoanalyst Jacques Lacan said that the human subject is less an entity with an identity than a being created in the fissure of a fundamental split. Every human being is the history of fusion and fission, of the fissures created by the civil wars of good and evil. Indeed, evil is, according to one contemporary theologian, nothing other than "the effect upon the network of relationships of an individual or systemic denial of interrelatedness itself."[3]

In first century Palestine, there was a ceremony to ritualize the breaking of relations and relationships called the *kezazah*, which literally means "a cutting off." The *kezazah* ceremony is described in the Midrash on the book of *Ruth*. It tells of a Jew who sold some land to an outsider. Whereupon the Jew's relatives would bring huge barrels full of nuts and parched corn and then would proceed to break them open in front of the children. During the breaking of the nuts, the children chanted "So-and-so is cut off from his inheritance." If by some means the land was returned to the family, the children would chant "So-and-so has returned to his inheritance." In similar fashion, if a Jewish man married a woman who did not fit into the family, his relatives would cart barrels full of parched corn and nuts and break them open in the presence of children, and the children would gather them and proclaim, "So-and-so is lost to his family." If the marriage were dissolved by some means, they used to say, "So-and-so has returned to his family."[4]

By custom, when a family member was disinherited, or a relationship was shattered, the member was publicly "cut off." In another form of the *kezazah* ritual, jars rather than barrels were smashed. A full jar would be broken in the streets before the gathered clan, who would then wail and lament the loss. Relationships are broken for a variety of reasons, psychological, financial, even theological. For example, when we misread biblical statements on the death and resurrection of Christ by asking what theory of atonement church members support rather than how they affect the community—its worship, its everyday rituals, its moral vision—we are breaking community with one another.[5]

There is the delightful story about the small town that was having an Easter pageant. The toughest guy in town, the town roustabout and heavy, and the least likely candidate, was selected to play the part of Jesus. Others were chosen to be part of the mob in the drama. As the man playing Jesus was carrying the cross, one man in the mob really got into it. He shouted, "Crucify! Crucify!" He got right up in the face of this man, hollered in his ear, and screamed so loud that some of his spit flew into the cross bearer's face. The man playing the part of Jesus turned to the other man and said, "I will see you after the resurrection."

The first words Jesus spoke to the disciples after his resurrection were "Peace be with you," after which he showed them his hands and side (John 20:19–20). In the words of the familiar Lenten hymn: "Crown him the Lord of love; behold his hands and side, / those wounds, yet visible above in beauty, glorified."[6] Did you ever notice that in Leonardo da Vinci's *Last Supper*, under Judas's elbow, is a spilt salt cellar? Salt is the symbol of friendship and hospitality. Spilt salt means the breaking of relational bonds and the consequent lapsing of protection, from the host and from on high. The wounds of Christ's side call us to repent of our ruptured relationships, be reconciled with one another, and become bearers of Christ's healing gift of peace and reconciliation in the life of the world.

The piercing of the Second Adam's side probably has been more written about than any of the other wounds of the cross.[7] Whereas the two men crucified with Jesus had their legs broken (*crurigragium*), to hasten death before the preparation for the Sabbath that officially began at sunset, the soldiers thrust the point of a "spear" or "lance" (the Greek word *logchē* can be either) into Jesus' side (John 19:31–37). This single incision released a gush of watery body fluids and blood, and the death of Jesus was complete. But the birth of the church had begun. From the open side of the First Adam, male and female were born. From the open side of the Second Adam, the Bride of Christ or "Mother Church" appeared.[8]

"The Holy Lance" has been the name of the spear with which the Roman soldier pierced the side of Christ. For early Christians, the holy lance was a symbol of both human cruelty and divine compassion. The armies of the First Crusade professed to have "discovered" this lance in the Antioch Church of St. Peter. They then rode off under the banner of the holy lance, point forward, and forced their way into Jerusalem where they wreaked such mayhem and destruction that, according to one chronicle, "the crusaders rode in blood to the knees and bridles of their horses."[9]

The holy lance can be either an instrument of warfare and death, or an instrument of medicine and healing. A contemporary artist tells of a vision that instructed him in the two-edged power of the lance—it sears as it heals:

Some years ago I dreamt that I was in jail, observing an execution. The prisoner was kneeling, baring his neck to the sword. Just before the sword touched the neck, it slowed and turned sideways and touched the shoulder of the prisoner gently with its flat side. What had begun as an execution turned into a ceremony of knighting, marking not the end, but an initiation into a new life. The sword, the very thing that can destroy us, became a source of learning and blessing.[10]

The question is: What do we do with the holy lance when we find it, or it finds us? Does the sword become a mechanism for execution or knighthood?

Paul's confession of a "thorn in the flesh" was more than just a metaphor. For him that "thorn in the flesh" was a sword in the side that became a holy lance:

Therefore, to keep me from being too elated a thorn was given me in the flesh, a messenger of Satan to torment me, to keep me from being too elated. Three times I appealed to the Lord about this, that it would leave me, but he said to me, "My grace is sufficient for you, for power is made perfect in weakness." So, I will boast all the more gladly of my weaknesses, so that the power of Christ may dwell in me. (2 Corinthians 12: 7–9 NRSV)

The Greek word for "thorn" is not prickly splinter, but spike or stake, which Paul says was driven straight through his flesh to impale him. This "thorn" in Paul's side was quite likely a person—a critical, vindictive, crippling, satanic spirit in his life that tore at him and tore him apart.

But this thorn in the flesh, this "broker," provided the Apostle Paul with the grain against which to carve out some of the greatest literature in the Bible. The splinters in George Ross's side also marked the grains against which he carved out some of his greatest sermons. Or to put it another way, thanks to the gift of the pearl-producing grit in the oyster, Ross was able to live some of his finest moments.

George Ross took up the "holy lance" as an instrument of healing. Ross was able to take his own thorny pain and crippling loneliness and use it as a vehicle of love and healing for those afflicted with similar pains. The principal force of healing in a suffering world, Ross proclaimed, is love. While trusting in the healing force of love, he was nevertheless as battered by life, torn asunder, and ripped by wounded sides as anyone.

In a W. H. Auden poem, there is a line about the failed caresses from which thought is born. Ross's own life, both physical and mental, was full of "failed caresses" from which much creativity and ministry was born.

There was the "failed caress" of his marriage to Joan Marie Ruda, a coruscatingly beautiful, dark-eyed, black-haired Italian whom he courted while at St. Stephens (Columbus). An intellectually gifted, giving, and vibrant young woman, Joan obtained a degree in nursing from Temple University and met George while doing graduate work in psychiatric nursing at Ohio State University. Stories still circulate of George coming home from their capers with lipstick-smeared face and shirt—to the amusement and applause of everyone. They were married in June of 1961 by the legendary Bishop of Southern Ohio, Henry Hobson, who had ordained George deacon and priest. Antoine de Saint-Exupéry once wrote that "there is no pain nor passion that does not radiate to the ends of the earth." If he is right, then the passion of the newly-weds was felt far beyond Florida, where they honeymooned.

But the passion cooled, and the pain radiated just as far. Ross knew very quickly what it meant to be taken up with the wrong woman, the reality behind Andy Warhol's cruel quip that "everyone ends up kissing the wrong person goodnight." No marriage today has a better than even chance of going the distance. No matter how good the marriage, there is the daily grind, the negotiations of living with another human being. The ties that bind unwind. This is not to mention the peculiar psychological pressures that issued from the mix of their hormones and chromosomes and from George's demanding personality and choice of profession, both of which no doubt exacerbated his wife's problems.

George could do nothing ordinary. He could not even have an ordinary bad marriage. Even in the best marriage, one must learn to live alone. But George and Joan lived so alone that each became a loner, unavailable and unreachable to the other. For whatever reasons, neither became an emotional partner for the other, and the marriage deteriorated into a raw wound full of anger and misunderstandings. By the time George arrived at St. Paul's in the early seventies, Joan wanted little to do with the church and even less to do with George. They were divorced in November of 1983. Shortly thereafter, Joan returned to the church of her birth, Roman Catholicism.

Marriage counselors Jack and Carole Mayhall tell about a sign on a church bulletin board that reads, "God can mend a broken heart, if you will give him all the pieces." They go on to write: "God can also mend a broken marriage . . . if you will give Him all the pieces."[11] George Ross preached that divorce is neither good nor godly. There is no relationship so shattered and broken that God can't glue it back together again. But Ross also preached that certain bone-crusher marriages are better buried than borne; that sometimes death, which like divorce is neither good nor godly, is the final healing act.

The Apostle Paul wrote, "If it is possible, as far as it depends on you, live at peace with everyone" (Romans 12:18 NIV). The realism in the apostle's words is striking: sometimes we can't be reconciled to everyone. This broaches a second "failed caress"—Ross's network of friends and colleagues.

The story is told of a college student who discovered that he needed a Bible for a course in religion, so he wrote home asking that his Bible be sent to him. His father wrapped it carefully and took it to the post office. The clerk took the package and shook it. "Anything in here that can be broken?" he asked. "Only the Ten Commandments," the father replied.

How easily the Ten Commandments can be broken. Why? Because all of them have to do with relationships, and relationships are fragile. They are easily damaged, bruised, and broken by one careless word, one stray act, one forgotten promise. How many relationships can survive the break of health, the wreck of reputation, the remove of riches, the stain of scandal? As precarious as relationships are, as many times as friends have clipped our wings, we also know that, in the words of Luciano De Crescenzo, "We are angels / who have but a single wing / and we can only fly / if we cling to one another."[12]

But how hard it was for George Ross to embrace another or to receive the gift of unconditional love. Although George Ross was a priest who spent his life listening to everyone else's troubles, he could not share his own. He was always more or less of a secret to everyone, even to his best friend Joseph Goetz, who became a Roman Catholic priest, theologian, author, and professor.

George and Joe went to the same high school together (Dayton-Oakwood), attended the same college together (Ohio Wesleyan), and pursued the same calling. Both had brilliant minds and shared interests in literature, the arts, and rhetoric. Both were Anglophiles. Joe received a Ph.D. from Oxford, and George became a self-appointed tour guide of English cathedrals, English gardens, and English country houses for generations of parishioners. Both were philologists in the original meaning of that word—"lovers of words." What survives of their correspondence—monuments of competitive insights and documents of affection—is filled with all the literary high jinks, prankish confections, and theological brio one would expect from the exuberant obstinacy of best buddies.

Yet even with this best friend, there were problems with intimacy. In almost forty years of friendship, there was never a frantic call for advice, a midnight cry for help, a luncheon confession about homegrown ghosts, a gabbing about hardships endured,

companionships shared, a back-to-the-wall, hand-on-heart declaration of emotion, a soulfelt letter that lays raw nerves as well as
rationalizations before a trusted confidante. If "bodies are united
by pleasure; but souls are united by pain," as Miguel de Unamuno
is often quoted as saying,[13] what prevented these two from becoming true soulmates were the unintegrated, unblended Picasso-like
colorings of life.

When Abraham Cowley, the seventeenth-century poet and essayist, got ready to retire, he gave this wish: "May I a small
House, and a large Garden have! / And a few Friends, and many
Books; both true."[14] George Ross's life was largely fallow and fea-
tureless of intimate friends. Books there were aplenty. Animal
companions, moreover, were abundant. Ross hated zoos, viewing
them not as contemporary arks but as cruel prisons. The place for
animals was in the wild or by one's side. Ross lavished affection
and attention on family pets. Indeed, in the obituary that ran in
the newspaper, George's pet dog Betsy and pet cat Grace, who
followed him everywhere after his daughter Mary found them in
a fraternity mailbox, were listed as surviving members of the family.

Because they were. George died at the time he normally took a
nap: on Sunday afternoon, at 3 p.m., with his cat at his side and
his dog under the bed. Grace refused to come out from under the
bed for one week—refused to eat, drink, or perform any other natural function. It was appropriate, but also weirdly sentimental,
that pictures of Betsy and Grace appeared in the newspaper the
day after the obituary.

The third "failed caress" was George's relationship with his
peers, especially the Episcopal diocese in which he resided. When
Ross first came to St. Paul's in 1973, he threw himself into the life
of the diocese. He was a deputy to the General Convention in
1974. He served on the Ecclesiastical Court (more about this later)
and became heavily involved in the financial affairs of the diocese.
He agreed to function as "Examining Chaplain," one of the diocesan academic examiners for people wanting to be ordained. He accepted the appointment of Bishop Burt as chair of the diocesan

Planning Commission, and he was a member of the department of Christian Social Relations. He was respected by his peers as a powerful preacher and a devoted pastor.

But then something happened to change his attitude toward the diocese. Not that he ever became totally estranged from it. St. Paul's parish continued to be one of its chief financial supporters. But Ross found in the diocese too much internal squabbling and political infighting for his taste. Just as the Bible portrays the disciples as murmuring among themselves when Jesus set off for Jerusalem, so Ross believed that when we look only at each other, we lose sight of Christ and get left behind. Christ goes on, while we stay and murmur.

The first sign something was awry was when Ross began rolling his eyes whenever someone mentioned the diocese, muttering under his breath asides about brain-dead bureaucrats in their closed worlds with shifting office alliances. One thing then led to another, or more precisely, to many others, as Ross began writing "shocked and appalled" letters to the bishop, some as long as three single-spaced pages, outlining what he felt was wrong with the administration of the Diocese of Ohio. Ross may have felt betrayed because nobody from the diocese was allowed to attend the seminary he was instrumental in starting. Or he may have resented the fact that, as he put it in a letter to the executive assistant to the bishop, "Over the last three decades I have presented 25 persons for ordination to the sacred ministry. The only ones rejected have been those nominated in this diocese."[15] Whatever its cause, his skepticism about the diocesan staff eventually became mere, even pure crossness. The barbed relationships with many of his peers were largely of his own making. He isolated himself from these colleagues by his unctuous, cynical mannerisms.

Yet there was no one in the diocese who generated more excitement or interest about ministry than Ross. The ultimate success symbol of ministry is not the size of the congregation or the size of the salary. It is, rather, the number of heads one has turned toward ministry. So many people went into ministry under Ross's influence and inspiration that the diocese dubbed his church the

"St. Paul's factory." In an ecclesiastical tradition that had little use for "recruiting" people into the faith, much less into ministry, Ross tapped people on the shoulder, pointed out their gifts for ministry, and shepherded them through the ordination process. Nothing made Ross more angry than when a bishop refused to support one of his protégés.

Ross had a far-flung reputation for hiring young clergy for a couple of years, mentoring them while they used the parish as their training ground, and then sending them off on their own. In his last sermon, he mentioned three things he was particularly proud of during his tenure as rector. One of the three was the number of people sent into the priesthood while he was at St. Paul's.[16] Yet as supportive as Ross could be toward those going into ministry, he also could be competitive, authoritarian, and iron-fisted toward those working with him, setting free associates to work within their sphere of assignment but reserving the right to make every decision worth making.

Orson Welles had a maxim: "When you are down and out something always turns up—and it is usually the noses of your friends."[17] It need not be that way, but it was for George Ross. When the ground started to shake and a chasm opened under his feet, he stood there alone, unable to ask for or receive the help that was available all around him.

If any denomination is at the forefront of ministry in the midst of the AIDS plague, it is the Episcopalians. Already well known for their work with HIV positive people and AIDS patients, the Ohio Diocese in 1989 adopted a position statement that prohibited discrimination on the basis of AIDS against anyone seeking employment; guaranteed full insurance coverage for AIDS-related illnesses; assured all employees of complete confidentiality; and stated unequivocally that no one can be dismissed for having the AIDS affliction. Although a member of the diocese having one of the most enlightened policies on priests with AIDS, Ross could not claim the gifts that were there and receive the care and support the diocese at least theoretically was prepared to extend toward him. One cannot say for sure, of course, but if Ross had been open and forthcoming about his illness with the congregation, many believe St. Paul's would have risen to the occasion, and Ross would have found himself surrounded by overwhelming support. Others believe just the opposite, and point to the way he was treated as proof of their position.

Ross's discomfort around displays of human affection, even at ritual moments of life, was acute. This story he enjoyed telling about an associate tells something about himself:

For many years Ralph Clewell directed our choirs and our music department and was one of the handful of men who shaped the Western Reserve Academy into the fine institution it is today. On his parish membership card, Dr. Walter Tunks had written this: "Do not send Ralph Clewell birthday cards and do not wish him happy birthday; he does not like it." When Mr. Clewell retired from his work here, there was not a little pomp and circumstance, as some of you may remember. On that occasion, one of the choristers greeted him at the door and said: "Mr. Clewell, we are surely going to miss you!" to which Mr. Clewell, with his usual sardonic tone replied, "*Miss* me? Young man, I didn't even know that you had been *shooting* at me!"[18]

If anyone ever exemplified the principle that the secret to a person's life hangs in the closet, and kept the location of the keys secret, it was George Ross. Yet if anyone ever preached that, in the words of the sixteenth-century Carmelite reformer John of the Cross, "God has so ordained things that we grow in faith only through the frail instrumentality of one another," it was also Ross. With no frosty reserve and with a tremendous capacity to suffer for others, Ross provided in-the-flesh ministry to those who felt lonely, in need, and without support.

The greatest suffering in the world at any given moment is most likely not the suffering of those who are diseased and dying, but the everyday suffering of ordinary, healthy, "normal" people.[19] What does one do when someone is suffering or in pain? Really very little other than to be present; to be there in the midst of another's suffering is enough, even if one can do or say nothing else. Ross believed that the sheer presence of a friend who elects to share another's load of pain was a ministry in and of itself. Feeling the pain of loneliness in others, Ross instituted at St. Paul's a pioneering program called "Tele-Care," in which singles and others living alone were called every day by someone in the congregation to see if they were all right and to make sure someone was there in case they needed to talk.

Like Coleridge's ancient mariner, surrounded by water but dying of thirst, Ross was encompassed by admirers yet engulfed with loneliness. His was not the loneliness of isolation but the loneliness of closeness—close enough to vibrant relationships to see what might be if only he could reach out beyond that which imprisoned him inside himself. It may have been that same imprisonment that caused George's father to take his own life in 1977 after a losing battle with Hodgkin's disease and a refusal to end his life plugged into a hospital wall. This tragedy haunted George after he learned of his own disease, even causing him to joke in a macabre way with his daughter Mary on their last trip together about hiring a "hit-bear" while climbing the mountains in Montana, Idaho, and Wyoming.

Ross's reticence about taking emotional risks is reminiscent of a wealthy entrepreneur who had never used the little red Radio Flyer wagon he was given as a boy. A few years ago, this same wagon was fought over by various Pennsylvania museums because it was in such pristine shape. The owner tells with pride how his childhood friends hauled things in their wagons, climbed in and out, and carried friends around, while he kept his shiny and clean. He never let anyone in his wagon or used it himself, because he didn't want it to get scratched or broken. He kept his wagon in a closet and saved it for eighty years. Now he has a museum piece.

But at what cost? The Australian poet Antonio Porchia has written that "every toy has the right to break."[20] The scratch marks and broken parts are signs that the toy has been loved and used, valued and appreciated. The baker in the MGM movie *Moonstruck* saw this clearly: "Love don't make things nice, it ruins everything, it breaks your heart, it makes things a mess."

Every heart has the right to break, too, and for the same reasons. The only hearts that never break are those that beat behind closed doors. Again, to quote Porchia, "To wound the heart is to create it."[21]

It was almost as if preaching a sermon with arms outstretched was the only way Ross could embrace others and risk the pain that came from the making, breaking, and re-making of relationships. With each sermon, delivered in an intimate, even confessional tone, he created an illusion of closeness to the congregation. Through his masterful use of understatement, Ross drew his listeners into a love relationship that was surpassed in his life only by the love he felt from his daughters.

Could this be why he preached so passionately about the ways in which radical forgiveness unleashes tremendous power—the power to resurrect life and restore relationships? Could this be why Ross loved to quote Frederick Buechner, especially this section from *Sacred Journey.* "You can survive on your own. You can grow strong on your own. You can even prevail on your own. But you cannot become human on your own."[22] Or why Teilhard de Chardin's belief that we are less human beings striving to become spiritual than spiritual beings struggling to become human so resonated in his soul?

Ross's stories about relationship, while not new, are fuller and fresher than can be found almost anywhere else. His stories about the rupturing of relationships caused by death were especially compelling. Ross liked to tell the story of the woman who was living in a nightmare of grief and anger after the death of her husband. For weeks she went daily to the cemetery to put flowers on his grave. In her despair she went to the doctor. She wanted to get a little pill to help her sleep. When she told her physician about taking the flowers to the cemetery, the doctor suggested, "Instead of taking the flowers to the cemetery, why don't you take them to the hospital? I have two patients in the hospital. Their families are gone. They have no friends. Your flowers would do them a world of good. Take them to them. And when you do, ask them how they are doing and give them some word of encouragement. See if there is something you can do for them."

The woman didn't think much of the idea, but she did it. She took the flowers to the hospital, instead of to the cemetery. That was the beginning of her recovery. Within a few months she became one of the most radiant and useful members of her community. I could tell that story a thousand times with a thousand different casts of characters. When we encourage others we drink of the fountains of life itself.[23]

To a world where love means never having to say you're sorry, or very much else, George insisted that love meant loyalty, sacrifice, and trust.

I used to live in Idaho. Once I went to a rodeo with a couple of old cattle ranchers in Pocatello. As we sat in the stands, a beautiful girl walked by. She had bought herself a blouse and embroidered it with every Idaho cattle brand she could lay her hands on. One of the cowboys turned to the other and, in a dry voice that could be heard for about a mile, said, "That critter certainly has changed hands a lot, ain't she?" That is funny—but it's not! That is the way it is with too many of us: we have changed hands so many times that we do not know who we are, where we are or why we are.[24]

Indeed, it seemed as if the deeper the thorns stuck in his side, the more devoted he became to his two daughters. The more withdrawn Ross became, the more he invested himself in them. They became his chief travel companions, and his daughter Mary became the closest thing to a best friend. When Ross disappeared from the parish after collapsing in the pulpit one Easter Sunday, only Mary knew where he had gone. It was she who cared for him when he was dying. Indeed, she may have been the only one who knew he was dying, although even she didn't know *why* he was dying.

Two of this century's most popular literary voices, Maya Angelou and James Michener, testify to the creativity that can come from scarred relationships. In an interview with Bill Moyers, Angelou described her early life in Arkansas:

She said she really had a tough childhood because she was not only black as a child, but she was also ugly. And to be black and ugly in Arkansas was to suffer tremendously. She said she was scorned and segregated by the whites and laughed at by the blacks because she was such a gawky child. She said that even at her mature age now, she still has those scars and lives with those scars, but she said, "At one time I was resentful of those scars, but now, before I write a poem, in order to prime my creative juices, I scrape my pen across those scars to sharpen the point."[25]

Michener tells a similar tale. He has made his mark in the publishing world by producing massive historical novels such as *The Source, Iberia, Hawaii, The Covenant, Texas,* and *Poland.* Ironically, Michener's style has drawn its strength and beauty from characters fleshed out with extensive genealogies and deep cultural roots. Yet he is a man without a birth certificate. Abandoned on a doorstep as an infant, raised as a foster-son in a family headed by the widowed Mabel Michener in Georgetown, Pennsylvania, James has never known his biological parents. While he claims to have come to peace with this vacuum in his own life history, it is easy to see why he finds pleasure inventing extensive lineages for the characters in each new novel.

Despite his generous spirit and kind nature, Michener was despised by one of his adopted-clan kin because of his accomplishments. In a rage of jealousy, mean-spiritedness, and sheer nastiness, some nameless relative—self-signed "a real Michener"—felt impelled to write hate-filled, hurtful notes to James A. whenever his name gained notoriety or newspaper space. Even after James Michener's Pulitzer Prize, this poison-pen writer would charge him with besmirching the good Michener name—which the writer said "You have no right to use"—and denounce him as a fraud. But the words this anonymous hatemonger thrust the most deeply under Michener's skin were "Who in hell do you think you are, trying to be better than you are?"

The final letter Michener received from his unknown "relative" came in 1976 after President Gerald Ford had presented him with the Presidential Medal of Freedom. The acidic note read, "Still using a name that isn't yours. Still a fraud. Still trying to be better than you are."

Michener testifies that the "seven words of that cry are burned into my soul." But he turned the negative power of that accusation into a life-challenge. Acknowledging that his relative "was right in all his accusations," Michener confesses, "I have spent my life trying to be better than I was, and am brother to all who have the same aspirations."[26]

Ross believed that religious traditions as well as persons should try to be better than they are. One way to do this is to get to know those who disagree with you. For this reason, Ross was one of the early leaders of the ecumenical movement and transformed St. Paul's into a center for reconciliation among religious traditions in the Ohio region. On the streets of any present-day city, people have painfully learned to pass by on the other side when encountering human need and abnormality. It hurt Ross deeply that Christians routinely pass by on the other side when they encounter those of a different theological persuasion.

Ross was active in movements to bring Roman Catholics and Episcopalians together, and early in his ministry fretted over whether the decision of the Episcopal Church to admit women to the priesthood, which he later would support enthusiastically, jeopardized these conversations. He was the first president of the Akron Area Association of Churches in 1979. He was founding president of the Akron Area Interfaith Council, which was comprised of one hundred churches, three Jewish congregations, and the Jewish Federation. He also began in the early 1970s a men's brotherhood program between the Episcopal parish and the Reform Jewish congregation in Akron. He worked with Protestants, Catholics, and Jews in organizing a local Akron chapter of Habitat for Humanity.

Tragically, Ross felt completely safe with no one, not even himself. We do not know what kinds of conversations Ross had with himself. But we do know that he loved the ending of *Music for Chameleons*, where Truman Capote holds this dialog with himself:

TC: . . . But I am not a saint yet. I'm an alcoholic. I'm a drug addict. I'm homosexual. I'm a genius. Of course, I could be all four of these dubious things and still be a saint. But I shonuf ain't no saint yet, nawsuh.

TC: Well, Rome wasn't built in a day. Now let's knock it off and try for some shut-eye.

TC: But first let's say a prayer. Let's say our *old* prayer. The one we used to say when we were real little and slept in the same bed with Sook and Queenie, with the quilts piled on top of us because the house was so big and cold.

TC: Our old prayer?? Okay.

TC and TC: Now I lay me down to sleep. I pray the Lord my soul to keep. And if I should die before I wake, I pray the Lord my soul to take. Amen.

TC: Goodnight.

TC: Good night.

TC: I Love You.

TC: I Love You, too.

TC: You'd Better. Because when you get right down to it, all we've got is each other. Alone. To the grave. And that's the tragedy, isn't it?

TC: You forget. We have God, too.

TC: Yes, we have God.

TC: Zzzzzzz

TC: Zzzzzzzzz

TC and TC: Zzzzzzzzzzz[27]

SERMONS

ꙅⱲꙅ

Forgiveness

Meanwhile the sinners were seeking his company, but the Pharisees complained.

Text: Luke 15:1–32

The humorist Robert Benchley once divided the world into two groups: those who divide the world into two groups and those who do not. The division I suggest to you may surprise you. The essential distinction is not between rich and poor, black and white, good and bad, wise and foolish, or friend and enemy. In the 15th chapter of St. Luke's Gospel, Jesus suggests that perhaps there is one distinction in the human race which is valid and that is this: there are those who know about forgiveness and there are those who do not. In this chapter from St. Luke, Jesus tells three short stories. He tells about a shepherd who lost and found a little sheep. He tells about a woman who lost and found a little coin. And then, rising to the climax of his sermon, he tells the story of a little boy who was lost and was found again.

Sermon preached at St. Paul's Episcopal Church, Akron, Ohio, on the Fifteenth Sunday after Pentecost, 11 September 1977. George Ross Papers, The University of Akron Archives.

The three stories are introduced by this text: "*Meanwhile* the sinners were seeking his company but the Pharisees complained." That first word interests me a great deal: "meanwhile." *Meanwhile*, the world was going on its way and business was being carried on. Life was unfolding. *Meanwhile*, as it was all going forward or backwards (as one might view it)—meanwhile two groups of people came to the attention of our Lord Jesus Christ. Now I would not suggest to you, and if you know me at all, you know that I would not suggest to you, that the political or economic affairs of the Roman Empire or of our contemporary society are unimportant or inconsequential or of no interest to the religious person. I would not suggest to you that the affairs of business and commerce, of education and homemaking—or of any other activity of the human hand or heart or spirit—are unimportant. St. Luke would never suggest it. Jesus would never suggest such a thing. St. Luke seems to set it all aside, all the world's frantic business and activity, with the word: "meanwhile." *Meanwhile*, as it all unfolds, there are two groups of people that come to the attention of God, and you are probably in one or the other. The two groups are these: the sinners and the Pharisees.

The theme of St. Luke's 15th chapter, clearly, is the theme of forgiveness, and that is the theme of the sermon this morning. The first thing I want to say about forgiveness you already know, and that is that it is sometimes very hard to find. If you read *Sports Illustrated*, you may have been amused, as I was, by the issue in which the Olympic runner Duncan MacDonald said that his *hobby* was "taking apart my Volkswagen." Then the reporter asked him what his *ambition* was. "Putting it back together," he said.[1] Well, yes! How easy, how very easy, to tear our lives apart, and how very difficult it is to put them back together again.

The difficulty with forgiveness is not only that it is hard to find. Sometimes, when we think we have found it, all we really experience is a painful kind of condescending toleration. That is not forgiveness. In his book *The Great Divorce*, C. S. Lewis pictures a number of departed souls who are allowed to look around heaven to decide if they can stay there. Heaven is so arranged that there is a commuter bus so that you can stay in heaven or you can take the bus back to the other place if you wish. You really get your choice. Lewis says that quite a few people decide that they do not really like heaven at all. One part of the book tells of a woman who learns that she will have to meet her husband in heaven—her husband whose adultery had led to their divorce on earth. She says, "Well thank you very much, but I think I will take the bus back." Then she says to St. Peter, "I am ready to forgive him, of course. But anything more is quite impossible."[2] There is, you see, a form of forgiveness that is, in fact, rejection, not forgiveness at all. Who has not met a mother whose forgiveness of an erring child is used as a chain to hold him forever? Who has not seen a marriage in which forgiveness is used as a device of manipulation and control?

There is a nobler kind of forgiveness which we know about, which has about it a certain sadness. This is the forgiveness which comes from our common awareness of our common human frailty. Do you remember this poem which John Greenleaf Whittier wrote one Sunday afternoon after strolling though the local cemetery?

> My heart was heavy, for its trust had been
> Abused, its kindness answered with foul wrong;
> So, turning gloomily from my fellow-men,
> One summer Sabbath day I strolled among
> The green mounds of the village burial place;
> Where, pondering how all human love and hate
> Find one sad level; and how, soon or late,
> Wronged and wrongdoer, each with meekened face,
> And cold hands folded over a still heart,
> Pass the green threshold of our common grave,
> Whither all footsteps tend, whence none depart,
> Awed for myself, and pitying my race,
> Our common sorrow, like a mighty wave,
> Swept all my pride away, and trembling I forgave![3]

We have all met the world-weary whose kindliness is born of such a tenderhearted but really sorrowful view of human nature.

It is about another kind of forgiveness that is not enslaving, not melancholy, but freeing and joyful that I want to speak to you this morning. Notice that each of the three stories in this chapter of St. Luke concludes in the same way. When the shepherd found his sheep, what did he do? He called in all his friends and neighbors and said, "Rejoice with me" (Luke 15:6). When the woman found the coin she had lost, what did she do? She went out and found her friends and neighbors and said, "Come home and rejoice with me, for what I had lost, I have found" (Luke 15:9). The father said, "Quick, bring out the best robe and put a ring on his finger and bring the fatted calf, for this my son who was dead is alive again. Let us rejoice" (Luke 15:22–23). All the neighbors came to the feast.

This is the kind of forgiveness which men and women, all of us, yearn for—not the reluctant and petulant toleration of our weakness, which in so many ways is worse than rejection itself; not the melancholy stoicism of those who accept human weaknesses because of their own weariness; not the controlling, manipulative forgiveness that enslaves and mortifies—but *this* kind of experience, this kind of forgiveness, full of joy and celebration and enthusiasm and excitement.

It seems to me that there are two consequences of Christian forgiveness. Notice the first one. When forgiveness occurs, a community assembles. They assemble to celebrate. The neighbors are called in. Surely one of the most terrible consequences of sin is the loneliness of its guilt. Forgiveness gives people back their friends and their neighbors. A community of friends rushes in to embrace us. Those of you who belong to Alcoholics Anonymous know what I am talking about; those of you who belong to deeply Christian homes know what I am speaking of; any of you who have had a truly religious experience of the Christian church entirely understand me. Christ offers us forgiveness, not as a general gesture from somewhere. He gives it to us by offering us a community of friends with whom we can celebrate the beginning of a new personal life. The "sinners sought his company" because he was speaking to the deepest need of our human nature.

The second result is that forgiveness multiplies forgiveness. Once you enter a forgiving community, you are ever thereafter a changed person. An illustration of what I mean is the story of a certain man. During World War II he was a navigator in the United States Air Force. After the war was over he revisited Japan. The only way he had ever seen it before was through the lens of his bomb sight. After the war, driving near Yokohama, he came to a group of hovels where people were living. Having lost his way, he asked in faltering Japanese, some directions from a teen-aged girl. During their conversation she showed him a picture of her former home that had been destroyed by bombs and a photo of her parents, who had been killed in a raid, and one of a grand piano on which she had been practicing in hope of becoming a concert pianist. On the verge of tears, the man tried to say how sorry he was. With a small gesture she silenced him and took from a chain she wore around her neck a little golden cross. Holding it before him, she said, "Me Christian." The experience changed his life. He is now a priest missionary in South America. Anyone who has been forgiven in the Christian community can tell you similar stories.

Yesterday, I had the great joy of joining two of our friends in Holy marriage in the Chapel. I read some words written by one who had discovered in his own heart the joy of forgiveness in a Christian community and whose life had been changed by that experience forever. This is how St. Paul said it: Forgiveness builds love with this result: you will become patient and kind, not jealous, not boastful or conceited, no longer rude or selfish. Love does not take offence and it is not resentful. You will no longer take pleasure in other people's frailties. You will be ready to excuse, to trust, to hope and to endure whatever happens to you (1 Corinthians 13).

Maybe Benchley was right, at least this far: you are either moving into a community that is celebrating human acceptance and Divine forgiveness, or you are moving away from it. Only you know. You are like some who came to him long ago, seeking his company, or you are standing in the meanwhile of your life, complaining about something or someone. May Jesus speak to each of us this morning to invite us into the forgiving community so that, as his universe unfolds, *meanwhile* we may have joy.

LET US PRAY:

Father, we bring our lives before your throne in penitence for our sins, in deep gratitude for the inestimable grace of your forgiveness and in joyful celebration with all our friends and families, both here and on the other side, who seek the company of your blessed Son, our Savior, Jesus Christ the Lord. *Amen.*

ᗧᐤᑫ

What Exactly Did Jesus Do—
And How Do You Know

I have always been thankful to God that I began my ordained ministry as a college chaplain. It was stimulating and it was fun to be a college chaplain at Ohio State University in 1958, and I was greatly blessed by the opportunity to serve under the wise and gentle leadership of Dr. Almus Thorp. Dr. Thorp has a keen sense of humor, and I think that is why he asked me shortly after I arrived to conduct one of the confirmation classes for college students. I began my lecture with great confidence. (How true is the observation that a minister never knows more than on the first day out of seminary!) I began with what I thought was a scholarly review of the history of the church. All my facts were right. I thought I was doing beautifully. Then, half way through it, one of the students raised his hand and with utterly innocent irrelevance he asked me: "I have been wondering," he said, "what exactly did Jesus do and how do you know?" I remember a feeling of panic as I fumbled through my notes and then I think I suggested that we take a coffee break!

"What exactly did Jesus do and how do you know?" Perhaps I would have been helped out of my panic (though I am glad I was left in it for a few years until I found the answers for myself) by something Karl Barth once said. He was asked by a communist professor from East Germany: "Dr. Barth, how is it that such a learned, civilized, intelligent, and brilliant man as yourself can believe in something like the Resurrection?" Dr. Barth looked at

Sermon preached at St. Paul's Episcopal Church, Akron, Ohio, on the Fourth Sunday after Pentecost, 15 June 1975. George Ross Papers, The University of Akron Archives.

him in his kindly way and then replied: "Because, my friend, my mother told me."

That answer might not have satisfied the professor anymore than it would have satisfied that Ohio State half-back in my first confirmation class, but as an answer it is very hard to improve upon. We believe as we do, we think as we do, we cherish the values that we do because we have discovered them in the important human relationships of our lives. We may discover the truths of geometry in the classroom, but we discover the deep values and beliefs that shape our lives only in our human relationships with one another.

"What exactly did Jesus do and how do you know?" The two questions go together. They are inseparable. Let me suggest to you this morning that Jesus did three things, or rather that Jesus *does* three things, whenever he enters a human life. First: where Jesus is, life is celebrated. On every page of the New Testament there is this message: with Jesus there is joy! How do we know that? Surely not simply because the Bible tells us so. How do we know? Let me tell you.

I know a man who was dead for all practical purposes. Morally he was empty, not evil, empty. He gave himself to nothing and to no one. He neither enjoyed his own life nor gave enjoyment to others. He was, to use a memorable image of Dr. George Rigas, a boarded up house with no light shining through, not even through the cracks. I have seen the light put back in that man's life when he knew that he was loved and had a purpose in life, as Christian neighbors loved him back to life again in the Spirit of Christ.

A married couple find their relationship once rich and fulfilling drying up into mere formality and courtesy, sometimes not even that. They listen but they do not see. Then one weekend they attend a parish conference on Christian marriage. Out of that experience of sharing in the spirit of Christ gradually, painfully a new relationship begins to develop, less intensely erotic than at first perhaps, but something deeper, more stable, more fulfilling. And one day as they kneel down to receive the Holy Communion they glance for just a split instant into each other's eyes and in that instant the spirit flows between them, and after all these years they know that at last they are married. What does Jesus do? How do we know? They can tell you.

A young couple experiences a terrible loss. The child they love dies of leukemia. That could destroy them. Instead, they reach out. They somehow penetrate in a moment of grief stricken prayer to Jesus Christ and find something there that is stronger than death, and through the doorway of suffering they enter into a larger life, a more generous and compassionate and consecrated life. You see them week by week in church and you know what Jesus does and how.

Here is a passage from the diary of a priest who was carried from his church to the hospital and came back slowly from death's door: "I was overcome with a sense of the freshness of life such as I had not known for many years. In the hospital I looked at the fabric of the bedclothes and at my own hands thinking how marvelously they were contrived. Every object on which my eyes fell, every experience was remarkable and new and later at home, to me the sudden flattening of a patch of grass in the wind could be the very footstep of God. To me the coming of spring that year was not the logical result of the ponderous wheel of earth, an annual occurrence scarcely to be noticed, but an enormous personal gift that brought tears to my eyes. And for the first time I knew what it was to thank God."

Where Jesus is, there is a celebration of life. How do we know that? Because in knowing him, we have rediscovered how to celebrate our own lives. That is not necessarily a convincing argument. That is necessarily the only convincing argument.

Among my notes, I have come across a wonderful passage but unfortunately I have lost the source, "Life's supreme tragedy is not poor health, lack of wealth or beauty or great gifts, a disappointment in marriage or having a boring job, grievously hard as they may be to bear. It lies in the fading of our youthful vision, and our greatest sorrow is always the death of that sparkling spirit of wonder we possess as children, that deep joy in the world and in living, that pure faith and believing heart, the bubbling of the divine joy within us."

Along with the celebration *of* life comes a new perspective *about* life. Where Jesus is, I have discovered, there is joy, and so there is also humor. A Christian without a sense of humor seems to me almost a contradiction in terms. Christians with the grace of humor born of a sense of joy are always recognizable if by no other means than by their ability to pass through conflict without losing their perspective. Their astonishing composure even as they were being thrown to the lions won over even the most hardened pagan persecutors in time. A few years ago Harry Emerson Fosdick was in the midst of a great fight over evolution and the Bible when he received a letter from a dogmatic fundamentalist. On the letter there was only one word: "Fool!" The next Sunday, Dr. Fosdick looked down from his great pulpit with a quizzical look and said: "I have often gotten a letter where the person had written a message and forgotten to write his name, but this is the first time I have gotten a letter where the person signed his name and forgot to write the message."

There was a man whose joy *in* life gave perspective *on* life and whose perspective gave birth to a gracious sense of humor, so that he could pass through great personal conflict with serenity. What does Jesus do? He gives people that kind of inward spirit. How do I know? I have seen him do it. Along with the joy and the gentle humor born of perspective, Jesus gives us a new love for people.

Jesus rescues us from the need to judge or manipulate or control, and he frees us for a new style of human relationship. That style for me is beautifully expressed in a book I am reading by Carl Rogers entitled *Freedom to Learn*. In it he writes: "I have come to think that one of the most satisfactory experiences I know . . . is just fully to *appreciate* [an] individual in the same way that I appreciate a sunset. People are just as wonderful as sunsets if I can let them *be.* In fact, perhaps the reason we can truly appreciate a sunset is that we cannot control it. When I look at a sunset as I did the other evening, I don't find myself saying: 'Soften the orange a little on the right hand corner, and put a bit more purple along the base, and use a little more pink in the cloud color.' I don't do that. I don't *try* to control a sunset. I watch it with awe as it unfolds. I like myself best when I can experience my staff member, my son, my daughter, my grandchildren in the same way, appreciating the unfolding of a life."⁴ Jesus said it even more simply. "This is my commandment, that you love one another" (John 15:12 RSV). "Judge not that ye be not judged" (Matthew 7:1 RSV). "In my father's house there are many mansions" (John 14:2 KJV).

What does Jesus do? How do you know? You cannot answer the first question correctly until you can answer the second question correctly. I did not know that when I taught my first confirmation class. I am only beginning to understand it. But of this I am growing more and more certain: where Jesus is there is joy; where Jesus is there is gracious, gentle humor born of divine perspective to support us through life's contradictions; where Jesus is there is unjudgmental love.

This is the message: "Life's supreme tragedy is not poor health, lack of wealth or beauty or great gifts, a disappointing marriage or a boring job. Life's supreme blessing is a sparkling sense of wonder, a deep joy in the world and in living, a faith, and a believing heart, the bubbling of the divine joy within us."

This is the message: Jesus gives such a blessing. That is what he does. How do we know? Because he has given it to us, and because never in all the two thousand years since his coming has he withheld that blessing from those who would follow him in faith. We do speak the things "we have heard" with our own ears and of the things "we have seen with our own eyes" (1 John 1:1 RSV), that we proclaim to you. *That* is how we know.

LET US PRAY:

Heavenly father, we pray for the blessing in our lives which your Son has so abundantly given to all who have followed him in faith through every generation: for the grace to celebrate with joy the life which now is and the life which is to be; for the grace of his own divine perspective in all our trials and conflicts, that with cheerful spirits we may go our way rejoicing; and above all we pray for the most excellent gift of charity, that we may cherish one another, without pretense and without judgment, and so manifest in our own walk and way your abundant love for all humankind. Through the same Jesus Christ our Lord. *Amen.*

Dying to Live

> *Great multitudes accompanied Jesus; and he*
> *turned and said to them . . . "Whoever does*
> *not bear his own cross and come after me*
> *cannot be my disciple."*
>
> Text: Luke 14:25–33

There are moments in our lives when God turns on us, as Jesus turned that day on the multitudes. There are moments when he tells us things we do not wish to hear—hard things. He says, "To follow me, you must die on your own cross." We are not told how those people reacted when he said that. Knowing ourselves as we do, we do not suppose that they were pleased. One is reminded of dear St. Teresa's complaint: "Oh, God," she cried, "it is no wonder you have so few friends—seeing how you treat them."

A wise saint once said that before God meets us as our friend, he confronts us as our adversary. I believe it. He looks into our proud hearts and says that something has to die there. He looks into our contorted, frowning faces, so fretted with anxiety, anger, annoyance and depression, and says, "Something here has got to die!" It is funny how he works. For years and years he lets us accompany him. I like that description in Luke: "Great multitudes *accompanied* him" (Luke 14:25 RSV). Cardinal Newman once

Sermon preached at St. Paul's Episcopal Church, Akron, Ohio, on the Sixteenth Sunday after Pentecost, 7 September 1986. George Ross Papers, The University of Akron Archives.

said that nothing is easier than to use the word "God" and mean nothing by it. That is the bald, unvarnished truth about much of church membership. It does not mean a thing. We are merely *accompanying* the Lord. It is possible to do that for years yet never for one entire day to have *followed* him. Thank God, if in some crisis of life or just out of the blue (who knows how he works?), Christ turns to us and says, "Enough of this! It is time for some straight talk between you and me. You have got to die, if you want to live." We may differ in many ways, but on one point we are all agreed: we do not want to die. Is there something wrong in our lives? Some trouble at home, some problem at work? Do we just suffer from a vague malaise we cannot specify? We will move heaven and earth to find any cause for it *except* a cause in ourselves.

Summer is over and I am glad to see some golfers back. Golfers will like this story. (I think that I should tell at least one golf story a year, so this is it.) A man who was being interviewed for a job in a large corporation was invited to play golf with his prospective employer. That sounded fine—except that he had not played golf since he was in college fifteen years ago. He wanted to make a good impression, and so he dressed up like Arnold Palmer, rented some snazzy golf clubs and went to the country club to golf. He teed up his ball, took a great swing at it, and completely missed. Nothing daunted, he laughed nervously, teed up the ball again, took a mighty swing and missed. He said, "Just a minute!" He teed up again, took a great swing, missed a third time. He mopped his brow, looked up at his fellow players and said, "Gosh, this sure is a rough course!" We laugh at that, but more often than we wish to admit, we blame our problems on our circumstances when what we need is a change in ourselves.

"You need to die if you want to live with me," says the Lord Jesus Christ. He says this to them, not because he is angry with them, but because he loves them. So it is generally: the only people who have a right to speak that way to us are those who love us and will stay with us. About twenty years ago a man came to my office to give a fairly large gift in memory of his wife who had died after a marriage of some sixty years. As we talked he said, "My wife told me a couple of years ago, 'There are three things about you that I like.'" He was glad that she could think of so many! "Tell me what they are," he said. She answered, "Well, you are a snob and you are weird and you are a pompous ass." "I saw the twinkle in her eye as she listed those great aspects of my character." As he told me this, on his face, the tears were streaming down; and I knew that those were tears, not so much of grief, as of an abiding inner joy. He said, "She had a great sense of humor, that woman. You know, it is awfully hard not to have someone who knows you all and all, and loves you still and all."

On the other hand, I suppose that there is really nothing more irritating in life than someone who says that he knows exactly how we feel. You have met people like that. "I know exactly what you are thinking, how you feel," they say. I am aware that the clergy are great offenders in this department. One of you passed along to me the other day a story about a priest who walked down a street lined with big Victorian houses. He spotted a little boy trying to reach the door bell on the porch of one of them. The doorbell was one of those old fashioned things set high up on the door. The boy was very small and was jumping up and down trying to reach it. "Poor little kid," thought the clergyman, as he walked up on the porch, patted the boy lovingly on the head and rang the bell vigorously with his other hand. "Little man," he said, smiling down like a god at the child, "now what?" "Now," said the boy breathlessly, "we run like hell!" God forbid that we should presume to know the secret life of anyone else. As blessed Evelyn Underhill once said, "Let us approach one another with discreet discernments."

Praise God when he works through someone who really cares about you and gives you an insight into that part of your life which has to die. It is not only our pride which has to die. Quite often, on the contrary, it is our low estimate of ourselves that has to die. Strangely enough we can cling to depression, guilt and low self-image because that, at least, gives us something to stand on, something to hide behind. We are reluctant to give it up. But it is a great moment when someone bids us die to that. For example, the other day I came across the case of Mary Ann Bird, who entitled her interesting biography *The Whisper Test.* She writes:

I grew up knowing that I was different, and I hated it. I was born with a cleft palate; and when I started school, my classmates made it clear to me how I looked to them: a little girl with a misshapen lip, crooked nose, lopsided feet and garbled speech. When schoolmates would ask, "What happened to your lip?" I would tell them I had fallen and cut it upon a piece of glass. I believed that no one could really love me. There was, however, a teacher in the second grade whom we adored. Mrs. Leonard was her name. She was short, dumpy, round, and a sparkling woman. Annually we would have a hearing test. Now, I was deaf in one ear; but when I took the test, I discovered that if I did not press my hand tightly on my good ear, as I was supposed to, I could pass the test. Every year, the teacher, sitting solemnly at her desk, would whisper something and we would repeat it. That was the test. In past years they would say something like "The sky is blue" or "You have new shoes." But not Miss Leonard. I waited for those words, which God must have put into her mouth, those seven words which changed my life. Miss Leonard whispered, "I wish you were my little girl."[5]

Something has to die if something is going to live. What was born was a beautiful woman who went on to become a great teacher. But first the self-hating little girl with the cleft palate had to die.

We are about to enter into a sacrament. How wonderful if we should meet Jesus even this morning as one who bids us die that we might live. Sacraments are generally celebrated in church with bread and wine. But I know one that was celebrated in a hospital with popcorn. The man I am thinking about was graduated first in his class at Harvard University Medical School. He went on to become one of the great obstetricians in the country, but on the way he served an internship in a burn ward of a children's hospital. That is where he died. Something died and came to life on the burn ward. He decided there that he would visit the burn ward on a regular basis, not as the great doctor he became, but as a visitor. Someone gave him a rubber nose, and a retired clown gave him a clown suit. So he dressed up as a clown. He would go over on Saturday afternoon to visit the children on the burn ward. He learned some corny jokes. He came up with some riddles to ask the kids as they lay face down on their striker frames.

One day he found a boy with his face so incinerated that there was not a feature that you could recognize. As he stood by the bed of this kid, another boy came roaring down the corridor using his IV carrier as a skateboard. That boy stopped and looked at this tragically deformed child and said, "You ugly." The doctor stood frozen, unable to move until finally he looked the child in the eye. Later he wrote: "It was like looking through a tunnel. I saw him as God must." The doctor always carried a bowl of popcorn when he went to see the children. As he looked deeply into the child's eyes, the child began to weep. So the doctor took a piece of popcorn and sponged up the boy's tears, and he ate the popcorn and the boy ate the popcorn. There is no pain in my life and there is no pain in your life that God does not look upon with infinite love and mercy. He makes of our own tears a communion with himself.

Does it hurt us when Jesus turns and says, "You have got to die"? Yes it does, and sometimes it makes us pretty angry as well because we really believe that if we die to ourselves everything will be lost. And that is true. But into the emptiness Christ comes to tell us that he needs disciples, that he has someone for us to love: a little sad girl, maybe, to whisper to; a little boy, perhaps, with whom to celebrate, with popcorn, a sacrament of life through death—things like that, which only those can do who first have died unto themselves.

Wow, this sure is a tough course! Sure it is. Or as Scott Peck says in the opening sentence of his great book *The Road Less Traveled*: "Life is difficult."[6] Sometimes at the heart of the difficulty, maybe when it is darkest, God turns to us in love and says, "All right—it is time to die." And then, instead of running away from that, we agree to it. Not long afterward, we will have moments of exhilarating usefulness, and the once incomprehensible words of St. Paul in the Second Letter to the Corinthians will begin to glow and to flow—like dawn after darkness or rain after drought. "Behold, we are afflicted in every way, but not crushed; perplexed, we are not driven to despair; persecuted we are not forsaken; . . . for we carry around in our own bodies the death of Jesus so that the life of Jesus may be manifested through us; as dying, behold we live; as punished, we are not killed; as sorrowful, we rejoice; as poor, we make many rich; as having *nothing,* we possess *everything!*" (cf. 2 Corinthians 4:8–9; 6:9–10).

LET US PRAY:

Eternal God, like the bread and the wine on the altar of this supper, we offer up our lives to you—that you may give them back to us, broken, blessed, and changed. Give us grace to love you in everyone to whom you send us. Give us courage to die to the way we have been dying, that we may live forever in you; through Jesus Christ, our Lord. *Amen.*

The Invisible Footprints of God

Text: Psalm 77:19

This past week, as you may imagine, I found myself a little puzzled. What text or topic should I choose for this next to the last sermon as your Rector? As I so often do, I turned to the Psalms for guidance. I was not disappointed. When I read the 77th Psalm, the 19th verse seemed almost to leap from the page: preach this; this is what you have always preached. And so this morning, I take as the text this 19th verse of the 77th Psalm: "The way was through the great waters, yet thy footprints were unseen."

It is an arresting phrase and a fascinating concept is it not: "the invisible footprints of God"? "Thy way was through the great waters, yet thy footprints were unseen." Upon the depths of life, Almighty God is walking with us; albeit to mortal eye, his footprints are unseen.

Thank God for the calm and happy moments in life when everything is going well for us; but thank God, also, for the times when we may feel alone and lost and at sea. Waves so often threaten to swamp our little craft; and yet, says the psalmist, invisible and unseen in those very moments, God is walking with us over the face of the deep. The psalmist touches the nerve of all great religion: that there are invisible realities that are known only by faith.

Sermon preached at St. Paul's Episcopal Church, Akron, Ohio, on the Fourteenth Sunday after Pentecost, 9 September 1990. George Ross Papers, The University of Akron Archives.

I. THE INVISIBLE

In the famous French story *The Little Prince,* a boy befriends a fox. When the fox must, at last, leave the little prince, he offers to tell him the most wonderful secret of life, if the boy will meet certain conditions. When the prince has met all of the conditions, the fox replies, "This is the greatest secret of life: only that which is invisible is essential."[7] Think about that for a moment. It is true: only the invisible is essential.

In the Second Letter to the Corinthians, St. Paul put it this way:

We never lose heart, for this slight momentary affliction is preparing for us an eternal weight of glory beyond all comparison, for we look not to the things that are seen, but to the things that are unseen: for the things that are seen are transient, but the things that are unseen are eternal. (cf. 4:16–18)

Some things we see; some things we see are better than other things: all the glory of the physical world, its gold and riches of every kind; and yet all those things that are seen are passing away. They are transient. They do not last, and those who put their trust in the things that are seen, one day, will lose hope. But Paul says: "We never lose hope because we live in the glorious presence of the eternal, invisible, imperishable things of God."

Paul is speaking here, of course, about the really essential things in life—in your life and in mine—which no one can see, but which are real, nevertheless. He is speaking about whatsoever things are excellent: about wisdom and courage, which are real though unseen; about hope and love; about loyalty and compassion. This we surely know: that the man who believes only in what he sees will lose even that.

There is an African legend about the Sky Maiden, a beautiful princess who rode down from heaven on a moonbeam. A young man saw her, fell in love with her, threw his net over her and asked her to marry him. She said, "Yes, I will. I will be a good wife to you, but first I must do something: I must go home for a moment." So when the Sky Maiden came back to earth, she was carrying a large box. She said to the man. "Take this and keep it for me. I will marry you and be a good wife to you; but you must promise me one thing. You must promise never to look inside the box." And so they were married and, for a while, all was well. Then, of course, one day, unable to curb his curiosity, the young man looked into the box. The box was completely empty. But when the princess returned she said to him, "Because you looked inside the box, I cannot stay with you any longer." "Why?" her husband asked. "What is so terrible? The box was empty." She answered, "I am not leaving you because you opened the box. I knew that you would. I am leaving you because you said that it is empty. It is not. It contains the light and air, the moonlight and the memories of my home in the sky. When I went home, I filled that box with everything that is most precious to me. How can I be your wife if what is most precious to me is emptiness to you?"

That story contains more than just wise guidance about choosing a mate. If we are insensible to the spiritual realities that give life its dimensions of joy and love, if we are empty of the magnificent unseen in life, we shall in the end lose everything that is dear to us.

II. THE GREAT WATERS

Consider also a second great truth in this text: "Thy way was through great waters. . . ." The "great waters" for the Jewish writer symbolize both life and death: what gives life and what brings death. The "great waters" represent also the adversities to which frail human flesh is subject from birth to death. "Thy way was through the great waters. . . ." We might translate this verse: "Though I was afraid and alone and at sea, you were with me. Though I could not see you, you were there." This is true faith.

Recently, I read a fine article by Professor Belden Lane of St. Louis University. It was entitled (wonderful title?) "Fierce Landscapes and the Indifference of God." Professor Lane was talking about the barren and deserted areas of the earth from which so many of our holy writings have come: the deserts of Sinai, the mountain passes of Tibet, the Highlands of Scotland, the horizonless sea. Could it be, he asks, that the revelations of God come to us most, not in the great peace of Eden, but in unfriendly landscapes, like Golgotha where we experience the apparent absence of God?[8]

A man by the name of Andrew Harvey, not long ago, made a pilgrimage to Tibet looking for enlightenment in the monasteries. He traveled from one sacred place to another, but the experience never came. One afternoon as he was walking through a lonely valley, he was distracted by the play of the sun on the ragged stones. He became so caught up in the austere beauty of the rocks and withered trees in that desolate place that he never reached the monastery. He was suddenly and mysteriously overwhelmed by the love and the peace and the joy of God. In the wilderness moments of our lives, often just as we feel despair over the futility of our search, there, precisely there, we find God. As someone has said: "We are saved in the end by the things that ignore us"—that free us from our self-centered seeking and thinking.[9] Only the invisible is essential, and in the wilderness God is near. He plants his footsteps in the sea and rides upon the storm. Therefore we never lose heart.

On this Sunday, as we begin a new year in our educational programs, let this be our goal: let us teach one another, in season and out of season, and let us teach our dear children, not from a book, not from hearsay, but from our own hearts and experience, two great truths of the Christian life: that only the invisible is essential and that upon the face of the great deep, there walks with us a God of everlasting love albeit, to mortal eye, his footprints are invisible. On these two points I felt called by God to preach to you today; and on them, indeed, I have endeavored by his grace, to preach to you often in these last eighteen years. From the abundant riches of his Word, may God bless us always.

LET US PRAY:

Eternal, invisible, God only wise: we ask thy grace for the education of our souls. Thou hast set us in a world of continual change and inevitable decay. Give us faith, therefore, that we may both perceive and embrace that love which fadeth not away. In the days of our life and at the hour of our death be thou our Guardian, Guide and Stay. Grant that we may so pass through the things temporal that we lose not finally the things eternal. If thou lead us through rough places, grant us thy sustaining graces; and, when life is o'er, open heaven's door; through Christ our Lord, *Amen.*

꧁ꙄꞶꙄ꧂

"Letter to Ann Elizabeth"

We think about our children at this time of year, as our schools open again. The children of our parish have been much on my mind as we have been reconstructing our facilities and our church school program in anticipation of a new year beginning September 16th. I remember a saying by the late James Agee. He once wrote: "To bring a life into the world is at least as serious a matter as to take one out." I suppose we all take our responsibility for our children seriously—whether as parent or teacher, pastor or doctor, or just as friend of the human race. In time I want to speak to you about our special responsibility as members of the church for the children whom God has given into our care, but this morning, I hope you will forgive a more personal message. It is a message for a special child: a letter, if you will, addressed to Ann Elizabeth, age four days, from her father. I share it with you because, though addressed to one little girl, I hope it might somehow convey the love and the hope we all share for every little child. The letter reads as follows:

Dear Ann,

As I write this letter, you have just concluded your fourth day upon the earth. I do not know when or whether you will read it. Maybe this letter will come to light wrinkled and yellowed by time among the long forgotten memorabilia of your father's life— found, perhaps, in some attic trunk as a dusty souvenir of an era, perhaps even of a world, you remember only vaguely and uncer-

Sermon preached at St. Paul's Episcopal Church, Akron, Ohio, on the Eleventh Sunday after Pentecost, 26 August 1973. George Ross Papers, The University of Akron Archives.

tainly. Whenever you read it, if ever you do, I pray that you will find in it some image of the joy and love which was in your mother's eyes today when she held you in her arms and of the joy and love which are in my heart as I write my first letter to you this morning. By the time you read this letter, perhaps you will have had children of your own. I hope so. If so, we need no further words to bridge the chasm of the years.

Perhaps the world in which you live as you read this is utterly estranged from the world in which I live as I write. So I must not write to you of any thing but the enduring things—and it is odd how few of them there are. Your world, no doubt, has as many passing troubles as the world into which you were born four days ago. Never the same, they are always the same, and so I will not speak of them: the wars, the businesses, the rise of states, the fall of empires, the passing scandals and the transient times and crimes. Let me write my first letter to you instead about soul-sized things that endure and have endured and will endure—ever since an un-named boy and an unknown girl stepped forth uncertainly from the primeval forest and prayed for God's grace to be the human race.

As I looked on you this morning, I prayed that God would grant you two gifts. First, I prayed that you would be free. You will not find it easy to be free. No one ever has. If you have learned to love the Bible as much as I do, you will have puzzled and pondered many times over the fact that there came a time when the Israelites wanted to go back to Egypt. The security of slavery was better than the difficulty of freedom. So it was and is and ever shall be, world without end for each of us. But: Ann, be free! No one can take your freedom from you. No insult, no illness, no judgment, no imprisonment—nothing whatever that anyone can ever do to you can rob you of the inward freedom of the spirit, for that freedom comes from God and no one can take it from you. Whatever else happens, never surrender your freedom to anyone for anything. Test everything by the test of freedom: does my marriage help me to experience it, does my country, does my church, do my friends? Of course, by now you will have learned the difference between a freedom that makes us joyful and mere selfish indulgence which makes us melancholy. No doubt by now you have heard me quote a saying by Hillel. Hear it again, nevertheless: "If I am not for myself, who is for me? . . . If not now, when?"[10] Jesus said: "Love thy neighbor *as thyself*" (Matthew 19:19 KJV). Take that always to heart. Love yourself earnestly, joyfully, robustly—and then, when you offer that self to others, you will offer a beautiful and precious gift. Always the first mark of those who love deeply is that they are themselves free and have placed the experience of freedom above all other values in their hearts.

Second, I prayed that you would receive the gift of sensitivity—that you would learn to listen to the essences of things. I pray that you will not be one who glides listlessly and vaguely across the slanting surface of this glorious world, but that it will be said of you that she was one who took time to listen to the birds at dawn, who noted the singular contour of a stone, the heave and roll of seas, the dart and glide of trout, the ooze of dew on forest moss, and such small things that mean nothing at all and everything altogether. I pray, Ann, that you will cherish all the little things—even as you, so small and beautiful, are to me this morning the express image of our heavenly Father's love.

These are my two prayers for you today, Ann, and I know that I shall offer them for you as long as I live—that by God's grace you shall be free and that you shall become ever more aware of the fair glory of simply being alive in God's good world. When you read this letter, years from now, I pray for something more. I pray that you will have, by now, become a person who wants to share your gifts of grace with others—and especially perhaps with those whose freedom has been trampled or whose perception of the beauty of the world has never grown as yours has (or as I pray it has). I hope by now that I will have shown you in a thousand ways how grateful your mother and I are for the priceless gift of your life. If someday you should transmit that gratitude through your own free and sensitive and generous life to your own children and to your husband and your friends, then—whether we are near or far—you will surely know that you have brought our lives, and not yours only, to fulfillment.

This comes with love and hope across the years from

Your devoted father.

I hope you will forgive the personal context of my remarks this morning. Beyond that, I hope that you have discerned somehow that while I was thinking of my own child, I was thinking of yours too—and of all the children of our parish as, in our Christian family here at St. Paul's, we pray and plan and work for a parish community in which each child will discover for him or herself that freedom and sensitivity and generosity which mark every truly Christian life.

LET US PRAY:

Almighty God, heavenly Father, who hast blessed us with the joy and care of children: give us light and strength so to love them that they may love whatsoever things are true and pure and lovely and of good report: we commend to thy continual care the homes in which our people dwell. Put far from us, we beseech thee, every root of bitterness, selfishness and anger. Knit together in constant affection those who in holy marriage have committed themselves to one another: turn the heart of the children to the parents and the heart of the parents to their children, and so enkindle fervent love among us all that we may be evermore kindly affectioned with brotherly love: following the example of our savior, Jesus Christ. *Amen.*

CHAPTER THREE

WOUNDED HEAD

ᕲᵂᑦ

Broken Thoughts

THE ROMAN SOLDIERS who mocked Jesus' claim of kingship twisted a crown of thorns to place on his head. Though the crown was most likely made up of the common thorny burnet, Matthew, Mark, and John use the Greek word *akantha*, which refers to any kind of thorny plant.

For a mock scepter, the soldiers put into Jesus' hand a reed (Matthew 27:29), which they also used to bludgeon Jesus on the head (Matthew 27:30; Mark 15:19). After beating him about the head with their hands and spitting in his blindfolded face, the soldiers knelt before Jesus and taunted: "Hail, King of the Jews." The pain that Jesus suffered from these lacerations, his skin already super-sensitive from the aftereffects of hematidrosis (sweating blood), must have been immense.

The wounds of the head—our broken thoughts and wrong-headed knowledge—are some of the severest wounds we can experience. Every one of us has unsanctified thoughts, mutters unspeakable words, thinks things that aren't so, even says things that aren't true. It is not only Chaucer's characters, or politicians, who can be found economical with the truth. Preachers also can call up reserves of "terminological inexactitude" (today's replacement phrase for "prevarication"). Everyone's life has some low-slung branches, some lowering of thoughts and standards, some wrong bents toward life, some mental debris.

George Ross contended that the mind of every person travels through various valleys of the shadow. "For some there is a valley struggle with addiction; for some, with depression," he said, and he backed up his words with this quote from the poet Gerard Manley Hopkins: "Oh the mind, mind has mountains; cliffs of fall / Frightful, sheer, no-man-fathomed. Hold them cheap / May who ne'er hung there."[1]

We are all products of prenatal dispositions, parental mistakes, and childhood injuries that blight us through life. Maybe the injury was committed by a mother or father, a sibling or friend. Maybe we are the harmed, or we may be the harmer. Characteristically, many of these injurious claims of habit and chains of thought are too weak to be felt until they're too strong to be broken.

The language Ross used to talk about our childhood mental wounds was "inner conversation." Citing the work of two University of Michigan psychologists, Ross argued that everyone has "inner conversations," and most often these conversations with ourselves are self-degrading:

We repeat the harsh words that we have heard from the intimate members of our own families, our father or mother, or perhaps our brother or sister. When these voices in the family are negative, when they are destructive, they speak of guilt or comparison or contempt. A young boy whose father is always critical and never affirming, will carry on a lifelong self-negating conversation with himself. When anything is broken, anything is missing, if there is a mishap or a failure the boy is blamed and for the rest of his life that boy wrestles with the temptation to blame himself for everything that goes wrong, not only in his life, but in life generally. That is why our inner conversations center so often on themes of envy, resentment and guilt. And that is why so many of us come to church, to listen to every word said and sung because we need the healing of our memories as well as the forgiveness of sins.[2]

Every Sunday morning, the undergoers and overcomers assemble. When Ross looked out at his people, he saw every one present as one or both. Some have overcome an obstacle; some are undergoing a problem; most are undergoing and overcoming simultaneously. Church is the place where those memories that sting, those thoughts that we just can't get right—all the crooked postures of mind and spirit—can be faced and outfaced, undergone and overcome.

An old Zuni parable tells about a kachina who emerged from a cave attached back-to-back to a person from an alien world—neither one could understand the other because neither could see the other. The only hope of turning the situation around was in turning around—to see each other as they were. Ross's preaching was based on this same principle: the only hope of turning alien, broken thoughts around is in turning around—to see them as they are.

Novelist John Updike, after listening to a United Methodist minister explain the pain of a difficult appointment in New York City, said, "I hope you don't get so bent out of shape that you don't recognize yourself."[3] The greatest challenge in preaching is to get people, who can't bear either to look at themselves or to look away, to look within and to see the shape they are in. We resist looking in because we shrink from pain. But a doctor cannot set a broken bone without inflicting pain. The pain of setting is worse than the initial break. Only by passing through the pain can healing begin and the bone get back in joint. Those who choose not to be in the midst of their pain can never be strongest in the broken places.

Three of Ross's favorite writers—Ernest Hemingway, Fyodor Dostoyevsky, and Arthur Miller—addressed this theme in very different but concurring ways. In *Death in the Afternoon*, Hemingway uses the metaphor of bullfighting to describe the artist's struggle for unity of soul and form. An amateur can be distinguished from a professional bullfighter, Hemingway argues, not by the articulation of form but by the articulation of function. The amateur's style may be spectacular, making the crowd gasp at his superb form. But the amateur uses his gifts to hypnotize the crowd into thinking he is fighting "close to the horns." The professional may have many fewer moves, and not nearly as dazzling a style. But the professional works as "close to the horns" as he can get.[4]

In a letter to his brother, Fyodor Dostoyevsky spoke of "holding the pain" rather than working "close to the horns," but the meaning is the same. Dostoyevsky wrote something that in our better moments Ross was convinced we know to be true: "In human life are infinite pain and infinite joy. . . . In it spring thorns and roses. It is necessary to hang on to both, to accept and hold our pain, even as we accept and hold our grace, for that is what it means to be human."[5]

Arthur Miller's play *After the Fall* has a character, Holga, who talks about a terrible dream that keeps repeating itself and finally is revealed as the "healing fact." Like a flare, Holga's words light up a theological wasteland:

The same dream returned each night until I dared not go to sleep and I grew quite ill. I dreamed I had a child, and even in the dream I saw it was my life, and it was an idiot, and I ran away. But it always crept onto my lap again, clutched at my clothes. Until I thought, if I could kiss it, . . . perhaps I could sleep. And I bent to its broken face, and it was horrible . . . but I kissed it. I think one must finally take one's life into one's arms.[6]

The child in Holga's dream points us toward some part of ourselves that we resist and avoid. But this broken part of ourselves is the salve that heals our wounds. The wounded healer lies in all of us.

About Jesus, Peter wrote, "He himself bore our sins in his body on the tree, so that we might die to sin and live for righteousness. By his wounds you have been healed" (1 Peter 2:24 RSV). It is also by our own wounds that we are healed. Our wounds can be healing passports to new directions and destinations. Our wounds can lead to the transformation of both body and soul. When we enter our wounds, walk into our weaknesses, face our broken thoughts and conceptual disorders, we find new pathways that lead to higher dimensions of living.

In this unusual Father's Day sermon in 1988, Ross challenged

his congregation (and himself) to enter each's pain and not waste
the experience of suffering:

> I have served in the ministry thirty years, almost thirty-one. I have come
> to understand that there are two kinds of faith. One says *if* and the other
> says *though*. One says: "*If* everything goes well, *if* my life is prosperous,
> *if* I'm happy, *if* no one I love dies, *if* I'm successful, then I will believe in
> God and say my prayers and go to the church and give what I can afford."
> The other says *though: though* the cause of evil prosper, *though* I sweat
> in Gethsemane, *though* I must drink my cup at Calvary—nevertheless,
> precisely then, I will trust the Lord who made me. So Job cries: "*Though*
> he slay me, yet will I trust Him." In another of the great psalms David
> sings: "*Though* the waters roar and swell, and *though* the mountains be
> cast into the midst of the sea . . . the Lord of hosts is with me, the God of
> Jacob is my strength."[7]

George Ross's valley faith lived in the cracks between a critical
mind and a believing heart. Some in the church maligned him for
an arch erudition. Some in academe, willing only to look at the
laity through a very long telescope, maligned him for grandstand-
ing and playing to the galleries. Ross could not comprehend either
charge, and the notes and responses he received from parishioners
were enough to encourage him *through* this valley of criticism.
Ross believed in both the chapel and the academy. He never lost a
scholar's commitment to the critical work of academe, but he
held it in tension with a commitment to the believing mission of
the church. Or in St. Thomas Aquinas's celebration of the endowment of both mind and heart, Ross's ministry was dedicated to the
pursuit of "the knowledge which breathes love."[8] Knowledge accompanied by love is precisely how Augustine defined the Logos:
"The Word breathing Love."[9]

The danger Ross fought in the church and in himself was the
danger of acquiring knowledge but never gaining wisdom. In Galatians 3:1-3 (NRSV), Paul exclaims: "You foolish Galatians! Who
has bewitched you. . . . Having started with the Spirit, are you
now ending with the flesh?" Or in the J.B. Phillips translation of
verse one: "Oh, you dear idiots of Galatia." The translation in the
Jerusalem Bible is even more blunt: "Are you people in Galatia
mad?" The Galatians, in Ross's mind, were like the Episcopalians.

They had strong financial capital, but their theological capital, their brainpower and intellectual endowments, had been depleted. Worldly folly held sway over divine wisdom. In the words of Archbishop William Temple, the Church of England was in danger of dying of good taste.

Ross aspired to the wisdom of the Spirit about knowledge. He struggled his entire ministry to find ways to turn knowledge, the unstrung beads of information, into the necklace of wisdom. An information junkie who listened to CNN while reading two newspapers, an inveterate learner who could not sit on the beach without clipping journal articles or making notes in the margins of books, Ross desired a theological education that ended in something more than information. Without wisdom, this era can be no more than what Bill McKibben has wittily called it, a "Missing Information Age."[10] In Abraham Heschel's prophetic words, "[Humanity] will not perish for want of information . . . only for want of appreciation."[11]

The English word "philosophy" is a transliteration of the Greek word *philosophia,* which is a compound of two Greek words: *phileo* ("to love") and *sophia* ("wisdom"). A true philosophy of education ends with wisdom, which can be defined as the knowledge that leads to acknowledgment. A Christian philosophy of education ends in the knowledge that acknowledges Christ as the secret and supreme source of all the treasures of wisdom (as Paul put it in Colossians 2:3).

Every year, at Christmas and Easter, George Ross sponsored special services for the children of the parish. At 5 PM on Christmas Sunday, children were invited to bring gifts to give to some other kids of the community, and hundreds of them responded. At 4 PM on Easter Sunday, children brought flowers with which they "flowered the cross." At both of these services, which were really educational events to help children understand the biblical significance of Christ's birth and resurrection, the children asked their priest questions about the holy days. Ross delighted in being put on the spot and answering these "children's questions."

Jesus said: "Wisdom is justified by her children" (Matthew

11:19, NKJV). To be "Wisdom's children," Ross believed, Christians must bend down to ask some children's questions—in this case, about wisdom and knowledge. What is wisdom? How do we get it and how is it different from knowledge? Why is it so important? What do we mean by "knowing"? How do we know? What kind of "knowing" should the Christian community promote? These childlike questions are the epistemological issues at the heart of the educational enterprise. For Ross, they also were at the heart of what it meant for the church to be a force for God and the gospel in the latter days of the twentieth century.

"This is eternal life," Jesus said, "to know you, the only true God, and Jesus Christ whom you have sent" (John 17:3 NRSV). What is the first reason for your existence? Every good Roman Catholic child is asked this question from the Baltimore Catechism. The first reason for my existence is "to know God," he or she replies. But what does it mean "to know" in the biblical sense?

The Hebrew word for "to know" is *yada. Yada* is one of those words with which preachers love to twit their congregations. The Hebrew term for coitus is also *yada*—the double meaning of "to know" demonstrates the intimacy of knowledge in the Hebrew mind. "And Adam knew Eve, and she conceived" (Gen. 4:1 KJV).

Aristotle described three kinds of knowing: *praxis, theoria,* and *poiesis.* Greek knowledge in all three senses is something detached and apart from ourselves. Attachment or emotional involvement is contaminating and distorting. By contrast, the Hebrew meaning of "knowledge" requires relationships. It insists on contamination and participation. Hebrew knowledge means mutual experiences that bring out the identity of each partner—that yield awareness of the mystery of each other. It was with this in mind that W. H. Auden claimed the ultimate purpose of education was to make one able to fall in love at first sight.

Yet this fundamental purpose of "knowing" or "intercourse" still is inadequate without the larger biological and theological components to this word "information." We must look at the larger creational purposes of "knowing" and the procreative functions of "intercourse"—social, economic, political, religious.

When you know something in the biblical sense of "knowing," you conceive. Ross "knew" this because of his acute aesthetic sensibilities. A lover of art, especially Oriental art and animal antiques (for example, bronze dogs), Ross filled his homes with objects of beauty. With a baron's soul but a butler's pocketbook, he was openly grateful for what little art he was fortunate enough to possess. Ross was also creative in making ordinary events into aesthetic experiences. Sunday dinner became a Ross family ritual of beauty for all five senses. The best food he could cook up was served on the family's finest china and silver amidst convivial banter and conversation. What was conceived at these dinners was a tradition of love, trust, and joy.

Is it any wonder art has sometimes been called in the Christian tradition "The Fifth Evangelist"? T. S. Eliot argued that aesthetic sensibilities and spiritual perceptions are closely linked. In fact, great preaching is an art. Like all artists, Ross had a side that was zany, what the world calls "crazy." Ross was crazy enough to actually believe that beauty could change the world. And because of that belief, he esteemed artists for creating the most beautiful things conceived by human brain, or achieved by hand, or spoken by mouth. He would have rejected E. M. Forster's case for the supreme uselessness of literature and art in *Aspects of the Novel* (1927).

When you know someone or something in the biblical sense of knowing, you conceive, you give birth, you create. In other words, knowing is ultimately an aesthetic concept. The Scriptures insist on an aesthetic epistemology.

When you know yourself, you conceive . . . and what is born is not narcissistic introspection, or the self's knowledge of its own peculiar needs and interests,[12] but wisdom about the purpose for living. When people know other people, they conceive . . . and friendships, and marriages, and children are born. When an artist knows a thought, a thing is born—a thing of beauty known as a poem, a play, a party, a musical piece, a dance.

To be sure, the birth process is a difficult one. The Australian novelist Patrick White describes the birth of his books as "a series of caesareans without anesthetics."[13] What was the cross but the birth pangs of resurrection? That is why one must enter and embrace the pain rather than eschew and escape it. Knowledge is not a laborless concept.

We are conceivers, all! Feminist critic Camille Paglia contends that "nature has tyrannically designed our bodies for procreation."[14] But it is not just our bodies that are designed this way. Our minds and our spirits are also designed for conception. Indeed, that is the *imago dei* in us. The more knowledge we bear, the more knowing we do; the more we bear our Creator's image, the more we do our Creator's will.

In the words of John Cheever: "Art is the triumph over chaos."[15] Similarly, Robert Frost liked to say that each poem he wrote "ends in a clarification of life—not necessarily a great clarification, such as sects and cults are founded on, but in a momentary stay against confusion."[16] Each sermon that Ross composed was one more momentary stay against chaos.

In terms of the Ross theological dictionary: God doesn't have beliefs. God has knowledge. God *is* knowledge, the consciousness of the cosmos—its energy, its information, its thought.[17] Beings capable of knowledge bear a greater resemblance to the Creator. The more the energy of knowledge is embodied and enacted, the more we are conformed into the image of God and transformed by the consciousness of our Creator. Metanoia is usually defined as a conversion or spiritual transformation. But metanoia means literally "after thought." What metanoia does is transform our consciousness so that it is connected to the divine consciousness. It gives us a Christ consciousness; it puts on us the mind of Christ.

This does not mean that everything we conceive is an image of God. William Golding once said on television that sometimes in moments of exuberance he knows he is acting in the image of the Maker; the rest of the time he just goes on writing his novels and going about his business. W. H. Auden dealt with the fact that art has more functions than the moral and aesthetic arousal of its audience by claiming, "There must always be two kinds of art, escape-art, for man needs escape as he needs food and deep sleep, and parable-art, that art which shall teach man to unlearn hatred and learn love."[18]

To be sure, Ross witnessed a lot of art that he deemed destructive of community and degrading of the spirit. "'Form follows profit' is the aesthetic principle of our times," wrote English architect Richard Rogers.[19] Ross could get cynical and ill-tempered when he saw aesthetics selling out to market, state, or church. Indeed, Ross felt that the church should worry more about its own shameful role in suppressing artists like Leonardo da Vinci, who had to watch as his works were mutilated and defaced, than about the National Endowment for the Arts's role in funding contemporary artists.

The twin nature of our role as conceivers was outlined in God's First Commandment: "tend the garden and till it." There are two functions to conceiving—*conserve* (tend, or keep, or care for the garden) and *create* (till the garden). Ross tells the story of when he first learned the double meaning of the First Commandment, and who taught it to him:

I remember an important invitation in my own life. My fourth grade teacher, as most people would have agreed, was not a beautiful woman. When the Lord passed out the ears and the teeth, He gave her more than enough. As the world reckons success, I suppose she did not rise high on the scale; no university or college ever invited her to go up higher. Yet I thought she was a beautiful woman, a great woman; and I have always been grateful to her. One day she invited me to come into the green house with her, a kind of lean-to attached to her classroom. She showed me the ivy and some other vines and a green turtle eating cabbage under a fern. "Come and see," she invited; and I have been accepting the invitation ever since. I remember another invitation, on a dark afternoon, in a planetarium. Suddenly all the lights went out. By this time I was in the eighth grade. When the lights went out, all the boys and girls commenced to tickle each other. (Never, never turn out the lights on a group of eighth graders!) From some recess a man's voice quieted us and drew our attention to a dim spot on the ceiling. The stars came out, one by one. The planets swam into view. Finally the earth, blue and beautiful, took its place, suspended gloriously in the sea of space. Through the clearing clouds, we could see the North American continent and Ohio and, down there somewhere, Dayton and us. It dawned on a very quiet congregation of eighth graders that we were part of something splendid. We belonged to it; we had been invited to participate in something fantastically, magnificently wonderful. We had been invited.[20]

It has been said that divine conservation is a form of continuous creation so that there is no difference between God's cumulative creating and God's continuous conserving. This is Descartes's argument:

> It is as a matter of fact perfectly clear and evident to all those who consider with attention the nature of time, that, in order to be conserved in each moment in which it endures, a substance has need of the same power and action as would be necessary to produce and create it anew, supposing it did not yet exist, so that the light of nature shows us clearly that the distinction between creation and conservation is solely a distinction of the reason.[21]

In order to be conserved, "it has need of the same power and action as would be necessary to produce and create it anew" if it did not already exist.

However much divine conservation and divine creation may be the same thing, from the human perspective the forming and re-forming of history over time are distinct but connected processes. You might call these two versions of conception the raw and the cooked version,[22] which is fundamentally a reconfiguration of the paradoxical relationship between tradition and innovation. Each one of us is the same person we were twenty years ago, and yet at the same time we are very different. We are at once old and new, an old-new organism that conserves and yet creates.

Ross believed in a church that transmits the tradition and an education that transforms the tradition. One is a re-working of the original formula, "In the beginning. . . ." The other is a re-working of the opening formula, "Once upon a time. . . ." Using an illustration from Ross's beloved world of classical music, we could say that the model that combines both might be called a kind of theological Saint-Saëns, a consolidator avowedly adhering to a classicist Christianity while at the same time a formal innovator of great creative resourcefulness.

Another way of putting it is to employ the distinction between nature (the raw version) and creation (the cooked version). When you know nature, you conceive and creation is born. This is why Ross had such a high sacramental theology and subscribed to the doctrine of "real presence" as it is found in grain and grape. In conserving nature and working with it, we cooperate with God in the ongoing cosmic processes.

God did not stop creating the universe on the seventh day. God rested, but the Sabbath work of creation is not shut up in the past. It still goes on into the future in a universe constantly and unpredictably evolving. God the Creator's unfinished work continues into the present. This is the "real presence" of the Eucharist: "My Father is still working, and I also am working" (John 5:17 NRSV). Our work is not done either:

> God, who stretched the spangled heavens,
> infinite in time and place,
> flung the suns in burning radiance
> through the silent fields of space,
> we your children, in your likeness,
> share inventive powers with you;
> Great Creator, still creating,
> show us what we yet may do.[23]*

The Great Creator is still creating. Creation is a continual process: it is a *creatio continua.* In fact, the Bible teaches that the earth, once created, itself becomes creator: "Let the earth bring forth" (Genesis 1:11 NKJV). And what it brings forth is, at the highest level, consciousness in creation. An apple tree takes nutrients from the air and soil and water and brings them all to fruition in an "apple." A cranberry bush takes ingredients from the environment and they mix together in that bush to form the fruit of the "cranberry." If an apple tree "apples," and a cranberry bush "cranberries," then this planet Earth "peoples." People are the fruit of the earth—the coming to consciousness of the very planet itself as the Earth lives its best learnings and yearnings, lives its best life in us.

Creation in nature and creation in art follow a similar process. Ross enjoyed poets who work in and work on the English language. But Ross loved poets in whom the English language was at work. These poets don't so much write in the English language as the English language writes itself in them. Similarly, Ross enjoyed visiting museums and galleries where artists who study an object, think about it, and then paint its picture display their creations. But Ross became ecstatic over artists in whom objects and people came to consciousness. The French painter, Paul Cézanne was asked why he could do what he did in his landscape paintings. He responded: "The landscape thinks itself in me." The purpose of the Christian life is not to be good and God-like, Ross insisted. The goal of Christianity is not the creation of lives of beauty, truth, and goodness. Ross taught that the purpose of the Christian faith is to so live that God comes to life in us; to allow beauty, truth, and goodness to come to consciousness in us and do their best work in us.

Russell Freedman is one of the most respected authors of children's books in the world today. He was awarded the Newbery Medal for *Lincoln: A Photobiography* and a 1992 *Hungry Mind Review* Children's Book of Distinction for *The Wright Brothers.* Before he begins any new book, Freedman likes to re-tell to himself a story his father told him. His father

was a small child when his family moved to a rock-bound farm near Windsor, Connecticut. One afternoon, as my father would tell it, he ran across a field to meet *his* father, who would soon be coming down the road with his horse and wagon. As my father waited and dawdled, he noticed a big stone on the other side of the field. He ran over, picked up the stone, which was almost too big for him to hold, and started carrying it back toward the road, stopping here and there to put the stone down and catch his breath, then picking it up again and carrying it a bit farther. When he reached the side of the road, he put the stone down for good.

When his father—my grandfather—came rolling down that dirt road and climbed out of his wagon, my father said: "Do you see that big stone? I picked it up and carried it all the way across the field."

"Why did you do that?" his father asked.

And my father replied: "God put that stone down over there, and *I* moved it over here!"[24]

Freedman's father was not tampering with the natural order of things or irreverently altering some divine plan. He was participating in the continual act of creation. God has gifted us with partnership in composing the unfinished song of creation. The gift goes by the name "Holy Spirit." It is the Spirit of God that invites and involves us in the ongoing project of composing a song known as "The Universe." Chaos theory evidences the mysterious, interconnected score of this universe, a universe where problems are less crossword puzzles to be solved, as Walter Brueggemann reminds us, than symphonies yet to be written.[25] In fact, worship "is to listen for the ancient song of creation and to recognize within that song our individual songs. To worship is to share these melodies and dissonances of our human condition. Our voices vary: some warble, some bellow, but the song is universal. It is our ode to God, and to the God within us."[26]

Unfortunately, almost the sole scholarly focus of the divine-human encounter has been history, an explanation of the world in which there is an extraordinarily high valuation of human responsibility. One biblical scholar after another has argued over the course of the past two hundred years that human beings are active participants in human history, creating that history for good or ill. Ross believed in extending this analysis beyond the bounds of human history to include all of creation.

The term "sensitive dependence on initial conditions" (or, more simply, "the Butterfly Effect") means that a butterfly flapping its wings in Brazil can create a blizzard in Boston. In other words, God made the world such that even the flapping of a butterfly's wings could eventually change the entire evolution of the atmosphere.

Ross did not totally reject the old Cartesian dualism between mind and matter. But he did know that we inhabit, not a causal universe, but a connectional universe, where everything is a part of everything else and where the chief property of spirit is creative power. That is why art is fundamentally a religious activity.[27] We have made art a human profession, and the first artist, as we know an artist, was probably a tribal priest.[28] In the words of Cynthia Serjak, "The word 'artist' became a job description rather than a naming of one side of everyone's life."[29] Not all cultures have made "the art world" a profession. In some cultures, art so overlaps with religion that there is little difference between the two. In Bali, for example, art is so pervasive in the culture that there is no word for it. It is a part of everything that the Balinese do, think, and say.

Many cultures have retained the spiritual purpose of art, and the artist has not become estranged from the educational or intellectual establishment. Ross was convinced that reading novels, if he got to choose the novelists, could provide almost as good a theological education as one might get in seminary.

Art is less a human profession than a religious enterprise. In fact, worship was for Ross the artistry of evoking experiences of the transcendent. Yet to see art as something some humans do to get spiritual is a mistake. Art is rather something spiritual all of us do to be human. St. Bonaventura called the Logos, Jesus Christ, "the art of the Father" (*ars Patris*). Jesus is God's art, and we are called to be God's art. As Paul reminded the church at Philippi, "Work out your salvation in fear and trembling; for it is God who works in you, inspiring both the will and the deed, for his own chosen purpose" (Philippians 2:12–13 REB).

When Paul says that "it is God who *works* in you" (emphasis added), he uses the present participle form of the Greek verb *energeo*—the creative energy of God in action. It is God who energizes our creativity. We are energized by the divine. Paul says literally "it is *God* who is at work in you" (NRSV). Or in better Greek form: "God is the one working in you." This is a stupendous claim, one that Ross believed.

All the primal energy of the universe now becomes the God unborn, living and breathing inside the womb of a woman, living and breathing outside the womb of the earth, so that we might be partners in the redemption of the world. The unborn God lives in us, and even the crumb we offer a starving bird is part of the same energy of redemption Christ unleashed on the cross.

The question then becomes: How do we participate with God in creation and redemption? First, Ross declared, we must know Christ. To know Christ means that there has been a transference of energy from the divine to the human. In other words, we would so open our lives to Christ that we would receive the life-giving, healing energies of Jesus Christ, that we would take all we need from the infinite divine energies of love and life that Christ offers.

Energy is transferred when the motion of two entities becomes synchronized over a period of time. This state of matching frequencies is called "resonance." We know what happens when we resonate with a playground swing—by kicking our legs randomly we go nowhere; by kicking our legs resonantly we fly. We know what happens when soldiers resonate with a bridge—that is why marching soldiers always break cadence when crossing a bridge, to prevent the bridge from vibrating to the point where it would collapse. We know what happens when an opera singer resonates with a glass—it explodes. It vibrates and pulsates to the point where matter returns to energy.

The same thing happens when a human being "tunes in" to the frequencies of the Spirit. In the words of the hymn, "Come Thou fount of every blessing, turn our hearts to sing Thy praise." Our problem is that we have become spiritually flat, tuned to God's Spirit only in spots, tuned most precisely to the material world. Yet material things do not yield the music of creation. In fortune, fame, and power are not to be found "the riches of life." Rather, the riches of life are found in the things of the spirit—gentleness, humility, endurance, compassion, love. When we resonate with these forces through the mind of Christ, we explode in energies of faith and hope and love. We fly into the future with strength and courage. We must "tune in" to the harmonies and frequencies of the Spirit—and in God's house there are many frequencies.

It does not take much to "tune in." In dynamic systems, infinitesimal inputs can have profound effects. Small changes over time can have amazing consequences. When we tune our energies to the divine frequencies, there is enough energy and nous to make us conceive things we did not dream we could. Daniel's windows were open toward Jerusalem when he prayed (Daniel 6). We also must open our windows and turn toward God.

Second, Ross declared that to continue the unfinished song of creation, we need to know an aesthetic mode of reasoning. The French painter Jean Antoine Watteau remained an artist even on his deathbed. A friend brought to his bedside a crucifix, but Watteau pushed it away. Did I offend your convictions? the friend asked. Not at all, Watteau exclaimed. "It's a bad carving."[30] Beauty was for Ross a key, if not definitive, category of the godhead.

Where mysteries abound, humans need rituals—the more beautiful, the more potent. Rituals are built around images and often mixed ones at that. Arthur Koestler once said that the essence of creativity is the bisociation of normally unrelated matrices, the mixing and matching of ideas.[31] In other words, metaphor is the very stuff of the conceiving creator mind.

In academic circles, metaphor is seen as a primitive and faulty method of communicating truth. An aesthetic mode of reasoning has been suspect. The modern world represented truth through propositions. It seriously believed that God thinks in propositions, in principles, in rules; that God would not think in models, in stories, in narratives. Ross believed that the story of Adam and Eve was true. But truth is not flat, one-dimensional, literalist. Literalism and truth are not one and the same thing.

In truth, we need more insights that are the product not just of critical observation but of "imaginative rationality." An artist absorbs material through images and then reproduces it in living form. Art is nothing more, nor less, than the production of images: in painting, in film, in poetry, in sound.

To continue the unfinished song of creation, we need to know a third thing: the boundaries of the human mind are not the boundaries of the universe. Philip Toynbee takes as the "primal religious statement of our time" this: "There is more than we can know." His second "primal" article of faith is this: "What we cannot know is better than anything that we can know."[32]

There is a cartoon picturing two college coeds, arms loaded with books, coming down the campus library steps. One says to the other: "Every day there are more and more things to be ignorant about." The more we know, the more we know we don't know. If we learn to rejoice at all we have left to learn, our melodies will be based not on fear and despair but on love and faith and hope. It is also for this reason that Christians should not be averse to having a song that sounds very different from that sung by others.

Finally, to continue the unfinished song of creation we need to know that our role as conceivers will not be directed to our own glory but to the glory of God. As John Calvin said, "sculpture and painting are gifts of God."[33]

Charles Wuorinen, the Pulitzer Prize–winning composer was interviewed on the radio after "Genesis" was premiered by the San Francisco Symphony. The interviewer noted that much had been written about the difficulty of the music, the delicate, polyphonic scoring for chorus and orchestra, and the problems many audiences have in grasping Wuorinen's work. Wuorinen was asked how he, as a composer, had come to a deep religious faith on his own when he had grown up in an agnostic family:

During the last couple of hundred or three hundred years or so we seem to have developed an attitude that art is for man alone. And I really don't believe that. . . . It seems to me that unless art is, to some extent, addressed to a higher power, higher purposes, in other words, if it is not in a certain sense . . . a kind of act of worship, it really doesn't mean very much.[34]

"My music," Wuorinen concludes, "is not necessarily intended for those who pay the price of admission. . . . It's addressed to God."

Each of us is an artist, able to participate in God's creativity. The art world is the whole world. In Ross's view, the true test of whether a Christian is living in the stream of the Spirit is this: What are you conceiving right now? What artwork is being born in you right now? The unfinished song of creation is being composed right now by our art. What kind of a song will it be?

SERMONS

ꙄꚖꙆ

The Worst . . . and Freedom from It

Text: Luke 18:9–14

In the seventeenth century there was an Anglican theologian who wrote a pamphlet entitled *The Inward Peace of the Christian Man.*[1] He lived in an era in many ways like our own, a time of tumultuous social change and conflict, and yet it was not about the events transpiring around him, which were turning world history upside down, that he spoke in his book. What he said, rather, was that in his day men and women were being torn apart by "the soul's conflict within itself." He went on to say this: "True peace arises from knowing the worst first, and then, our freedom from it." Many people I know have one of two problems: either they know the worst and that is all they know, or else they know their freedom and that is all they know.

In the second lesson this morning our Lord Jesus Christ told a strange story. "Two men," he said, "went up to the Temple to pray, one a Pharisee and the other a publican, a tax collector. The Pharisee stood by himself and this was his prayer: 'I thank you, O God, that I am not like other people, weak and sinful and adulterous. I am especially glad that I am not like that man over there.'"

Sermon preached at St. Paul's Episcopal Church, Akron, Ohio, on the Twenty-first Sunday after Pentecost, 23 October 1977. George Ross Papers, The University of Akron Archives.

123

"The other man," said Jesus, "stood afar off, and this is what he said, 'Dear Lord, I have come here to face the worst that is in me, and it is bad. Have mercy on me and help me to find grace to live beyond this brokenness, to reach beyond these limits, to find healing for my sickness and faith where I doubt.' That man," said Jesus, "went down to his house with grace" (cf. Luke 18:10–14).

There are three points to the sermon this morning and they are these: (1) knowing the worst, (2) finding the freedom, (3) going home justified.

I. KNOWING THE WORST

First: knowing the worst. I hesitate to talk about it. I know some of you very well, and you do not need to be told about the worst. You know all about it. Tragedy strikes down a beautiful young girl or takes away a wonderful boy on the very birthday of his manhood. Some of you have failed in your business; some, in your marriage. Some of you are sick. Some of you are dying. Imagine, therefore, how hesitant a preacher who loves and knows his friends must be when it is necessary for you to know the worst, whatever it is, to face it, to accept it, to grieve it, and, in fact, embrace it before you can be set free of it. I would not dare to say such things to you, were it not for the fact that I testify of what *I* know.

The pathos of our day, surely, is that many people know the worst; they have found it out; they are in it. Dorothy Parker once wrote a poem that I read every so often as middle age creeps up on me at a not so petty pace:

> When I was young and bold and strong,
> Oh, right was right, and wrong was wrong!
> My plume on high, my flag unfurled,
> I rode away to right the world.
> "Come out, you dogs, and fight!" said I,
> And wept that there was but once to die.
>
> But I grow old; and good and bad
> Are woven in a crazy plaid.

I sit and say, "The world is so;
And he is wise who lets it go.
A battle lost, a battle won—
The difference is small, my son."
Inertia rides and riddles me;
The which is called Philosophy.[2]

That is what passes for philosophy, for wisdom, among a few of us, perhaps among a lot of us today. Poor Dorothy Parker died a broken hearted, lonely woman, lost in alcohol and drugs, in a New York apartment. She was one of us who had found the worst, but not the freedom from it. George Bernard Shaw wrote that for many people this must be the epitaph: "Died at thirty, buried at sixty." Well, of some of us, I guess it is true. At some point we find the worst, but it destroys us, and we die before our time.

He stood afar off and faced the worst, but, said Jesus, *he did it in the Temple; in the Temple he did it, and in prayer he did it.* Therein lies the explanation of the grace he found. It is not enough to be able to discern what is wrong, either with oneself or with one's world. It matters *where* you make the discovery and *how* you make it. He made it in the Temple at prayer, and so he was freed of it.

Someone once said that the North Wind made the Vikings. Well, I think something like that is true of every mature personality. The tragedy in the church today is not found in the people who are discouraged or dismayed or depressed even, but in those who are complacent about themselves and about this world for which our Lord gave up his life. Phillips Brooks hits the point right on dead center, with these words: "Sad will be the day for every man when he becomes absolutely contented with the life that he is living, with the thoughts that he is thinking, with the deeds that he is doing; when there is not forever beating at the doors of his soul some great desire to do and to be something larger, which he knows that he was meant and made to do because he is a child of God."[3]

Jesus saw in the man who knew the worst and faced it in prayer the possibilities of grace and new life. It is when we begin to see ourselves in the perspectives of our needs and not in the presumptions of our successes that God can do something with us, when we can begin to take those giant steps that lead to personal maturity.

In one of Peter de Vries' novels there is a character by the name of Tillie Seltzer, who offers this prayer to God: "Give us courage for our fears, the wisdom to survive our follies, and charity to bind up the wounds we inflict on one another."[4] The Gospel is this: God hears prayers like that; God hears them and he answers them.

II. FINDING THE FREEDOM

Second: finding the freedom. Freedom from the worst is the gift he offers each of us in prayer. G. K. Chesterton offers us the ultimate wisdom in a simple sentence about the theology of Lewis Carroll, a small sentence on that topic: "Alice must grow small if she is to become Alice in Wonderland."[5] Or to put it in our biblical way: God must be born a baby in Bethlehem in a dirty stable because there is no room in the inn, and die upon a cross among criminals, taking all the worst and embracing it and accepting it and enduring it and transforming it through his personal prayer to God.

To the Temple with our pain. In the Temple with our Lord. From the Temple to our houses with his power. There, if you will, is the pattern and sequence of everybody's Christianity. It is Christ's way beyond the pathetic inertia of the self-righteous and of the self-defeated alike.

III. GOING HOME JUSTIFIED

Third: going home justified. "He went down to his house justified," the Lord says, but he does not tell us exactly what that means. I think it means this: that whereas once the man's awareness of his trouble defeated him, now God empowers him in his humility to go home again with grace. He moves from self-disgust through the door of humble prayer into the life of service back home. That is the story of everybody's pilgrimage in Christ. Dr. Leslie Weatherhead in so many of his sermons has helped me to see the point more and more clearly as my own experiences seem to converge upon the same truth. This is one of the illustrations of it that he offers and which I have found helpful and which I hope you will find helpful. It is a very simple story about the time when Albert Schweitzer came to visit at their home in London. At that time their daughter was quite small, just beginning to take piano lessons. They had a piano, not much of a piano, old and slightly out of tune, and the little girl was doing her exercises when this great man arrived at their humble home, so they told her to stop. But Dr. Schweitzer said, "No, no, no! Let me sit down beside her." So he sat down and took the little girl's hands in his own and they felt out the notes. Between them they played a sweet, simple little melody. Here was the greatest living exponent of the music of Johann Sebastian Bach, one of the world's greatest men, and yet he had time to sit down with a little girl who was just learning to play the piano and to help her with it. Now you may think it a homely, perhaps even trivial, story, but it is an image I carry about in my heart of what it means for a man to go to a house, his own or anybody else's, justified by the grace of God. For it is also the story of our dear Lord Jesus Christ, who takes our clumsy fingers in his and on the old, out of tune world we live in, teaches us in great humility how to play some songs of faith and love and joy. Justified.

Now this is Altar Sunday or Stewardship Sunday or Commitment Sunday. We have called it all these things as we present our annual pledges to the work of Christ in and through this parish. Let us remember that once there was a man who said, "I tithe of all that I get" . . . yet there followed this graceless, in fact, a tragic statement: because he exalted himself he went down to his house unjustified. So can every pledge be to any church. My prayer this morning is this: that when we offer our pledges on the Altar of God for the work of God, each one of them will be a sacrament of a certain personal experience which we wish to share with others, namely, this discovery in Jesus Christ: that true peace arises first from knowing the worst and then our freedom from it as we offer our lives in humility in the Temple. Jesus leads the way. Let us follow from confession through forgiveness to self offering. So shall we all go down to our houses justified.

LET US PRAY:

Gracious heavenly Father, we pray for our dear parish family and congregation and for all who seek to find here with us forgiveness for their sins and healing for broken hearts, and to be strengthened through grace for mature lives of Christian service. Open the hands of our loyal people in generous commitment that the good work which you have begun among us through years past may be continued with eagerness and steadfast purpose in our generation, through Jesus Christ our Lord. *Amen.*

Paracletos

To speak *of* the Holy Spirit it is necessary to speak of one's own life *in* the Spirit. And so I do not hesitate to speak about my experience with the Holy Spirit. Yesterday I administered the rites of Christian burial to one of our brothers in one of the beautiful cemeteries near Akron. Standing at the grave side, waiting for the family to come from the cars, I looked around and saw little clusters of people bearing their small bouquets of Memorial Day flowers. (We used to call it Decoration Day, when I was growing up.) I watched them wandering among the stones and saw the flags flying throughout the cemetery, marking the graves of those who had fallen in the wars. For a moment, as I waited there, I found myself lost, looking at a linden tree, all its leaves dancing in a breeze. After I had spoken the words of final benediction, I found myself acutely aware for a moment of my own breathing. As I closed the book and embraced the family and made my way back home, it suddenly came to me that the breath which came from inside me and shaped itself into those prayers and the wind which blew through that linden tree were the same. I suddenly, for a fleeting moment, felt myself one with the dead who yet live and with the living who yet die. Not for the first time in my life (though every such moment is always the first time), I understood what T. S. Eliot meant when he said of the Holy Spirit: "The fire and the rose are one."[6]

I realize very well that such an experience is personal. Your experience with the Holy Spirit may be, and probably is, completely

Sermon preached at St. Paul's Episcopal Church, Akron, Ohio, on the Day of Pentecost, 26 May 1985. George Ross Papers, The University of Akron Archives.

129

different. You may wonder, "What in the world is he talking about?" But anyone who has known the Spirit of God surely knows somehow what Wordsworth meant when, above Tintern Abbey, he wrote that he had felt this disturbing presence of God:

> Of something far more deeply interfused,
> Whose dwelling is the light of setting suns,
> And the round ocean and the living air,
> And the blue sky, and in the mind of man;
> A motion and a spirit, that impels
> All thinking things, all objects of all thought,
> And rolls through all things.[7]

As I read the Bible, that is the first thing anyone must say about the Holy Spirit: something that rolls through all things, an invisible power that pervades everything, the source, the ground, the origin, the destiny of all that is and has been and yet shall be.

An ancient Jewish prayer for Pentecost, the "Atta Nimisa," says it well: "O God, Thou art! the hearing of the ear, the seeing of the eye cannot reach Thee; no How or Why or Where can lead us to thee. Thou art! Hidden is thy secret, deep, so deep; who can find Thee?" The seeing of the eye, the hearing of the ear cannot search out the Holy Spirit; but, as the Bible says: "Deep calleth unto deep."

To understand what the New Testament means by the "Holy Spirit," we must examine a word, a word strange to our ears, but common in the first century. Jesus said to the disciples: "Beloved, I must leave you, but I will not leave you comfortless. I will send to you the Holy Spirit, the *paracletos*" (cf. John 14:16-18). The word *paracletos* has a fascinating double meaning in the Greek language. On the one hand it means an advocate or a counselor, a defense attorney who stands at your side when you are accused of a crime. I think that Jesus promised the *paracletos* because he knew that his church would soon be on trial, that these men who had left their homes, their boats, their all, to follow him would in just a few days be catapulted into a hostile environment and their lives would stand at hazard. So he promised to them the *paracletos*, the advocate who would stand beside them in all those trials, to be at their side and to see them through. So I believe the Holy Spirit comes to us when we are in the trials of life.

A man kneels down in a hospital room to pray for his wife in surgery. He is not ordinarily a man of prayer; he does not even know how to go about it. The only prayer that comes to him is one that does not seem quite right, "Now I lay me down to sleep . . ." So he sits and waits and suddenly, he knows not how, four words form in his mind and he offers them to God: "O God, help her." St. Paul reminds us that sometimes we are not able to pray—even those of us who often pray are just not able to pray. It is just then, says Paul, that the Holy Spirit comes and stands within you and helps you to pray "with sighs too deep for words" (Romans 8:26).

I remember an experience with the *paracletos* of God a few years ago. A faculty member of a college in my parish was struggling with many fears. He feared that his marriage was coming apart, and it was. He feared that his career as a scientist and teacher was floundering, and it was. He feared for his children's future in the kind of world he read about in the daily paper. And he took to drinking—heavily—until, by and by, he was full of all the fears of an alcoholic. One day he woke up in his automobile on a lonely, back-country road and had not the slightest idea of how he had gotten there. That was very frightening. He wondered how long he had been driving in that condition. Had he reached the point of no return? He told me that in the midst of these fears words came to him and he cried out to God, "O God, if you exist, if you are there, please help me!" There were no tongues of flame, no rushing, mighty wind, no glossolalia; but in that moment, he said, he felt a sense of calm within himself, and he knew that he was at the turning point. So the Holy Spirit comes to us, the *paracletos*, our advocate, the one who intercedes for us when we can no longer help ourselves.

That is one meaning of the word, but *paracletos* has another meaning in Greek. In the ancient world when an army was preparing for a decisive battle, especially if the outcome was in doubt, the commander might summon a man called "the *paracletos*."

The *paracletos* was an orator who was unusually skillful in the gift of encouragement and morale building. The trumpeter would sound and the army would gather and the *paracletos* would speak. If he was effective, by and by, the nearly mutinous, disorganized, dispirited rabble would become an impassioned, confident army. Away they would go as one man to battle. Jesus said, "I will give you the *paracletos* to summon the disparate and divided energies of the church and to give you courage and encouragement as you go out into the world in my name to do my work."

William James, speaking at Columbia University, once characterized our modern age with one German word. He said that we today are the victims of *Zerishensheit,* which means "torn-apartness." But if ever any group of people suffered from *Zerishensheit* it was the church of Christ in the city of Jerusalem on Pentecost Day. Guilt about their past and all of its betrayals, fear about the future and all of its dangers, alienation from everyone else in the city of Jerusalem—that was the condition of the church of Jesus Christ before the Spirit came. But when the Spirit came, that torn-apart community was healed and united and made strong and confident. They went down from that upper room and out into the street to minister the healing and the power and the love and the joy that they themselves had just received. The *paracletos* empowers the church for its healing and its prophetic mission. Remember when Jesus took the Book from the attendant in the synagogue He read from the prophet Isaiah to clarify the mission of the spirit-filled people of God in the world: "The Spirit of the Lord is upon me, because he has anointed me to preach good news to the poor. He has sent me to proclaim release to the captives and recovering of sight to the blind, to set at liberty those who are oppressed, to proclaim the acceptable year of the Lord" (Luke 4:18–19 RSV).

From this we learn that those in whom the *paracletos* is at work are not those who are passive and quiet and placid and withdrawn in private mysticism. The Holy Spirit anoints Jesus and us as active, energetic, public advocates for peace and justice and brotherhood and the righteousness of God in the world. St. Augustine spoke of the Holy Ghost as *deus rerum tenax*: "God, the persistent energy of life." The Holy Spirit is known not only in the gentle breeze in a linden tree; the Holy Spirit is the consuming fire, which would burn the bones of Jeremiah if he should keep silence before injustice and evil in the world.

How does the Holy Spirit speak to us today? To my way of thinking, one of the most moving passages in all modern literature is a single page from the prison journal of an unknown German resistance fighter. It was written on the eve of his execution by the SS about the Holy Spirit:

I vividly recall my night of torture in the Lehrter Street Prison and how I prayed to God that he might send death to deliver me because of the helplessness and pain and the violence and hatred to which I was no longer equal. How I wrestled with God that night and finally in my great need I crept to Him, weeping. Not until morning did a great peace come to me, a blissful awareness of light, strength and warmth, bringing with it the conviction that I must see this thing through and at the same time the blessed assurance that I would see it through. Solace is woe! This is the Holy Spirit, the Comforter. This is the dialogue that he conducts with us. These are the secret blessings he dispenses which enable a man to live and to endure.[8]

Jesus said: "I will not leave you comfortless. I will send to you the *paracletos*."

How do we know the Holy Spirit? Some people tell us that *their* way to know him is the only way. But the Scripture tells us that, as it was in the days of Paul, so it is today: The Holy Spirit is known in *many* ways, but in all his work there is a persistent energy of life and that is the energy of the Divine Love. Bishop John Taylor concludes his book on the Holy Spirit (which he entitles *The Go-between God*), with these words:

A West Indian woman in a London flat was told of her husband's death in a street accident. The shock of grief stunned her like a blow, she sank into a corner of the sofa and there she sat rigid and unhearing. . . . Friends and officials . . . came and went [but no one could reach her]. Then the school teacher of one of her children, an Englishwoman, called and, seeing how things were, went and sat beside her. Without a word, she threw an arm around the tight shoulders, clasping them with her full strength. The white cheek was thrust hard against the brown. Then as the unrelenting pain seeped through to her the newcomer's tears began to flow, falling on their two hands linked in the woman's lap. For a long time that is all that was happening. And then, at last, the West Indian woman began to sob. Still not a word was spoken and after a little while the visitor got up and went, leaving her contribution to help the family in its immediate need.[9]

Sometimes the Holy Spirit comes in tongues of flame; he has come in ecstatic speech and with a rushing, mighty wind that shakes the pillars of the house. And sometimes he comes to us, Bishop Taylor continues, "in the straining muscles of an arm, and the film of sweat between pressed cheeks, the mingled wetness of the back of clasped hands. He is as close and unobtrusive as that and as irresistibly strong.[10] *Deus rerum tenax!*

LET US PRAY:

We pray for the church today and especially for this congregation of St. Paul's that we may be filled with the love and the power of the Holy Spirit of God, in all our members and in all our work. Come, Holy Spirit, come and make our hearts your home. *Amen*

Saved by Surprise

Someone said to Jesus, "Who will be saved?
How many?" Jesus answered, "Some will say,
'We used to have dinner with you; you know
us well.' But the Lord will say, 'I know you
not.' Meanwhile men will come from far
away and sit at table in the Kingdom of God.
Behold some who are last will be first and
some who are first will be last."

Text: Luke 13: 23–30

Nothing is psychologically more normal than the desire to be certain about sacred things. And yet the Bible from the first to the last book unfolds the disquieting truth that salvation comes more by surprise than through certainty. Outside his tent Abraham listened, astonished as the angel told him that his one hundred-year-old wife would bear him a son. Sarah, you remember, was eavesdropping inside the tent as the old men talked. When she heard the angel's promise, she laughed out loud (Genesis 18:1–15). Down the centuries, we hear her old woman's cackle over the absurdities of God's grace. By his bedroom door, the Praetorian guard stood watch as Caesar slept; meanwhile, beneath strange starlight, a baby was born with only the friendly beasts to guard him in a sta-

Sermon preached at St. Paul's Episcopal Church, Akron, Ohio, on the Fourteenth Sunday after Pentecost, 24 August 1986. George Ross Papers, The University of Akron Archives.

135

ble. Now great Rome has crumbled and great Caesar's bones with it, but that little child has brought us here today. A cranky clergyman, stewing over the terrible and general decline of things, set out one day in his worried way to set things right. Filled with resentful wrath, he rose to fight till victory. That night he went to sleep defeated, blind, and troubled—broken, yet somehow healed, utterly naked yet clothed, he knew not how, with mysterious joy—and here we are, two thousand years later, assembled in a church which bears the name of Paul.

How strange it all is and how evident in all of it that humanity is saved by Divine surprises and not by human certainties. "Who will be saved?" they asked. "You'll be surprised!" he answered. It is evident, however, even to the casual student of history, that the church which began as a surprise of Divine grace often forgets how it began. The craving for dogmatic certainty is nowhere more alive than in the Christian church. Church people not only require certainty in sacred things, they become surly when challenged by the not-so-certain. Bishop Fulton J. Sheen once visited a parochial school and found himself discussing Jonah and the whale with a group of sixth graders. (Fools walk in!) There was one boy who questioned and questioned the Bishop. No answer from the Bishop was satisfactory. Finally the boy said, "I don't believe any of this. I just don't think that the whale ate Jonah." The Bishop said, "Well, young man, if he goes to the other place, *you* ask him!"

The urge to excommunicate those who challenge our certainties is deep set in the human heart and is clearly evident when the religious climate is supercharged and overheated, as it is today. In the state of Michigan recently a television evangelist announced that God has anointed him to become president of this country. At prayer meetings he speaks in tongues and cries, "Satan, be gone" as he lays hands on the sick. When Hurricane Gloria threatened Virginia Beach, where his headquarters is located, he claimed credit for the deliverance of the community, proclaiming, "We rebuked that thing; we commanded it." (One thrills to imagine what such a man might do with the national debt.) For the first time in American history voters may find themselves challenged to vote for a candidate or else oppose the will of God. Last week Fr. Charles Curran, Professor of Theology at Georgetown University, received a letter from Cardinal Ratzinger, prelate of what used to be called the Holy Office or "Inquisition." Fr. Curran was to cease his university career because of heresies discovered in some of his books. At the same time across the country in Los Angeles, a Jesuit priest received a letter, also from Rome, commanding him to burn an unpublished book in which he reports that 25 percent of the bishops of the Roman Catholic Church in this country favor the marriage of priests. Someone in Italy has decided that no one in America ought to know that. So at one extreme we have unbridled claims of private inspiration, while at the other there are extraordinary assertions of institutional authority to suppress private opinion.

The religious atmosphere in which we live is supercharged and overheated. We need not, when we assemble here, comment on the internal controversies of other religious bodies; that is unnecessary and even wrong. But as Episcopalians, do we not need in such a moment to reflect upon our own approach to religious truths?

I. THE PRINCIPLE OF FREE SPEECH

The first principle in this matter can not be too often restated: namely, that we hold that freedom of inquiry and freedom of speech are always to be maintained. The burning of books and the persecution of heretics is still an issue; perhaps never in the history of the world has it been such a frightful issue as it is today. Amnesty International reports that ninety-one governments imprison religious and political prisoners; dozens of regimes murder and torture their own dissidents. According to a survey by Freedom House, three billion people in one hundred and seventeen nations live under governments which suppress free speech. To champion free speech and the freedom of inquiry is not to be indifferent to the truth. John Milton, who was as convinced and steady a Christian as one can imagine, fell out with his Puritan colleagues on this very issue. In his great book, *The Areopagitica* (*On Freedom of Speech*), John Milton wrote:

Though all the winds of doctrine were let loose to play upon the earth, so truth be in the field, we do ingloriously by licensing and prohibiting to misdoubt her strength. Let her and falsehood grapple; who ever knew truth put to the worse, in a free and open encounter![11]

That idea sank deep into English thought and into Anglican Church practice. The Inquisition became as abhorrent to us in religion as the Star Chamber was to us in politics. For people who have been saved by surprise, Christianity does not admit intolerance of free discussion. Who knows, God may have some surprises still to spring on us!

II. THE PRINCIPLE OF
MENTAL HUMILITY

The second principle is like unto the first. It may be stated very simply as the principle of mental humility. I had a seminary professor who said of our systematic theology class, "Students, when you say the Nicene Creed, don't forget to smile." I did not know what he meant for a long time until it dawned on me that the Nicene Creed is not so much a serious utterance of an amazing idea as it is a joyful response to an amazing grace. Every bold statement about God's greatness ought to be accompanied by a humble awareness of our frailty. It's rather like the elderly man who fell in love with an elderly lady. He approached her, got down on his knees, and said, "I have two questions for you. The first is, 'Will you marry me?'" She said. "Yes. And what is the second question?" He said, "The second question is, 'Will you give me a hand getting up off my knees?'" So should boldness be joined with humility when man speaks *to* God *about* God.

III. THE PRINCIPLE OF
EXPECTANT OPENNESS

The third principle to guide our conversation about God, in addition to free speech and mental humility, is the principle of expectant openness. Jesus said, "I am the truth." Whatever else that means, at the very least it means that truth is personal and that, therefore, we approach truth not as an intellectual proposition to be mastered, but as a beautiful person to be loved. We meet the truth, not at the end of a dogma, but in the face of a friend. That being so, all our conversation about God will have about it less a mood of arrogant completeness than a cheerful expectancy. I love the way Paul puts it in the Epistle to the Romans. "Give blessing when you are persecuted, rejoice with the joyful, weep with the hurting. Always lift up what is noble and be aglow with the Spirit" (cf. Rom. 12:15). J. B. Phillips translates Philippians 4:5 as "Beloved, delight yourselves in God." What a wonderful way to speak of our approach to religious study. "Delight yourselves in God!" The theologian after my own heart is Anglican divine, Richard Hooker. Please excuse his old-fashioned language and do listen to his cheerful counsel.

Whatsoever either men on earth or the angels in heaven do know, it is as a drop of that unemptiable fountain of wisdom; which wisdom hath diversely imparted her treasures unto the world. As her ways are of sundry kinds, so her manner of teaching is not merely one and the same. Some things she openeth by the sacred books of Scripture; some things by the glorious works of Nature: with some things she inspireth them from above by spiritual influence; in some things she leadeth and traineth them only by worldly experience and practice. We may not so in any one special kind admire her, that we disgrace her in any other, but let all her ways be according unto their place and degree adored.[12]

Freedom of speech *always*, humility of mind and heart *always*, openness to the manifold surprises of grace *always*—perhaps such an approach to sacred things will not satisfy those who crave supernatural or ecclesiastical dogma; but let us make no apology as Episcopalians for who and what we are. We are what we are by the grace of God. I know that some will be surprised to see the muddle-headed Episcopalians wandering into heaven; and for that reason I take much comfort in our text this morning. It reminds us that God has a vast sense of humor and that when the gates are opened, from west to east, from north to south, most surprising (and surprised!) folk will be admitted.

We may go from church more certain than we came. That may be good—provided that we are mainly certain that God is great, that his mercy passeth human understanding and that he has prepared for us, and for all humankind, amazing surprises of still unfolding grace.

Who is That on the Other Side of You?

Text: Mark 8:31–38

The Indian poet and mystic Rabindranath Tagore has said that each of us has two persons within: the conscious self, who is always getting in the way, rather a stupid fellow, and the other person, the unconscious self, who is really the creative spirit. T. S. Eliot asks the haunting question which we all find difficult to answer: "Who is that on the other side of You?"[13]

The text for the sermon is from the Gospel just read: "Jesus began to speak about his suffering and his resurrection, and Peter took him aside and rebuked him (cf. Mark 8:31,32). St. Peter is a *locus classicus*, a case study in the duality of human personality. On the one hand there is the brave, bold man of wonderful faith, trusting where he cannot see, learning humbly how to pray, casting his net for mysterious fish, launching out into the deep. But the same man who walks upon the waters averts his eyes from Christ to watch the waves, and so he sinks. The one who confesses, "You are the Christ," takes Christ aside to rebuke him. In one moment he protests, "You will not wash my feet," and in the next beseeches, "Lord, wash me head to toe." In other words: if not in minute particulars, then in the major essentials, the man on whom the Christian church is founded is just like you and just like me. There is the self-assertive, egocentric personality, all fumbles, follies, wild gestures, fantastic schemes, getting in the way; yet eventually, out steps a man of faith, of vision, dreams,

Sermon preached at St. Paul's Episcopal Church, Akron, Ohio, on the Second Sunday in Lent, 3 March 1985. George Ross Papers, The University of Akron Archives.

141

courage, and self-forgetful love. G. K. Chesterton's conclusion ought to encourage us, when he writes:

When Christ established his great society, he chose for the corner stone neither the brilliant Paul nor the mystic John, but a shuffler, a snob and a coward, in a word, an ordinary man. And upon this rock he built his church, and the gates of hell have not prevailed against it. All the empires and kingdoms have failed because of this inherent and continual weakness: that they were founded by strong men for strong men. But this one thing—the historic Christian church was founded on a weak man, and for that reason is indestructible.[14]

St. Peter's life offers three instructions: First: Don't rebuke unavoidable suffering. Second: Don't lie down in inevitable mistakes. Third: Do listen to Christ.

I. DO NOT REBUKE
UNAVOIDABLE SUFFERING

First: Don't rebuke unavoidable suffering. When Jesus began to speak about suffering, Peter rebuked him (Mark 8:32). When the soldier stepped forward in Gethsemane, Peter cut off his ear (John 18:10). We do the same thing. Rebuke is our characteristic way of handling contradiction. Anger, even to the point of violence, is our typical and usual reply. We rebuke our circumstances. "It is just not fair that I have to go through this." "Why is this happening to me?" Anyone with an illness, even the sniffles, is a practiced expert at rebuke. We rebuke both our friends and our adversaries, our parents and our children, our spouses, the well known and the unknown, who jostle, arrest, or frustrate us. Jonathan Edwards said it well: "If you would have a mind to test the strength of the house, observe it in the storm." It could have been about Peter or about us that the jingle was written: "When things went well, he looked swell; / But, when things went bad, he looked sad." Peter wanted no cross in his program for world reform. He was like the man in the Rubáiyát whose journey to Utopia omitted Jerusalem:

Ah Love, could you and I with Fate conspire
To grasp this sorry Scheme of Things entire,
Would not we shatter it to bits—and then
Remould it nearer to the Heart's Desire?[15]

If we were Christ, we would do something like that, don't you think?

In his rejection of the cross St. Peter was saying in effect, "O God, save me, but don't hurt me." But anyone who knows anything about being saved knows that it can't be done without being hurt. Marcel Proust, out of the long pain of his life, wrote somewhere that it is from the heartaches, chastening, sufferings and pain with humiliation that we grow our souls. We recall the well-loved words of Paul: "We rejoice in our troubles for troubles make for fortitude, and fortitude produces the veteran, and out of the veteran's character and tested experience comes hope, the kind of hope that does not disappoint us" (cf. Romans 5:3).

The maxim is well worn, but like a holy grail it holds a precious truth: that the only way *out* of a difficulty is *through* it. Jesus always, from the very first day on the road, knew that; but Peter forgot it more than once, as we do. Jesus had to rebuke him for that forgetfulness; perhaps, he must rebuke us as well. Can we not hear him asking, "Simon, who is that on the *other* side of you? Suffering is what love is willing to endure when it must to gain its goal. Suffering is the universal experience all of us share and that is why our Lord embraced his cross, so that from within our pain, our loss, our loneliness, our utmost physical and spiritual distress, he might share without avoidance the sufferings of humankind in order to redeem them. God can lead us through to the other side, not to the easy victories we would like to enjoy, but to the glory he has prepared for those who unfeignedly love Him. St. Peter wanted to omit the cross. Jesus loved us too much to leave it out, for if he leaves out the cross, he leaves out suffering, and if religion has nothing to say about the dark subject, it has nothing to offer us. "So, Simon, standing there in your indignation, your rebuke, your superior attitude, who is that on the other side of you?"

II. DO NOT LIE DOWN IN
INEVITABLE MISTAKES

The second instruction is like unto the first: Don't lie down in your failures. Read the twenty-third Psalm slowly sometime and get it right please. The valley of the shadow is something to walk through, not something to lie down in. God hears us when we pray, "Yea though I walk through the valley, thou art with me." But we are not invited to lie down by the shepherd until we reach the green pastures.

Judas Iscariot and Simon Peter make interesting case studies, don't they? They were alike in one way: they both made mistakes. But on the other side of Peter there was a man of humble faith who walked through his mistakes, while Judas lay down and died in them. One man made mistakes. Mistakes made the other man. How is it going with you today? Sometimes this question is addressed to us in angry confrontation by those who really love us. Who is that on the other side of you? Don't turn away from this rebuke if it comes sometimes with sharpness from a friend or relative. Don't turn away in resentment and petulance. Always remember that whom the Lord loveth, he chasteneth. "Who is that on the other side of you?" Maybe you came to church this morning discouraged. You know that you have betrayed the best and you may also know that you have been betrayed. But who is that on the other side of that aspect of your life? Make no mistake about it: someone *is* there. A man of faith is there, a woman of courage is there. Commence to walk through your valley, and you will find on the other side of you a Shepherd who has been this way before and knows the way through.

Someone once asked Socrates why Alcibiades, a brilliant, charismatic Athenian, was such a deeply unhappy man. Socrates replied, "Because wherever Alcibiades goes, he takes Alcibiades with him." Jesus Christ entered Simon Peter's life and he broke that spell and a new man with a new chance emerged. Perhaps someone here this morning is lying down in the failures of life. Maybe the mistakes have piled up on you and you are lying in the valley. Wherever you go, you take your failure-self with you. Christ is very near to you if that is so. He is very near to you this morning. Maybe he has never been closer to you than he is right now; and if you listen, you can hear him asking you a question that you really ought to answer: "Who is that on the other side of you?"

III. DO LISTEN TO CHRIST

This leads us to the third and final point: Listen to Christ; he is not farther away than the other side of you. Listen to him when he calls you as he called Simon from trivial life to great life. Listen to Christ when he tells you that not all suffering is avoidable, but all suffering *is* redeemable. Peter listened to that and so can we. Listen to him when he tells you that you will betray him more than once in your life, but you can be forgiven; and life can expand for you again through the straight and narrow gateway of repentance. Peter listened to that and so can we. Listen to the Lord when he asks to wash your feet. Let him do it, for your salvation really depends upon your acceptance of your dependence. Peter learned that and so can we. Don't lie down in your dark valley; walk through it with the Shepherd and listen to him as you go.

Most of the time Simon Peter and the others didn't know where they were going or how to get there; they didn't have the foggiest idea about it. Just a handful of unarmed men against a hostile and indifferent world—no wonder in their anxiety they make so many mistakes! No wonder we do! But they became wonderfully and radiantly sure about one thing, and in the glory of that one certainty they blazed a trail of glory across the face of the earth that is still widening and lengthening. They became confident, as they put it (in one magnificent sentence) "of the light of the knowledge of the glory of God in the face of Jesus Christ" (2 Corinthians 4:6 RSV). The healing, the joy, the hope, the peace that faith gave to them can be ours. We can trust where we do not see. We can endure the unavoidable cross without denial. We can hope for a brighter day when the present world seems a dim diminished thing "And when the strife is fierce, the warfare long, Steals on the ear the distant triumph song."[16] And we know that Easter is shining on the other side of whatever cross we have to bear.

IV. THE PURPOSE OF LIFE:
TO FIND THE REST OF IT

If you find yourself leading a life of rebuke, if you are lying down in a dark valley, if you are all but dead to a side of you that has been crusted over by trouble, then this is the Word of God for you this morning: on the other side of you as you are there is a self that is and can be; and God is saying to you this morning, as he said to Peter in his dismay at Caesarea Philippi: the purpose of your life now is to find the rest of it.

Who is that on the other side of you? On the other side of Simon, St. Peter. On the other side of Levi, St. Matthew. On the other side of Saul, St. Paul. Who is that on the other side of you? Let no mistake or sorrow of the past bar you from the glorious adventure of finding the answer to that question.

CHAPTER FOUR

WOUNDED BACK

Broken Promises

SAMUEL JOHNSON REPORTEDLY shook his head and muttered, "This is not the kind of life to which heaven is promised." Cannot every one of us say the same about our own lives at times? Each of us has memories that, when we revisit them as Dr. Johnson did, make us wince at "open wounds, shrunk sometimes to the size of a pin-prick," in F. Scott Fitzgerald's words, "but wounds still."[1] Mary McGarry Morris, in her novel *Vanished*, talks of how "remembering was too much like grave digging. Every stone-clang on the shovel struck cold and hard through his bones."[2]

In our journey through life, sometimes we do everything right, and nothing good happens. Sometimes we do everything wrong, messing up right and breaking down left, and everything good happens. It is a strange universe in which we sojourn, but never so strange that suffering is a stranger.

The truth of the matter is that every one of us will suffer. We will suffer because of things we have done. We will suffer for things others have done. A Christian actually takes on responsibility for fellow human beings, even the irresponsible ones. In *The Brothers Karamazov*, Saint Father Zossima gives Aloysha this disturbing reminder:

Remember especially that you cannot be the judge of anyone . . . until [you have] perceived that [you are] every bit as much a criminal as the man who stands before [you], and . . . may well be more guilty than anyone else. . . . You yourself are guilty, for you might have brought light to the evil-doers, as the only sinless one, and you did not shine. If you had shone, then with your light you would have illumined the path for others too, and he that committed the evil deed might not have committed it in your light.[3]

This for George Ross was the double meaning of the Cross. First, the one most sinless bore the greatest sin, even the most heinous sins of the world. In the shadow of that sacrifice, those eyes that are keener see for the rest of us; those bodies that are stronger are called to lift for the rest of us; those minds that are sharper are called to theorize for the rest of us.

Second, the one most broken heals the greatest brokenness. Sunday after Sunday, Ross proclaimed from the pulpit in a variety of ways that there is no cross so great but that God cannot use that cross as a fulcrum to lift others' lives. Is Satan crushing you under a heavy load? Christ can transform those burdens on your back into a Santa's bag of gifts that distribute healing and hope to a world in need.

The transformation of backbreaking burdens into life-giving gifts may not happen in one's lifetime. We live in the overlap of the past and future. God lives in the eternal now. There is, for example, the story of Anna and Susan Warner. Their father was deep in debt. The children had to do something to save him, and them. So they took to writing novels, poems, even hymns. For one hymn Anna wrote she never did get proper copyright control, so she did not receive the significant income to which she, the composer, was entitled. But how many people have been blessed, even ushered into eternity, singing her simple hymn "Jesus Loves Me"?

Ross's favorite parable of how the baggage of broken promises can become luggage for an abundant life was the story of one of the greatest saints of the twentieth century, Dorothy Day. Ross's preaching demonstrates that no story is so often retold that it cannot be made new by its telling. The following rendition made new for his congregation the story of Dorothy Day. She started out her life living as some "Hollywood butterfly," as he put it.

Then she moved to New York. Perhaps it was inevitable that a young, attractive woman, alone in a big city, soon found herself pregnant. Unprepared for motherhood and single, she married, but in less than a year she was divorced and alone again. Then she went to work at a few odd jobs in New Orleans, and later returned to New York. Once again she found herself pregnant, but this time she decided to bring the child to birth. Her lover absolutely refused to marry her. In a few days she attempted to take her own life. Then followed long weeks of pain, sorrow, frustration and loneliness. In her autobiography she wrote later: "I know what remorse is, what shame is. I know the bitter aftermath of sin." In those days she almost went under; but then, as sometimes happens, something mysterious touched her and transformed her character. As day by day she lost herself in her baby, the child gave her a new life. Later she wrote: "No human creature could receive or contain so vast a flood of love and joy as I felt when I held my child." So it was that Dorothy Day came at last, one fateful afternoon, to a New York church to kneel before a crucifix. And she understood—and was baptized a few weeks later. Five years later she published the first copy of *The Catholic Worker*. She established hospitality houses all over the world for poor people and pregnant girls and the sick, the helplessly sick especially. With a tenacity that surprised everyone who knew her, against tremendous odds and opposition, she prophesied to an indifferent, secular society the sacrificial love of God in Jesus Christ. She made no peace with oppression as long as she lived. Why? Because one afternoon at the foot of a cross, her cross and Christ's cross, Jesus Christ transformed her character by the awful witness of His sacrifice. She saw that love *is* sacrifice and that sacrifice *is* the way of Christ and that the way of Christ, and that way only, leadeth to eternal life.[4]

The beating and mockery of Jesus have been the subject of much debate and confusion. John uses the Greek word *mastigoo* (which means "whip," "flog," or "scourge") to describe the kind of beating Jesus received. Matthew and Mark use the word *phragello* ("to flog" or "scourge"). Jesus did not receive the severest form of beating that often preceded crucifixion, known as *verberatio* and designed to prolong the agony of death. Yet the hema-

tidrosis that Jesus had suffered in Gethsemane left his skin especially sensitive to any form of flogging.

The scourge usually had a short handle with several long
leather thongs, at the end of which were attached sharp pieces of
bone or small metal balls. The victim being flogged was stripped
of all clothing, tied to a post, and beaten severely on the back, buttocks, and legs. Scourging cut deeply into the muscles and ripped
loose ribbons of flesh. Many victims went into shock from the
loss of blood and severe pain.[5] The weight of the cross afterward
on their raw backs only added to the immense agony of the flogging.

No one has yet gotten out of life without a back battered and
beaten by broken promises, forgotten responsibilities, and unful-
filled duties. "The good that I would I do not, but the evil which I
would not, that I do" (Romans 7:19 KJV), confessed the Apostle
Paul. No one has yet gotten out of life untainted. No one has yet
cut an innocent swath through the world's evils and horrors and
temptations—except Jesus.

George Ross largely shared the ecclesiology of Thad Garner, a
Southern Baptist folk preacher and musician, who said, "The
Church is one cat in one ditch, and one nobody of a son of a bitch
to pull him out."[6] Ross's way of describing the state of the church
was more elegant: "The most pressing issue in human life, in my
opinion, is the broken connection between our poetry and our politics. We are broken and sundered in those very parts of the soul
where we most yearn for unity and connection."[7]

In his ministry Ross worked hard to heal three broken "parts of
the soul": the broken promises we make to each other, the broken
promises we make to ourselves, and our broken promise to creation.

I. BROKEN PROMISES TO EACH OTHER

In Thornton Wilder's 1940s drama *The Skin of Our Teeth*, a
man named George comes back from the war to his wife Maggie,
only to inform her that he has decided to leave her for another

woman. Maggie counters with the announcement that she has a few words for him:

I didn't marry you because you were perfect. I didn't even marry you because I loved you. I married you because you gave me a promise. . . . That promise made up for your faults. And the promise I gave you made up for mine. Two imperfect people got married, and it was the promise that made our marriage. . . . And when our children were growing up, it wasn't a house that protected them; and it wasn't our love that protected them, it was that promise."[8]

The first set of broken promises that Ross dedicated his ministry to mending and re-membering were the broken social promises we make to each other—to people of different gender, color, and class. Ross felt deeply the pain of a world whose peoples are so unequally joined together.

A former president of Kenya, Jomo Kenyatta, "hypnotized" huge gatherings with the parable of the prayer and the land. He said that when the missionaries came to Kenya they gathered their converts and told them "let us pray with our eyes closed." By the end of the prayer, when they opened their eyes, the land was gone. And what have we lost while we kept our eyes closed to the suffering of other people? One question that drove Ross's ministry was this: How can we keep our promises to each other? How can the human heart be thawed into compassion and commitment?

USAmerica's broken promises around the world, as well as its 408 broken-treaty promises with the native Americans and its daily broken promises to overworked and underpaid citizens, the laid-off and the in-debt, nettled Ross. Our nation's twisted priorities—spending more money to feed its lawns than many countries spend on food for an entire population—could work him into a rhetorical frenzy:

Some thirty million people in this country live in substandard housing—or without housing of any kind at all. Somehow we can find two hundred billion dollars to subsidize a venal, graft-ridden and corrupt savings and loan business, but fifteen billion dollars for decent housing for our people must be squeezed a penny at a time through the Congress.[9]

Through his preaching, Ross endeavored to raise to more activist levels the double-breasted, blow-dried daring of a socioeconomic and cultural elite that pressed the edge of the envelope by driving by a homeless shelter. For Ross, it was more than the world's salvation that was at stake in getting the church outwardly mobile rather than upwardly mobile. It was also the church's. "If it is God's plan to save the world by giving it the Church, it is evidently also God's plan to save the church by giving it the world."[10]

Ross saw himself of one clay with the marginalized and oppressed, the deserted and the disappointed. In one memorable Christmas message, Ross demanded that his power-tie wearing, mobile-phone wielding congregation answer this question: "What difference does this celebration make? The hungry, the poor, the needy, ask: 'Is there any hope or must we go on waiting?' Not by what we claim, but by what we offer; not by what we stand on, but by what we stand for; not by what we say, but by how we serve; not by what we get, but by what we give, will our Christmas be tested by God and a message of hope sent or denied to the world."[11]

An anonymous pharmacologist, when asked by the Food and Drug Administration to define a drug, replied: "Any substance which, when injected into a rabbit, produces a scientific paper." It was not enough for Ross to theorize in the public arena about the thinness of our moral air. He had to show concrete ways in which high finance and low morals didn't have to go together. It was not enough for Ross to theologize in church about the thirsts of Christ—the thirst for justice, the thirst for peace, the thirst for truth, the thirst for righteousness—thirsts that continue down through the ages. Jesus, no matter how much he thirsted, refused the sponge of easy sedatives and sedate palliatives. Ross refused to quench the thirst of Christ with cheap answers to the causes of poverty, urban blight, drug abuse, or issues of class. He also mobilized his well-heeled congregation to do something about them. Ross preached that when "faith spills over into love, people can be transformed; communities can be transformed; the world itself can be transformed." Ross never lost his nineteen-sixtyish belief, expressed nearly two hundred years earlier by Thomas Paine, that "we have it within our power to begin the world all over again."[12]

"If someone should knock on your door or call you on the telephone to ask you to support the Church," Ross told his congregation, "simply say, 'I *am* the Church! What can I do for you?'"[13] Although few of Ross's sermons were without a jab in the social kidneys, poking his congregation to take up the cross of the world's pain and set their feet on the road to justice, he also placated their consciences with hefty doses of realism about the intractable and ineradicable nature of the world's thirstiness. A Christian must do something; a Christian can't do everything.

Ross fixed especially tightly the sights of every church he pastored on its urban mission. He believed that the city was the layout of the soul. As the city fared, so went the spirit. Ross was an early advocate and architect of Habitat for Humanity, sensing instinctively its potential in getting boomers involved in hands-on social justice ministries. He committed St. Paul's to the formation of ministries to the homeless in the Akron community. To a cultural elite who gets its religious news from the leisure and relaxation section of the newspaper, Ross offered this reality check and invitation to a life of rewarding disappointments:

A few lively people from this parish and from a few others have been energized by the power of a great expectation. It is easy to be despondent about poverty. The magnitude of the housing and hunger problems overwhelms us. There are tragedies enough on every side to dismay the most dauntless. But whenever Christians enter the pictures—and I don't care what the picture is—they enter dancing. That is the secret of our invincible vitality, our perennial youthfulness and our continual appeal to the heart and soul and mind of man. Perhaps we cannot build a decent house for everybody in the world, but we can build a decent house for *someone* in Akron, and we expect to do it. That expectation can transform a city.[14]

He inaugurated and funded at St. Paul's a program whereby anyone in the community who had a problem could call a certain number and find an advocate and friend on the other end of the line. This program, dubbed Crisis Answering, was so successful it became a United Way agency.

Ross was an early leader in the civil rights movement. He castigated the nation's moral drowsiness over racial malice and prejudice at the same time he showed a patriotic devotion to the ideals of the nation. Some of his colleagues found the mix a bizarre confection. But when he brought out the flag and sang "America the Beautiful" at every national holiday, it was part and parcel of his deep commitment to the nondiscriminatory principles of the Constitution and Declaration of Independence. The Sunday after NAACP leader Medgar Evers was shot on Wednesday 12 June 1963, Ross mobilized the Delaware County Ministerial Association to conduct an inter-racial and interdenominational service at St. Peter's Church. In his sermon that Sunday afternoon, Ross compared the reasons for the segregation of African-Americans to the reasons for the savagery of Hitler's Germany.[15]

After the assassination of the Rev. Martin Luther King, Jr., Ross was "alone among the clergy of the state," as Senator Frank Church put it in a later tribute to his friend, to welcome the protesters. He opened up his church, St. Michael's Cathedral in Boise, Idaho, for a prayer service by the candlelight marchers who processed through that capital city.[16] Throughout his life, Ross could hit all the "leftier-than-thou" notes of holiness found in the church's official literature on social justice while sounding like a retro-Barthian when it came to theology or a retro-Buckleyite when it came to church politics and brain-dead ecclesiocrats.

Ross registered strong support for women in ministry and women's issues. He began one sermon by contrasting the pay raises Congress gave themselves with Congress's denial of funds to poor pregnant women who were victims of incest or rape.[17] He publicly criticized President George Bush's stance on women's issues and argued a pro-choice position from the pulpit. Even though he was worried about whether St. Paul's was ready for a woman minister, he brought Nancy Rich to Akron to become St. Paul's first woman assistant rector. His withdrawal of support from Trinity Seminary was precipitated in part by what

Ross perceived to be a hardening stance against the ordination of women.

Ross was at the center of the storm that divided the Episcopal Church over the ordination of women. He was a member of the Ecclesiastical Court of the Diocese of Ohio that found L. Peter Beebe guilty in 1975 of disobeying a "godly admonition" of his bishop. Bishop John Burt gave Beebe the godly admonition not to allow the "irregularly ordained" Episcopal priests Alison Cheek and Carter Heyward to celebrate Holy Communion on 8 December 1974 at Christ Church, Oberlin, Ohio. Beebe disobeyed, arguing that such an admonition was not a "godly admonition" because it was not a "godly judgment."

In June of 1975, the diocesan Ecclesiastical Court convened the first trial in the diocese in fifty years.[18] Beebe was unanimously convicted of charges that he violated his bishop's godly admonition, even though Ross and other jurors on the Court supported the ordination of women. Beebe was dismissed as rector of Christ Church by Bishop Burt on 13 March 1975. Beebe then asked to have a new trial to continue debate on the priesthood of women in the Episcopal Church. The appeals court reversed the guilty finding of the Ohio diocesan court.[19]

Ross was not as public or as daring in his support of women's ordination as he was in support of racial justice. Yet he set his feet and the feet of his churches on the road to justice for women, and he summoned his congregations to take up the cross of their sisters' pain. Margit Sahlin, the first woman priest to be ordained in the Lutheran Church in Sweden, received a letter saying, "You are another wound in the body of Christ."[20] The letter-writer spoke more profoundly than he knew. Ross believed that Christ not only bore our wounds in his, but that only the wounded body of Christ can make whole the divided church.

Ross was hardly what would today be called a "politically correct" liberal. His favorite political commentator was William F. Buckley. Ross was downright conservative on matters of law and order (he supported capital punishment), on governmental intrusions in the private sector, and on fiscal policy. There may not be any "good" wars, Ross argued, but there may be necessary ones sometimes.

The Vietnam War, however, was not a necessary war. Ross was an early opponent. His prophetic address to the convention of the Diocese of Idaho, which condemned America's role in the war and called for immediate withdrawal of troops, was placed in the *Congressional Record*. There one can still read these words: "America cannot really withdraw from Vietnam. We will live on for centuries, in the barren soil, the deformed children, the memories of hatred and disgust of a ruined people."[21]

II. BROKEN PROMISES TO OURSELVES

At one time or another, every one of us has walked down that boulevard of broken dreams. There one finds lost opportunities, lapsed resolutions, wasted yesterdays swallowed up in wallowing self-pity and depression—what the Bible calls "the years that the swarming locust has eaten" (Joel 2:25 RSV). Yet the verse also promises that God "will restore . . . the years which the swarming locust has eaten."

God restores to us our broken years, Ross believed, by encouraging us to do what we can do rather than focus on what we cannot do or should not have done. "Of all the things that I have learned in the ministry," Ross proclaimed, "I put this down as one of the most useful: that the antidote to the discouraged life is not the successful life but the eventful life."

When nothing seems to be happening in your life, make something happen. Fill your life with events, not sentiments. Make the bed. Visit the sick. Pay the bills. Put one foot in front of the other. If that is all you can do today, do it! Write a sonnet. Say a prayer. *Do* something. The sure cure for the resentful life is the eventful life. Paul did not slip into resentment or outrage simply because for seventeen long years he was not permitted to preach in the prestigious pulpits of Athens, Rome or Jerusalem. He did what he could where he was; he preached in Syria.

Paul's apostolic greatness "depended entirely, not on what he did in the spotlight of his success, but on what he did in the interval fourteen years in Syria. Humor, laughter, the grace to see beyond present troubles to eventual outcomes and the resolve to do what we can where we are and not to give up, *never* to give up, *never, never* to give up—that is how we shall not only endure our troubles, but also how we shall find our way to God."[22]

Real heroism, wrote Dwight D. Eisenhower in a wartime letter to journalist Ernie Pyle, is the "uncomplaining acceptance of unendurable conditions."[23] For Ross, real heroism was gallantry under fire and the uncomplaining struggle to do what one can do about unendurable conditions. In one of his last sermons at St. Paul's, Ross quoted from this letter written by a nurse for AIDS patients in a New York hospital. The priest she describes is one of "the astonishing people which the astonishing Gospel creates":

Today a priest came to visit. He walks to the bed rail, holds his hand palm down about twelve inches over this man's head and begins to pray silently. Minutes later he makes a sweeping, slow cross over the top part of my patient and quietly fades from the room. I am aware of tears in my eyes. Why does this touch the heart and soul within me so? This little priest, looking to be in his sixties, salt and pepper hair, no taller than 5'3", walks around the hospital blessing the dying. Here he is today, praying over and loving an unconscious man who does not even know him or know that he is there; but this is his work in the world and he does it with great dignity and compassion; and seeing him, I feel the nearness of God.[24]

III. BROKEN PROMISES TO CREATION

Ross was a member of the world's oldest profession. He was a gardener, and, as such, a healer in our third broken promise—to creation. At every rectory, he put in a garden where herbs and vegetables flourished in fragrant abundance. For him mosses were more than, in Peter Dunwiddie's words, "biological widgets—useless inventions of a creator inordinately fond of the color green."[25] Rather they were biological wonders, passports of insights into the mind of the Creator.

Ross loved the oceans and mountains above all (the desert never touched him as deeply), and his daughters believe he felt closest to God while he was fishing (or listening to classical music). Ross liked to quote the British journalist Arthur Binstead that "the most serious doubt that has been thrown on the authenticity of the biblical miracles is the fact that most of the witnesses in regard to them were fishermen."[26] More seriously, he saw the Christian religion as an "outdoor spirituality," and he got his people outdoors whenever he could. At the end of the service on Rogation Sunday, bagpipes at the back of the church led the people outside to dedicate foliage and trees planted in honor of members of the congregation.

The people of Israel transformed three agricultural festivals in Canaan into historical festivals. The Feast of Unleavened Bread, a spring festival at the beginning of barley harvest, became the Feast of the Passover to celebrate deliverance from slavery. The Feast of Harvest, a second spring festival at the beginning of wheat harvest, became the Feast of Pentecost to celebrate the giving of the Torah at Sinai. And the Feast of Ingathering, a fall festival celebrating the grape harvest, became the Feast of Tabernacles to celebrate Israel's wanderings in the wilderness. Israel changed festivals celebrating what God was doing in nature to what God had done in history. The church was born at the Hebrew harvest festival—the feast of the ingathering or Feast of Weeks—and Rogation Sunday became one of Ross's favorite celebrations in the life of every parish he served.

Like his Celtic forebears, Ross displayed a bardic sensitivity to the presence of God in nature. He used nature in his sermons, and he lifted up a Christ who was present in creation. Rogation Sunday became one means of taking these stands and helping his congregation not repeat the mistakes of their forebears. What was the first recorded observation by one of the Pilgrims on the land they had discovered? What did they say of its breathtaking natural beauty? Only this comment by William Bradford, who called the New World "a hideous and desolate wilderness, full of wild beasts and wild men."[27]

One Rogation Sunday, Ross announced the addition of an Eleventh Commandment to the Ten Commandments: "Thou shalt rejoice in every good thing which the Lord thy God hath given thee." In this sermon, he quoted the thirteenth-century Persian poet, Gulisstan of Saadi, words worth remembering especially on days "when the sorrows of life might warp our personalities or ruin our possibilities":

> If of thy mortal good thou art bereft,
> And from thy slender store,
> Two loaves alone to thee are left,
> Sell one and with the dole,
> Buy hyacinths to feed thy soul.

So we say: bring on the pipes and drums, the balloons and the begonias! Let us rejoice, let us rejoice in every good thing which the Lord our God hath made. We celebrate as Christians today, not because we are un-aware—God knows we *are* aware—of the pain, the sorrow and the strug-gle of the world—but because in Christ Jesus we have also touched the central joy of the universe, which nothing shall ever overwhelm. Let, therefore, no frowning spirit come to this house today. Let our halls echo with happy voices. Let our courts ring with praise and on our lawn let there be May dance and song; for such festivity well becomes the people of God and is, we think, well-pleasing to the laughing Christ of everlast-ing joy.[28]

Whenever Ross read the injunction in Genesis for humans to "have dominion" over the four-legged, two-legged, winged, and finned creatures, he heard God telling us to be "foster-parents" of creation. Leviticus states: "The Land is mine. You are my ten-ants."[29] This biblical passage carried much meaning for Ross. The two great creation hymns in the Old Testament, Job (especially chapter 12) and Psalm 104, were some of his favorite passages of Scripture, as was this section from Deuteronomy: "When you are trying to capture a city, do not cut down its fruit trees, even though the siege lasts a long time. Eat the fruit, but do not destroy the trees; the tress are not your enemies" (20:19 TEV).

A cartoon captures in abbreviated form how well we have kept our promises to creation. It shows God sitting up in the clouds, looking down on the mess that humans have made of creation. God is mumbling and complaining: "One week of work and an eternity of worry."

Why is God worrying? Perhaps some random examples will

suffice. Twenty-five million buffalo have been wiped off the Great Plains in fifty years. We wiped them out pretty much just for the hell of it. The same is true with alligators in Louisiana, where they were slaughtered almost to extinction thirty years ago, but are now making a comeback thanks to state and federal protection. We do not begin to know how many plants and animals exist in the world—1.4 million have been identified so far—but some believe another 30 million are there yet to be discovered—that is, if we don't drive them into extinction first. The only eagle some people want to protect is the one on the back of a dollar bill.

A child asked the rector after a sermon: "Why don't Christians believe God created the world?" The rector replied: "Why, they do believe God created the world. In fact, they believe that God did not only create it but loves it so much God sent Jesus to die for the world." The child replied: "Then why don't they take better care of it?"

To "take better care of it" means more than to "preserve" planet Earth. To the extent the language of "preservation" is the language of technological control, Ross wanted nothing to do with "preserving" the earth. You "preserve" a peck of pickled peppers. You "preserve" body parts for transplant. You "preserve" little patches of wetlands that die a slow death because the dying life around them leeches their life right out of them. "Preserve" is a control word that resists the continuing forces of creation.

The First Commandment instructs us to "tend the earth and till it" (Genesis 2:15). The language is one of conservation and co-creation, not preservation of the mess we've already made of planet Earth. Ross invited his people to trust God's creative spirit to surprise them with new manifestations of what God can do here on this planet. He never argued that now it was a *status confessionis* moment for the environment in the history of the church—a moment when the church must decide to be a part of the confessional struggle on behalf of creation or to sit this struggle out. Nor did Ross even remotely share the radical spirit of poet Gary Snyder, who urged Reed College graduates in 1991 "to go into the twenty-first century lean, mean, and green."

What he did do was remind his congregation that all of creation is involved in the work of redemption. And he raised unsettling questions about toxic tailpipes, the subsidizing of the destruction of the planetary environment through foreign aid, and the use of tax money to pay for dams that destroy tropical forests and displace indigenous people. Why should USAmerica subvent agricultural practices in South America and Costa Rica that ruin the land, destroy wildlife, and impoverish people? When it came to humans' treatment of nature, Ross didn't have a chip on his shoulder. He had an entire forest.

One of Ross's favorite ways to help his congregation think of redemption in more than humanocentric terms was the annual Easter tradition of "Flowering the Cross." At 4 PM on Easter, there was a children's service, and everyone at St. Paul's was invited to bring bouquets of flowers. In the course of the service, the children would come forward and slip their flowers into rubber bands on a large cross. The congregation would watch as the wooden cross was transformed into a flowered cross. A poem written in the early part of this century, "I See His Blood Upon the Rose," well expresses Ross's cosmic christology:

> I see His blood upon the rose
> And in the stars the glory of His eyes,
> His body gleams amid eternal snows,
> His tears fall from the skies.
> I see His face in every flower;
> The thunder and singing of the birds
> Are but His voice—and carven by His power;
> Rocks are His written words.
>
> All pathways by His feet are worn,
> His strong heart stirs the ever-beating sea,
> His crown of thorns is twined with every thorn,
> His cross is every tree.[30]

In Ross's theology our relationships to animals provided a key indicator of our moral standing. "You save humans and animals alike," the Psalmist praises God (36:6 NRSV). Every "Blessing of the Animals" service Ross conducted was based on the fact that the line between humans and animals is both large and small. Literary naturalist Barry Lopez recounts the story of a polar bear mother forced by bored and sadistic sailors to witness the killing of her cubs.[31] Her horrifying cries of pain and anguish resurrect in the Christian's ear sounds of the slaughter of the innocents through the ages.

It is not nature versus humans. We are nature: we are nature come to consciousness, the cambium of nature.[32] Many of the early church fathers Ross read so eagerly understood this clearly. Origen advised his audience, "Understand that thou has within thyself flocks of cattle . . . flocks of sheep and flocks of goats . . . Understand that the birds of the sky are also within thee."[33]

In the Garden, Adam and Eve speak the language of the beasts—they live in harmony with creation. God's first covenant with Noah was with every living thing, not just human creation. In fact, Noah stands as a savior figure for the whole planetary ecosystem. Jesus continued this tradition, countering the establishment religion's animal taboos by making positive animal connections—Jesus' manger birth; Jesus' adult vision quest spent in the wilderness with wild beasts.

For Ross, the whole earth is part of the redemption story. That is one reason why the eucharistic host is shaped in a circle—to symbolize the redemption of the entire cosmos. The whole creation awaits transformation, transfiguration, and transubstantiation with eager longing and expectation. In both the Old and New Testaments, redemption returns balance, harmony, and beauty to creation: "The wolf shall live with the lamb, the leopard shall lie down with the kid" (Isaiah 11:5 NRSV); God brings "the universe, all in heaven and on earth," into unity with Christ (cf. Ephesians 1:10). In words that some believe belong in the liturgy of the church:

> All Gloria *in excelsis* cry!
> Earth, air, fire, water, man and beast
> He that is crowned above the sky
> *Pro nobis puer natus est.*[34]

Everything in the cosmos is covered by the cross (Colossians 1:20), and the new community in Christ breaks down all barriers: cultural, sexual, economic, social, ecological (Galatians 3:27–28). Our horizons are wrongly limited to the human world (Romans 8:19–23). Perhaps it is time for a more literal reading of Jesus' command to "preach the gospel to the whole creation" (Mark 16:15 RSV). As the poet Henry Vaughan suggests so powerfully in a couple of passages, the whole creation preaches to us:

> Walk with thy fellow-creatures: note the *hush*
> And *whispers* amongst them. There's not a *Spring*,
> Or *Leafe* but hath his *Morning-hymn*; each *Bush*
> And *Oak* doth know *I AM*; canst thou not sing?[35]

> Birds, beasts, all things
> Adore him in their kinds.
> Thus all is hurl'd
> In sacred *Hymnes* and *Order*, The great *Chime*
> And *Symphony* of nature.[36]

IV. FROM JERICHO TO JERUSALEM

An Akron reporter covered one of Ross's Sunday sermons in which he argued that everyone walks the same road in life, "from Jericho to Jerusalem." Ross pointed out how in Jesus' day that road symbolized the historic pilgrimage of Israel from its beginning struggle to its ultimate victory. "Every devout Jew wanted to walk upon it at least once in a lifetime."

Let Jerusalem stand for the fulfillment of our life's plans, whatever they may be. You and I want to get on with them, but on the road from Jericho to Jerusalem, things happen which we did not plan, which have nothing to do with our own goals and plans.[37]

We will meet on our way beggars crying out for mercy, just as in Jesus' time. "Children come out of nowhere, it seems, asking to be loved. Strangers fall victim to other people's greed and lie mutely in the ditch, unable even to ask for help but needing it desperately." Then there is the blind beggar Bartimaeus, whom Ross compared to "an educational system that does too little to remove the blindness of our corporate ignorance." In the midst of all this need, "Jerusalem beckons us. Shall we hurry on or will we stop to help?"

One of the problems we have on life's highway, Ross argued, is that today the road from Jericho to Jerusalem may be a superhighway built on stilts, high above the city's clamor:

We ride on it with 300 horses at our command, air conditioners humming, windows shut tight. We are on our way to some destiny, we suppose. Below, the slums, squalor and suffering are real as they were when Jesus walked the way. But do we hear, do we see, do we care?[38]

To a church preoccupied with its own life and success, to a nation lost in dreams of glory, to a people who can only form circles looking inward, never outward, there are many perils on the road from Jericho to Jerusalem. "But the greatest peril of all is that those who travel on it may lose their own humanity."

The road from Jericho to Jerusalem runs right through Akron, Ohio, and you and I are walking on it. My question to you is this—"Are you stopping along your way to help somebody?"[39]

To help the broken person on the way, we must admit to being broken ourselves. As the inscription on sundials reminds us: "Omnia ferunt, Ultima necat." It means, "They all wound, the last one kills." Time doesn't just heal all wounds. Time wounds all of us. Only when we share in the brokenness of others can we be made whole.

SERMONS

꩜

The Parable of the Farmer and the Seed

> *Jesus said, "The Kingdom of Heaven may be*
> *likened unto a farmer who went out to sow*
> *his seed, and after he had scattered the seed,*
> *he went to sleep, and when the wheat was*
> *fully ripened, he rose and, taking his sickle,*
> *went out to the harvest."*

> Text: Mark 4:26–34

In this brief text there are three great truths of our faith. Anyone can learn these truths. You do not need to be a Ph.D. in religion; you need not practice yoga in a monastery. The three truths
of this text are easily grasped and understood and put into practice
by any simple farmer who goes out to sow his seed and waits until
the harvest comes and then goes out to bring it in.

Sermon preached at St. Paul's Episcopal Church, Akron, Ohio, on the Third Sunday
after Pentecost, 16 June 1985. George Ross Papers, The University of Akron
Archives.

I. REST

Herein is the first truth: after he sowed the seed, he went to sleep. He went to sleep; he trusted God to work beneath the surface of the soil until the wheat was ripened for the harvest. He went to sleep. Without such inner confidence and such interior serenity, there can be no good life. "My peace I give to you," said Jesus to his friends; "not as the world gives, do I give to you peace" (John 14:27 RSV). Before and after every healing ministry or decisive encounter, we read in Scripture that our Lord went to a secret place of prayer to be in communion with the peace of his Father, with what Goethe called "the peace that lieth over the mountain tops." When the storm was raging on the lake and the disciples were frightened and filled with dread, Jesus went to sleep. If you have ever suffered from insomnia, you know that sometimes such sleep is very difficult because every sleep is a giving up of control. Every time you go to sleep, you surrender; you let go, and for some of us that is exceedingly difficult. A friend and I were chatting not long ago about a wedding. She said, "I haven't slept a wink in a week!" I confess that I was not very sympathetic; in fact, as I recall, I laughed. Soon she smiled and said to me, "Well, maybe I ought to relax a little." I said to her, "My dear, not a little, but a lot." Sometimes others must give us this sermon and preach this word to us when we forget that without sleep there can be no work. I well know, believe me, that there are times in life, many times, which require our utmost effort and our intense concentration. I marvel sometimes when I see mothers and fathers disembarking two or three children in the parking lot. I say "hello" and ask how things are going. Almost always back comes a cheerful, "All clear!" I don't believe it for a moment! You know as well as I do that, before that door opened, Suzy was biting Angela's elbow, and Franny was assaulting Zooey; and though some of the words sounded like it, Mom was not exactly praying when she was trying to get the chewing gum out of her dress. Dad's knuckles were turning white as he gripped the steering wheel. Then, they all unfold from the car, like flowers in bloom. I say, "Hi, how's everything?" and they all smile and say, "Oh, just great!" Have you ever noticed how in a church parking lot everything is always JUST GREAT! You don't believe it; I don't believe it! Nobody believes it. Life is not all serene and relaxed. If you are planning a little refutation of my sermon, to be delivered at the coffee hour, please be advised that I know all about the *Sturm and Drang* of life! It is precisely *because* we work so hard, *because*, we have such tensions and stress, that we need our Sabbath rest. When we do what has to be done, then we ought to go to sleep. It is then that God goes to work for us, as the text says "in ways we know not." "While he slept the seed grew; he knew not how." That's the faith; that's the truth. "While he *slept*, the seed grew."

> Thou life within my life, than self more near,
> Thou veiled Presence infinitely clear,
> From all illusive shows of sense I flee,
> To find my center and my rest in Thee.[1]

How can you get through this life without experiences like that! Or listen to this prayer from the great tradition: "Let my soul take refuge from the crowding turmoil of worldly thoughts beneath the shadow of thy wings; let my heart, this sea of restless waves, find peace in thee, O God."

Who said that? A recluse, a naive religious, a delicate person? By no means. Those are the words of St. Augustine of Hippo, praying out of his daily struggles as one of the most active and energetic men that this world has ever seen. You sow the seed and then you go to sleep; such is the pattern of the good, the healthy and the noble life. Every Calvary requires a Gethsemane garden; every Pentecostal mission requires an upper room of hidden gestation; every Exodus has a burning bush in some far desert, for it is in the hidden places of the heart, when we relax to God, that the seeds of the Spirit are sown and take root and "grow we know not how."

II. WAIT

The second truth is like the first: that the Kingdom of Heaven is filled with people who have learned how to wait. Next to resting, waiting is all important to a farmer. There is a great verse in the Bible: "He who would master the morning and imprint the day with the seal of his intentions must learn to walk in the pace of God."[2] That is a wonderful passage. In farming, timing is everything. If you plant too soon or harvest too late, all your love's labor will be lost. That is the way it is in everyone's life. Recently a book was published with the title *The Hurried Child*.[3] It is tragic today to see so many boys and girls whose childhood is being cut short by teachers too eager for geniuses or parents too eager for trophies and society too eager for consumers. We are robbing our children of the precious seedling years of natural and God-governed growth. We should stop this. Fathers, mothers, will you slow down sometimes and let the flowers bloom in due season? Do not try to harvest seedlings and do not think that it is unnecessary to hear this. It is a mad and sad society we are living in where many people would abolish childhood. Don't *you* do it. Some of us need to apply this text quite personally, I suspect, because some of us are trying far too hard to grow ourselves too fast. Our shelves are filled with self-improvement books. Every ache has a corresponding pill in our medicine cabinet. We want it easy; we want it all; we want it now. The Kingdom of Heaven is filled with people who have learned how to wait for it. Someone has said that the church is an anvil that has out-worn all the hammers. Wouldn't you like to say that about your life and the tensions and problems and frustrations that you face in it? I would. But let me tell you: you can never have that kind of life until you learn how to acquire a kind of agricultural patience.

Religious philosopher, Eric Butterworth, once faced a private tragedy. He felt the whole weight of the world fall on his shoulders. He was looking everywhere for help, he asked everyone for guidance, trying to get some golden thought that would lead him through the mess he was in. One afternoon he started to leaf through his long-neglected Bible and his finger came to rest on the words "It came to pass." That phrase means absolutely nothing in itself. But God focused Eric Butterworth's attention on it. "Suddenly," said Butterworth, "a light dawned in my mind, that this experience that I am having is not forever. It came to pass; and I began to realize that the problem hadn't come to ruin me, but had come to strengthen me. It had come to bring me something that I needed just then for my growth as a human being. It came to pass." There are strange interludes in everyone's life. We have to learn how to live in them, don't we? When the farmer scattered that seed, it was a wrinkled, brown, shriveled, unpromising, little thing. Then it disappeared beneath the ground. Then the clouds gathered and the rains came and the wind blew and the weeks passed. Absolutely nothing seemed to happen for a long time. Then the green bud broke through all resistance, like Easter, and so *it came to pass!* Think that through, will you, as it applies to your own life? Allow this tremendous insight to light up your life as it has lightened the lives of countless Christians before you: that God is working his purpose out when nothing in your life seems to be working out and that just when he seems most absent he is most active. If ever you are tempted to forget that, just remember the cross.

III. WORK

Finally this word. Sleeping and waiting are very important—they are all important—but they are a prelude to something else. The something else is *working.* "When the harvest came, at once he put in the sickle and went to work." There comes the hour in anyone's life when the self-same Power which gave growth to the seed gives energy to you. "When the harvest came, he went to work." Faith without works is dead. I will not belabor that point this morning. I don't need to. In just a moment I shall commission six members of this parish family to begin a mission of love and service on the island of Haiti. I don't know when the seed was planted; I don't know who planted it. I certainly don't know how the seed took root. Perhaps a story at a mother's knee planted the seed; maybe an offhand remark by Dad at table one night; maybe a hymn one day in church; perhaps a prayer grandmother taught in the nursery. Who knows? We just don't know when the seeds were planted or how they grew, but *that* the seeds were planted and *that* they have grown we know because this morning we see young men and women with sickles in their baggage going off to work! That's the parable; that's the message and the model of the good life as Christians see it.

Wordsworth said, "Poetry is the harvest of the quiet eye."[4] So, indeed, is friendship; so is the mission of the church; so is success in any field of endeavor. God makes the seed to grow. He leaves it to us to plow and plant and gather in the harvest and therein, do you see, are the two strong principles of every strong life: "activity and receptivity, tension and relaxation, working hard and resting back. . . . He who cannot rest cannot work; he who cannot let go cannot hang on; he who loses serenity within loses everything without."[5]

When I say goodbye to those young men and women at the Hopkins Airport on Tuesday and as you keep them in your prayers through these next two weeks, let the mind drift back to the text: "The farmer sowed the seed; then he went to bed and rose and went to bed and rose and, while he slept, the seed grew, he knew not how, but God gave it the increase. And when the harvest came, the good man went to work."

LET US PRAY:

Lord, you make this world and all that therein is. You are the Lord both of the seed-time and of the harvest. In that faith we repose in confident rest and peace, for we know that beneath the surface of everything, you are always at work to bring new life from old; refreshed in this confident faith, give us energy in all our work that while it is yet day, we may work with joy, knowing that in you, O Lord of the harvest, our labor is not in vain. So give us inner serenity, patience with ourselves and with one another, diligence in work until the evening comes and the fever of life is over and our work is done. Then in your mercy give us a safe lodging and a holy rest and peace at the last. *Amen.*

⊰W⊱

Tempted by Satan (or God?)

Text: Mark 1:9–13

In every development of the human personality a mysterious linkage is forged between frustration and fulfillment. Your biography, in fact, is the story of the experience in which that linkage is forged. Hidden in every victory are the constituent elements of a subsequent defeat. At the meridian of every success, the shadow of failure falls. As we grow older and pass through the states along life's way, we discover that every birth involves a death. A child dies a reluctant and painful death as the adolescent is born. No sooner do the chaotic contradictions and ambiguities of adolescent life attain momentary equilibrium than suddenly we are face to face with a whole new set of uncertainties and challenges as we make fateful decisions about marriage and work and having children. The midlife crisis, about which we read so much nowadays, inevitably arrives not at the point of failure for us but at the point of success. The Bible tells fascinating stories about this mystery. A successful Exodus weekend is followed by many years of difficulty, as the people wander through the desert. The glittering civilization of King Solomon's empire is succeeded by an era of contradiction, collapse, and fraction. Jacob woos and wins a bride and then come years of frustrating servitude as he discovers, as many do, that the girl he courted is not the girl he wed; and she, likewise, discovers that the husband is not the same as the groom! St. Mary gives birth to a beautiful baby; the Magi kneel; the shepherds come; the angels sing; and then, immediately, the flight to

Sermon preached at St. Paul's Episcopal Church, Akron, Ohio, on the First Sunday of Lent, 24 February 1985. George Ross Papers, The University of Akron Archives.

Egypt, the rage of Herod, the tragedies. At the height of a successful career as a preacher, healer, exorcist, leader of women and
men, Jesus the King of Glory goes to Golgotha. The Palm Sunday
parade eventuates in the Via Dolorosa. The chapter after Pentecost is entitled "Martyrdom." And so on and on.

Unless the profound meaning of this paradoxical account of the
human story has somehow dawned on you, you will find the text I
have chose baffling: Jesus was baptized in the River Jordan and the
dove appeared and above him the Voice from heaven was heard
to say "I love you, dear Son." And immediately the Holy Spirit
drove Jesus into the wilderness to be tempted by the devil (cf.
Mark 1:9–12).

I. GOD OR SATAN OR BOTH?

If the river and the dove and the Voice signify a configuration of
magnificent attainment and transcendental joy for Jesus, then the
wilderness represents the lonely struggle of the soul to make fundamental decisions about itself. In this struggle, we read, certain
thoughts come to mind, but whether these thoughts are from God
or from the devil, it is not always easy to say. The Bible is coy
about this. It is the *Holy Ghost* which drives Jesus to be tempted
by Satan. We are reminded of the experience of Job. It is not just
the devil's will that Jesus be tempted, but also *God's*—indeed,
God's will most of all and first of all. The temptations of our Lord,
in other words, arise as a part of God's plan and not apart from it.
This is something we must definitely wish to reject if we can. We
prefer light and darkness, sin and holiness, the good and the evil
neatly separated. We think that sickness and health are opposite
things. We think of our good times as sent by God and our bad
times as originating in something else; but the Bible says that
what happened in the wilderness and what happened in the river
are all part of a seamless robe of experience in Christ. The moment when we know that we are loved, when the sun is shining
and the dove descends and all goes well with us, is incomplete until the shadow of the wilderness hour creeps over us and we must

decide who we really are and what we will do with the rest of our lives.

I suggest this as our first consideration this morning, as we think about our lives and Lent and the baptismal and wilderness moments of our own experience (this is the *first* and great consideration, although we may arrive at it quite late in life and in our reflections). Eden without expulsion, the baptismal moment without the wilderness temptations, Exodus success without the years of wandering, the faithfulness without the temptation, the Olivet without the Gethsemane cannot lead us to that wholeness and fulfillment which is God's great plan for the human soul.

II. THE PARADOX OF THE FALL

The second point is simply that all temptation is a temptation toward and in and from the human ego, which is why sometimes we have difficulty knowing whence it comes. You see that clearly enough in the Garden of Eden. The temptation there is to become master, to reach out and to take for yourself that which might forever free you of any necessary connection with God or with the rest of life. "Eat this," something whispers, "and you will be like God." "Turn these stones to bread." St. Augustine said of the fall of Adam that it was "a fall upward," that is into a more complex state of consciousness. Until the ego had had its fling, so to speak, it had not come fully into its own self-awareness. Only after the fall can the ascent begin. (Some of you know this exceedingly well!) And so the early Fathers of the Church used to speak of the *felix culpa*, the happy fall of man into self-consciousness. But in the wilderness of which we read this morning Jesus came to the second decisive moment in human life when the question arises with an intensity, conceived, I believe, by the unsettling Holy Spirit: is the apple really enough, is that all there is—this mastery, this sensuality, this Godlike existence in which my own insatiable ego knows all, enjoys all, controls all, does all? Is that all? Every temptation in the spiritual life of the personality is a temptation, finally, to choose between the apple and the cross. Will we grab what we can for ourselves; or do we at some point make the Holy-Ghost-decision to live for others, to let go of the grasping ego in favor of an embracing self and to move beyond the known, controlled and dogmatic world of superior Adam into the mysterious and free and joyful world of self-giving Jesus?

III. THE FIRST TEMPTATION

In the wilderness our Lord heard something say, "You are hungry. Turn these stones to bread." That is the temptation you and I have every day: become a consumer of the world; that's what counts; you've got the money; you've got the means; why not do that—turn the world into something you will consume? I need not rehearse for you the nightmare which results when, unlike Jesus, you and I decide to go that way. Our planet is being heartlessly polluted and plundered and raped as the consumer psychology dominates and paralyzes all the other human sensibilities.

IV. THE SECOND TEMPTATION

The second temptation was to master the mind of man through shrewd techniques. "Climb up to the Temple top," says the devil. "Throw yourself down, and you will win the minds of men." This is the temptation of technique, and in our century we know all about it. Don't bother with people. Don't bother to get to know them. Don't bother to share your life with them. Don't take time to love them. Don't go to the commitment of a cross. Don't go to the frustrations, conflict, fatigue, and occasional exhilaration and hard work of a parish church. Find a short cut (a technique of mass media, let's say) and you might be amazed at the results. All of us struggle every day with the temptation of technique, which is the temptation to avoid personal life in favor of technical craft. Technique-ridden leadership in the church, in the professions, in the business world, and in the state leaves a hungering humanity yearning for some personal experiences which will convince them that they count, that someone cares deeply about them, that not everyone is out to win their vote with clever advertising or to get their money to keep the "wonderful world-wide ministry" going, that there is more to Christianity than the success frenzy of the religion that reaches them via the wizards of the electronic church. Jesus refused to manipulate the mind of man with techniques. He chose the only way he knew—the cross and love and an appeal, which far from manipulating people, allowed itself to be manipulated. Perhaps our civil politics and our religious communications and our interpersonal lives have become so decadent in this latter day that our Lord must plead in stark loneliness on his cross of Love. One thing he will not do is to jump from our temples to impress us with his success or his power or to require from us loyalty which only love can win.

V. THE THIRD TEMPTATION

The third temptation is politics. The devil took him up to a very high mountain and said, "Now, take control; take control of these nations and you will be Lord indeed." This is the ultimate and most insidious temptation of humanity—to build a new world order by any means available, to put things right by the exercise of the superior will and vigorous outbursts of ego. Our century may not survive this last temptation. For the first time in all human history, perhaps, the wilderness experience of the soul will lead not on to mission but to Armageddon.

VI. THE OUTCOME

After the baptism of self-discovery comes the wilderness of self-surrender and then the ministry of consecrated life. At least that is how it went with Christ. How it goes with you, how it goes with me, remains to be seen. Will we settle for a consumer's life, turning the world into our own private pile of bread? That would be sad! Will we forsake the personal for the technique-ridden career as the manipulator of other people's opinion, doing what we must to make them think highly of us? That would be sad! Will we turn to the strategies of power and control, having despaired of the problematic and difficult ministries of love? That would be sad! These are the questions which the ego in each of us must face every day of our advancing or regressing lives as spouses, parents, children, citizens, church members, persons. The Lenten exercise, as I understand it, is, at its best, the effort to be honest about one's besetting temptations, not as if they were something to be denied or suppressed or regretted, but as something sent by the Holy Spirit into our lives as essential elements of our emerging personalities. What we do in our wilderness with our temptation and the Holy Ghost and Jesus Christ and the world is the story we will tell the saints one day about our lives. Let us pray that when they tell us their stories, we will not be completely ashamed!

I will conclude with the haunting words of Dietrich Bonhoeffer on this subject:

The Bible is not like a book of edification, telling us many stories of men's temptation and their overcoming. To be precise, the Bible tells only two temptation stories, the temptation of the first man and the temptation of Christ, that is the temptation which led to man's fall and the temptation which led to Satan's fall. All other temptations in human history have to do with these two stories of temptation. Either we are tempted in Adam or we are tempted in Christ. Either the Adam in me is tempted—in which case we fall. Or the Christ in us is tempted—in which case Satan is bound to fall.[6]

We must decide. Tempted by God (or is it by Satan?), let us use Lent as a time to clarify our fundamental choice about the meaning and direction of our lives: that what we really want from life is not just our little ego and its pleasures, its wisdom, its mastery, its power. What we really choose is Christ, Christ's joy, Christ's commitment to others and to the world, Christ's suffering and patient love. Then ensues the great adventure, not of Eden and innocence but of Easter and joy.

LET US PRAY:

O God, as we experience temptation in both the fulfillments and the frustrations of our lives, sustain and strengthen us in the decisions we make. In our anxiety, we withdraw into ourselves, and that way lies death. Give us, rather, the faith which opens us to Christ's decision in the forty days: to trust you with his future and so to enter it with joy and freedom and love. We know, Father, that in that choice our salvation is at stake. *Amen.*

ॐ

The Prize

*I strain forward to claim the prize of the up-
ward call of God in Jesus Christ until I attain
unto mature adulthood.*

Text: Ephesians 4:11–13

That verse raises two questions, at least. The first question is:
Is there really such a prize, is there such a goal and upward call, as
Paul thinks there is? The second question is: What does he mean
by the phrase *mature adulthood*? I think those two questions, if
unanswered or if inadequately answered, raise yet a third question: If we do not know that there are a prize and a goal and if we
do not know what the maturity of our own adulthood might be,
why strain forward?

One of my enthusiasms of the present moment is a Welsh poet
by the name of R. S. Thomas. In one of his poems he describes a
Welsh peasant by the name of Iago Prytherch, who has few graces
or possessions, but can still be viewed as a "winner of wars, / Enduring like a tree under the curious stars."[7]

It may seem a long way to you from the bleak Welsh hills and a
hopeless, earthbound peasant to the bustling streets and canyons
of Wall Street; but Walker Percy, who has become in a way the
chronicler of what is perhaps unfairly called the "Yuppie Genera-

Sermon preached at St. Paul's Episcopal Church, Akron, Ohio, on the Twentieth Sunday after Pentecost, 25 October 1987. George Ross Papers, The University of Akron
Archives.

tion," asks in his novel *The Second Coming* these soul-troubling questions:

Is it possible for people to miss their lives in the same way one misses a plane?" . . . Where are we? Deep in the woods, socking little golf balls around mountains, rattling ice in Tanqueray, riding $35,000 German cars, watching Billy Graham and the Steelers and *M*A*S*H** on 45-inch Jap[anese] TV. Out of fear, out of greed, out of curiosity, out of boredom, we lash ourselves to these and other pieces of the American life style. . . . And each lash is like one of the thick hairs which knit Gulliver to the ground; and their sum total keeps us solidly tied down.[8]

You don't have to talk to a Welsh peasant to meet the earthbound human!

I. THE UPWARD GOAL?

The first question before the house, this house and every house, is this: Is there or is there not an upward goal for human life, a prize to be won; or are we helplessly tied down to the things we own which own us, the habits we have formed, the little ideas, which like hardening plaster, have solidified our minds? Some might say, "Well, *once* there was a prize in my life, an upward goal, I guess, but it's gone. The girl I loved married the wrong man, not me. The job I hoped for went to another. My loved one left me—or died. The stock market crashed and took my money with it. Once there was a prize, a golden dream. Not now."

What does Paul mean when he says "mature humanity"? Now, some would say—quite a few would say—that maturity is coming to accept things as they are. For them "maturity" is just another word for "disillusionment." The older you get, the more disillusioned you get. I read the other day about a man who had just won 2.8 million dollars in the New Jersey lottery, but he didn't go get it for six months. "Why didn't you go get the money?" all his friends asked. He said, "Because I was afraid it might change my life." Now, that is a tragedy! That is a tremendous tragedy, and it is happening all the time among us—a tragedy endlessly repeated—people on the very threshold of magnificence, of wonderful lives, who don't claim it because, as they have grown older, they have grown more fixed and, therefore, more fearful.

Add to this disillusionment, experienced by countless folk today, the curse of loneliness, which is epidemic in this society and you realize how many people are holding onto their lives by very thin hairs. Not only priests and prophets but also artists and poets are saying that just beneath the thin, glittering surface of modern secular life there is a profound loneliness, emptiness, and pointlessness that is making people both tired and sad. Secularism has not delivered its promised treasures!

Loneliness, lost dreams, earthbound lives—all these spiritual calamities lead many today to say: "No, there is no upward goal; no, there is no prize to be claimed; maturity is cynicism; therefore cease to strain forward; abandon the spiritual struggle."

II. MATURE ADULTHOOD?

"I strive, I strain forward to claim the prize of the upward call of God in Christ Jesus until I attain unto mature adulthood." What a strong and wonderful voice we hear in these words, the voice of a Christian faith! What a radical alternative the Christian faith offers to the melancholy and secular culture in which we are living today. It is a radical alternative, but to claim it you must make, and I must make, a radical choice. We cannot have it both ways—half secular, half Christian—in the twilight of undecided and uncommitted lives. The goal and the prize of which St. Paul speaks are real because Jesus Christ is real and because Jesus Christ is Lord. Maturity is not skepticism but ever widening compassion; and to strive for love, for peace, for justice, and for the Kingdom of God demands our very best—our life, our love, our strength, our souls, our all. Don't ever think, if you are not a Christian, don't ever think that Christians are meek and weak! We are tough—we Christians—tough in ways which the secular and merely worldly cannot even begin to imagine.

With the stock market crash this past week and with the gathering storm of an uncertain economic future casting long shadows over the country, and indeed over the world, this is a great hour for Christians. While the pen of secular despair writes "lonely" for many, many today, the pen of God's word for us writes "community and friendship and love." Our humanity is not measured by the rise and fall of the Dow Jones average. Our humanity is not measured by the rise and fall of gold. Our humanity is hid with God in Christ, by whose teachings, by whose life, by whose love held high upon the cross, by whose resurrection to life eternal, gives us the model and the image and the hope of true mature adulthood. It's a wonderful time for Christians to live! The worse the times get, in many ways, the better it is for us. In a world on the brink of spiritual prostration, it is a great thing to believe in God and to stand for God, when people no longer know what to stand for—or if they can even stand at all. In a time of aching, private loneliness, what a splendid opportunity opens to us in the family of God: to fling wide the doors of our friendship and to discover the joys and power of our love!

In a word, we who strive and strain forward to claim the upward call of God in Christ unto mature adulthood have marvelous opportunities today. Don't let the long-faced and grim and dour and sour words you hear ever take away from you that joy. We ought to be thanking God every day for the privilege of being alive in tough times. By our faith, our hope, our love, our Lord, we can show the best of spirits in the worst of times. Voltaire said it very well: "The burning of a little straw may hide the stars, but the stars outlast the smoke." This we know: we are Christians. Sometimes only the rough times teach us what that means, so let us rejoice. Let the whole church of Christ rejoice to be the church today. In the darkest night our Star is the brightest. Therefore, by all means, let us continue to strain forward to claim the prize that others may see that there *is* a prize to claim.

The One Talent Recipient

He who received the one talent came to the master and said, "Master, I was afraid and went and hid your talent in the ground." The master answered, "You wicked servant!"

Text: Matthew 25:14–15; 19–29

Look where you will in all the world, it is evident everywhere that God is not evenhanded. Those who would level society to a bland equality are offended everywhere they look. God appears to revel in disparities. If he digs a deep valley, immediately beside it he throws up a high mountain. On the Amazonian forest he pours superfluous floods while, with scorching heat, he desiccates the Sahara. In the central mechanisms of the cosmos God implants vast and implacable forces of inequality and disequilibrium. And thank God! If every atom in the universe was equal in temperature to every other, immediately a darkness and a chill would fall on all, and everything alive would die.

He whose keen eye observed the flight of the sparrows, the spinning of the lilies, the coming and the going of the seasons of life and death, reminds us today that by Divine Wisdom one person had five talents, another, two, and a third, only one. We cannot say why that is so, any more than we can explain why the

Sermon preached at St. Paul's Episcopal Church, Akron, Ohio, on the Twenty-third Sunday after Pentecost, 15 November 1987. George Ross Papers, The University of Akron Archives.

Maker delights as much to make a flea as to fabricate a whale. The fact of unequal gifts is not, in other words, either for us to lament or to explain. It is God's will. It is God's way. It is as absurd, as laughable, for us to regret or pity the modestly talented as it is for us to praise and laud the individual with many gifts. To one person five talents, to another two, to another only one. God's will. God's way.

Jesus warns us, therefore, not to make invidious comparisons between our gifts and those of others. He invites us, rather, to ponder the problem of the one talent individual. The other stewards in the story all made fruitful use of their talents, but the one talent recipient stood condemned before God of a crime for which only a pathetic excuse could be offered: "I was afraid and went and hid your talent." So that person stood condemned of great wickedness: "Thou *wicked* servant!" said the Master. What is the wickedness of the wicked servant? Simply this: the servant stood condemned of leading an *unproductive* life.

Here we touch a nerve at the heart of the Gospel. For Jesus Christ the purpose of life was what he called "fruitfulness." His cousin, John the Baptist, struck at the rotten core of society when he cried in the wilderness: "Repent" and "bear fruit that befits repentance, . . . [for] even now the ax is laid to the root of the trees; every tree therefore that does not bear good fruit will be cut down and thrown into the fire" (Matthew 3:8, 10 RSV). When people came to Christ to inquire about the essence of true religion, he answered them with utmost simplicity: "You will know them by their fruits" (Matthew 7:20 RSV). In John, chapter 15, verse 2 (RSV), we hear this clear word from Jesus: "Every branch of mine that bears no fruit, [God] takes away, and every branch that does bear fruit, [God] prunes that it may bear more fruit." And in verse 8: "By this my Father is glorified, that you bear much fruit, and so prove to be my disciples." In the 13th chapter of Matthew, verse 23 (RSV), Jesus said "that he who understands the word is like the seed, which, planted in the good soil, yielded fruit a hundredfold." Again he said: "The kingdom of heaven is like a [tiny] grain of mustard seed, . . . the smallest of all the seeds, but when it has grown, it is the greatest of shrubs and becomes a tree so that the birds of the air can come and make their nests in its branches" (Matthew 13:31–32 RSV). Jesus is speaking about the church. Our Savior built his church almost entirely on one talent men and women. It was not upon their great gifts, but upon their great faithfulness that Jesus built his church.

Have you ever noticed that the first commandment of God and the last commandment of Christ are the same commandment? Do not think that the first commandment was delivered to Moses on Mt. Sinai. The first commandment of God was given to Adam and Eve in the Garden of Eden. In Genesis, chapter 1, verse 27 and 28 (NRSV), it is written: "God created man in his own image; in the image of God he created them: male and female he created them. God blessed them, and God said to them: '*Be fruitful and multiply*'." That is the divine law of life: "Be fruitful!" When he ascended into heaven, Jesus said to the disciples: "Go, therefore, [into all the world] and make disciples of all nations, baptizing them in the name of the Father and of the Son and of the Holy Spirit, teaching them to observe all that I have commanded you; and lo I am with you always" (Matthew 28:19–20 RSV). Is that not the self-same word of God to our first parents: "Go, be fruitful and multiply!"?

Do you sometimes wonder what God wants from you? Do you ever ask, in the quiet of the night, "What does God want from me and my life?" This is the answer: "Be fruitful!" It is not what we *possess*, but what we *produce* that counts with him. Life is God's gift to us; what we do with life is our gift to God. The greatest wickedness is summarized in this lame excuse: "I was afraid and I went and hid." Is that not the essence of sin since the beginning? God said to Adam: "Adam, where are you?" And Adam answered: "I heard the sound of thee in the garden, and I was afraid . . . and I hid myself" (Genesis 3:10 RSV).

Everyone is afraid. We are *all* afraid; we are *born* afraid. Think of all the things we fear! We are afraid of making mistakes, of being foolish, of loving and losing, of stepping out onto life's bright stage and making a mistake and then hearing—God forbid!—

someone *laugh*. We are afraid of losing what we have; we are afraid of losing our youth, our beauty, our security, our money, our self-sufficiency. Everyone has something deep in the heart of which he is most profoundly afraid. Have you ever awakened in the middle of the night, trembling from a dream in which you failed some great life test? I have. I used to have one often. I dreamt that I was taking a university examination to which I knew not a single answer! A good friend of mine in the priesthood told me about a dream he often has—of finding himself in church, fumbling through the Prayer Book, unable to find the right service—and all the people laughing! You may have such a dream. There is absolutely nothing wrong with being afraid; it is the most natural experience in life. Do not you think that the five talent and the two talent persons were just as afraid as the one talent recipient was? Of course they were! Every time they took risks with the master's money, they were afraid. Acceptance of being afraid, of having fears, is the beginning of wisdom. Our fear is the furnace in which our faith is forged. Do not think that faith is the conquest of doubt. Faith is the conquest of fear through trust. The words of Job strike a mystic chord in every soul: "Fear came upon me, and trembling, which made my bones to shake; then a spirit passed before my face, and the hair of my flesh stood up" (Job 4:14–15 KJV). It was when he was most afraid that the power of God became most real to Job.

Some of you know that I regard Vincent Van Gogh as one of the spiritual giants of our fear-racked time. The other day someone bought one of his paintings for fifty-three million dollars. Incredible—how do you explain it? In a letter to his brother Vincent Van Gogh wrote: "In a picture I want to say something comforting, as music is comforting. I want to paint men and women with that something of the eternal which the halo used to symbolize, and which we seek to give by the actual radiance and vibration of our colourings."[9] Those words were written from a mental hospital in the south of France. Vincent Van Gogh agonized with terrible, horrible fears, greater and more terrifying than, pray God, most of us in a lifetime will experience. In lonely pain, longing for friendship, in the dark night of his soul, Van Gogh continued, nevertheless, to reach out, to contribute, to be fruitful, to paint. He refused to bury his talent in his fear. Perhaps that is why, in this frightened generation, people will pay fifty million dollars for a bouquet of blue irises on a madman's table—because somehow we know with Jesus that it really does not matter if a man has five talents of happiness or one talent of pain. All that matters is that we live fruitfully and try, within the limits of personal capacity, to bring beauty, joy and hope to others.

As you know, I was in India just a few days ago. I want to share many things from my trip with you sometime, but this morning I will share just one precious moment. I sat in the dingy classroom of a school for evangelists in the city of Bombay. After a few preliminaries, a tall, frail man by the name of Abraham Shivinga stood up and, through an interpreter, told his little story. Abraham had come to know the Lord Jesus Christ five years ago when he surrendered his life to the Lord and was converted and baptized. Four years ago the Holy Spirit called him to preach the Gospel and to establish churches in the little villages around Bombay. When he began this work, the villagers, wary always of strangers, stayed away. Gradually some of the children came to his hut to listen to Bible stories at night, and then some of their older brothers and sisters came, then a few of their parents. After five months of his telling them about God's great love in Jesus, two old men were baptized, and a widow accepted Jesus as her savior. Not long after that, a monsoon struck, and a flood devastated the village. Abraham's house was blown away, and in the aftermath his wife and little girl died of pneumonia. He said, "It was then that I sat down in the middle of the village and wept and asked God why. The villagers came to me and said, 'Why do you go on preaching? Give it up; go back home. What kind of God could it be who has taken your wife, your daughter, and washed away your house? What kind of God is he?'" Abraham said, "I went to sleep that night resolved to give it up. But in my sleep I dreamt, and the Lord spoke to me in that dream. He said, 'Abraham, your wife is with me and your baby is with me and they are safe. I will help you. Do not give up.'" Abraham Shivinga said, "A wonderful thing happened the next day. God gave me a tree, and I sat under the tree and I slept under the tree and I cooked my meals and I began to tell my stories again under the tree and the children came back. After a while the church grew and we had a hundred members, and I went on to the next village to preach. Now, I have five churches. I thank God for his mercy."

Does Abraham Shivinga have five talents? Does he have even two? No. Only five years ago he learned to read. He has no college education; he has no seminary training. He is not ordained. He is a layman and one of the poorest human beings upon the face of the earth; he is a man of sorrows and acquainted with woe—but what a man! He has given what he has—all of it—to God, and God has blessed him with a miraculously fruitful life. I do not know how many churches he will plant before he goes home, but I do know that wherever I go that man will be alive in my heart. I will pray for him whenever I pray; and I will pray for myself, that I might somehow be as faithful where I am as he is where he is. How strange and great is the mystery of God's grace, that a seed planted in India bears fruit a world away in Akron!

Life is God's gift to us. What we do with our lives is our gift to God. "I was afraid; so I hid my talent." Fear can do that to us all; but when faith meets fear, when we give our lives in faith to Jesus Christ and when his love embraces and enfolds us, anyone, *anyone,* can have a magnificently fruitful life.

LET US PRAY:

Dear God, give us grace to offer, to give our lives entirely to you. With your perfect love cast out our inmost fears; then set our feet on the path of Christ unto abundant life and make us fruitful in his service, who with you and the Holy Spirit lives and reigns forever and forever. *Amen.*

CHAPTER FIVE

WOUNDED HEART

ꟲꟳꟲ

Broken Faith

BEGINNINGS AND ENDINGS are important. George Ross's main spiritual guidebook, The Book of Psalms, begins "Blessed is the one . . ." and ends "Praise the Lord."[1] In between the blessing and the praise is every emotion of the heart, every motion of the soul, every tendril of the spirit imaginable.

In this passage from *Zorba the Greek*, a saintly old Turk, Hussein Aga, took young Alexis Zorba on his knee and placed a hand on his head as though he were giving him his blessing.

"Alexis," he said, "I'm going to tell you a secret. You're too small to understand now, but you'll understand when you are bigger. Listen, little one: neither the seven stories of heaven nor the seven stories of the earth are enough to contain God."

But there is more:

"But a [person's] heart can contain [God]. So be very careful, Alexis—and may my blessing go with you—never to wound another person's heart."[2]

Our greatest wounds are the heart wounds, the scars of the spirit. Dr. Maxwell Maltz is a plastic surgeon whose research into psychology led to a popular self-help book called *Psycho-Cybernetics*. Maltz's plunge into psychological theory began with encounters with patients:

Consider the salesman who suffered a facial disfigurement as the result of an automobile accident. Each morning when he shaved he could see the horrible disfiguring scar of his cheek and the grotesque twist to his mouth. For the first time in his life he became painfully self-conscious. He was ashamed of himself and felt that his appearance must be repulsive to others. The scar became an obsession with him. He was "different" from other people. He began to "wonder" what others were thinking of him. Soon his ego was even more mutilated than his face. He began to lose confidence in himself. He became bitter and hostile. Soon almost all his attention was directed toward himself—and his primary goal became the protection of his ego and the avoidance of situations which might bring humiliation. It is easy to understand how the correction of his facial disfigurement and the restoration of a "normal" face would overnight change this man's entire attitude and outlook, his feelings about himself, and result in greater success in his work.

But what about . . . the others who acquired new faces but went right on wearing the same old personality? Or how explain the reaction of those people who insist that the surgery has made *no difference whatsoever* in their appearance? Every plastic surgeon has had this experience and has probably been as baffled by it as I was. No matter how drastic the change in appearance may be, there are certain patients who will insist that "I look just the same as before—you didn't do a thing." Friends, even family, may scarcely recognize them, may become enthusiastic over their newly acquired "beauty," yet the patient herself insists that she can see only slight or no improvement, or in fact deny that any change at all has been made. Comparison of "before" and "after" photographs does little good, except possibly to arouse hostility. By some strange mental alchemy the patient will rationalize, "Of course, I can see that the . . . scar may not show any more, but it's *still there*."[3]

Wounds and wrongs stick like burrs to the soul. They can disable the spiritual systems until the mind shuts down, the body loses its defenses, the soul becomes cratered in scar tissue. In July of 1986, fifty-year-old author Andre Dubus stopped to help a stranded motorist and was hit by a swerving car. After a brush with death and ten operations, one of which took his left leg and disabled his right leg with permanent neurological damage, he was confined to a wheelchair. Hence the title of his collection of autobiographical essays, *Broken Vessels*, which looks at life's hardships, failed marriages, severed limbs, and fractured bonds.[4] But the world that Dubus finds most painful to enter is the spiritual world within, where old wounds become fresh injuries in an instant:

After the physical pain of grief has become, with time, a permanent wound in the soul, a sorrow that will last as long as the body does, after the horrors become nightmares and sudden daylight memories, then comes the transcendent and common bond of human suffering, and with that comes forgiveness, and with forgiveness comes love.[5]

In the last of H. Richard Niebuhr's manuscripts can be found some of his most profound reflections on the nature of "faith." The most powerful chapter in *Faith on Earth* for me is chapter five, "Broken Faith," where Niebuhr explores the way faith can go wrong. Faith can "fall" into destructive spirits of disillusionment, fear, forgetfulness, and isolation as the believer breaks faith with God, with one other, and with one's community.[6] The "reconstruction" of a "broken" faith begins when an affirming spirit replaces a scoffing spirit.

As The Book of Psalms makes clear, God asks for a lot of praise in the Bible. God does this, not because God is like some dictator who needs a claque of people around saying "How wonderful you are," but because *we* need to tell God how good God is. *We* need a posture of praise in relation to the divine in order that we might have a "right spirit" (Psalm 51:10 NRSV). C. S. Lewis, one of Ross's spiritual guides,[7] wrote a classic essay on the Psalms entitled "A Word About Praising." In it, he points out that good art or music isn't poorer for our failure to recognize and appreciate them. But we are. It's that way with God. *We* need an affirmative, grateful spirit. Healthy, modest and happy people do a lot of praising, "readers [praising] their favorite poet, walkers praising the countryside, players praising their favorite games—praise of weather, wines, . . . colleges, . . . children, flowers, . . . rare beetles, even . . . politicians or scholars." Cranky, unhappy people don't praise much of anything. "Praise almost seems to be inner health made audible."[8]

For Ross, as for the Psalmist, faith *originates* in praise and affirmation. Biblical scholar Walter Brueggemann, whom Ross read studiously, calls for a praise-constituted church where praise is not so much responsive as constitutive: "The words with which we praise God shape the world in which we shall live."[9] If something doesn't begin in a "right spirit," it doesn't end in one. If our walk with God doesn't originate in praise, it doesn't end in praise. Or in the more poetic words of Jewish theologian Abraham Heschel, "It is man who is the Cantor of the universe, and in whose life the secret of cosmic prayer is disclosed."[10] In another passage, my favorite, he states: "The beginning of prayer is praise. The power of worship is song. First we sing, then we understand."[11]

With Moses came the law. But the commandments, the anointings, and the crownings needed to be ratified with an affirmation, a yes, an *Amen*. With the new Moses, Jesus of Nazareth, came grace. But the grace, and the community built on that grace, also needed to be ratified with an affirmation. The *Amen* was not some rubber stamp or automatic stop. It was rather the spiritual ratification of the statement. The Bible is filled with a chorus of affirmations, of *Amens*.

Indeed, an *Amen* is how the Psalms begins. Poet Marianne Moore renders the first Psalm as "BLESSED IS THE MAN / who does not sit in the seat of the scoffer—/ the man who does not denigrate, depreciate, / denunciate."[12] In a radio broadcast, English literary critic Max Beerbohm once said something that Arthur Koestler later used as a frontispiece to one of his books: "Ladies and gentlemen, I am afraid my subject is rather an exciting one and as I don't like excitement, I shall approach it in a gentle, timid, roundabout way." Add "scoffing," and one has a shorthand statement of how "moderns" came to approach life. The modern period has been an Age of Criticism plagued by a scoffing spirit. The Western tradition of philosophy, created by the Enlightenment, is predominantly skeptical, negative, and scoffing. Faith in negation did not begin with Descartes's radical doubt, nor did it end with Derrida's radical deconstruction. But it did achieve dominant status in the modern era. Roger Scruton, in *The Philosopher* on *Dover Beach*, argues that the central inadequacy of much modern philosophy is that, at the end of the day, there is "nothing" to espouse.[13] One of the foremost architects of the modern era, Sigmund Freud, apologized at the end of *Civilization and Its Discontent* because he had no explanation for the agonies of existence: "I have not the courage to rise up before my fellow-men as a prophet, and I bow to their reproach that I can offer them no consolation."[14]

Psychologist Erik Erickson liked to tell the story of a rabbi who felt inhibited when asked to make a speech in heaven. "I am good only at refutation," he said. The rabbi is not alone. Many of us are trained to define ourselves by what we oppose rather than what we advance. As one of my mountaineer ancestors put it, "Whatever it is—I'm against it." In the classic Groucho Marx film *Horse Feathers*, Groucho prances around in his academic cap and gown, singing this ditty: "Whatever you do, / Whatever you say, / However you may amend it—/ I'm against it. / . . . Even when you've altered and condensed it, / I'm *against* it."[15]

Little wonder, then, that the modern age and its rigorous imperative of objectivity created an educational system addicted to objections, a culture of criticism with acute literary and artistic self-consciousness. Modernity made an art form of criticism, and critics have become some of our most celebrated artists. Northrup Frye's widely cited *Anatomy of Criticism* (1957) is a theory of literature *and* a theory of criticism—as if they were one and the same. Some deconstructionists have been known to kill off the author, with Roland Barthes announcing in 1968 that "writing is the destruction of every voice, every origin. Writing is that . . . black-and-white where all identity is lost, beginning with the very identity of the body that writes."[16] When the reader both plays the text and is played by it, texts or works of literature are theoretically unnecessary. All one needs to study literature is literary theory.

"All criticism tends too much to become criticism of criticism," warned G. K. Chesterton.[17] Remove the crabbed matter from many academic tomes, and they would become paper-thin volumes. Criticism has almost come to be regarded as more important than the work it criticizes. One literary critic wrote this about Robert Frost, then about himself: "Robert Frost defined a liberal as someone who can't take his own side in an argument. In more than thirty years of teaching and writing about history, I have not succeeded in developing a single, consistent theoretical position of my own or, for that matter, in embracing anyone else's."[18] The reviewer in the *Times Literary Supplement* told how his heart "warmed" when he read these words, and he congratulated the author on his being such "a brave, as well as an intelligent and civilized man, to admit to what most of us suspect about ourselves."

Ross was the product of an educational system that specialized in "critical thinking," where the prestige goes to those who "sit in the seat of the scoffer" rather than to those who "sit under their vine and fig tree and live in peace and unafraid" (to quote another First Testament author). Mary Midgley points this out with force: "Scholars who reject something are always one up on scholars who accept it, and it pays to raise very small issues because this makes it easier to avoid accidentally appearing to have accepted something after all."[19] Academe is a conflictual contest where, Midgley observes, the negative always wins. Has an "oral defense" ever been made by a candidate who celebrated rather than cut down someone else's thesis? How many Ph.D.'s in the sciences have been granted for designing rather than dissecting?

Of course, the negative vote decides in areas other than the academy. Ninety-five people may be *for* something, but the five that oppose it get the biggest hearing and sometimes stop the project. Or look what gets admitted into pride of place in our marriage ceremony. The last word goes to the critic—"If anyone here has any objection, speak now. . . ." We give the critic the final say. We aren't about to let anyone sweep us off our feet, even when we're being swept off our feet.

Chief Justice Earl Warren gave a clue as to why sports enjoys such enormous popularity within the ivy towers of academe. He said he always turned to the sports page first, because he wanted to start the day reading positive accounts of people doing "their best." Ohio State football, Duke basketball, Stanford volleyball permit even the most critical, the most skeptical among us, to be unabashedly and unashamedly *for* something—although Warren would be appalled to the degree sports headlines are now about brawls, drugs, flubbed passes, team quarrels, and teammates wanting to be traded, and sports critics hindsighting the big game.

As a good student, Ross learned the lessons of modernity well. Ross's seminary training and continuing education in biblical studies taught him higher criticism, historical criticism (which lost its predominance at the end of the 1970s), literary criticism and social world criticism, redaction criticism, aesthetic criticism, and so on. One mainline seminary even had a faculty position entitled "Professor of Homiletics and Christian Criticism of Life." The picture of the person who once held that position greets students to this day as they enter the Dean's office.

Throughout his life, Ross enjoyed reading critical reviews (the *New York Times Book Review Supplement* and the *Times Literary Supplement*, to name but two). He also enjoyed providing critical reviews of books for his congregation. He could and did at times render judgments in an idiom not unlike that of the high Victorian slang which would "introduce my bootmaker to the gent's tailor," or could evaluate an argument in terms not unlike this low Pennsylvania Dutch vernacular, "see the mistletoe in my coattail." But he tried never to be mean or nasty in his judgments. Why be mean to people, even if they're wrong or stupid?

The worst people in the world to listen to sermons are clergy. Why? Because we can't hear a sermon without critiquing it and figuring out ways we would have preached it differently. Yet any artist can take the greatest painting by Rembrandt—and can bring the viewer up so close that the brushmarks, the imperfections, the bad places all show—and on that basis can provide textbook reasons why Rembrandt's painting cannot be a great piece of art. There is not one artist, or architect, or musician, or preacher, or disciple that can withstand that level of scrutiny. Not even George Ross. The late Anthony de Mello, an Indian Jesuit priest and psychologist, liked to tell the story of two taxidermists who stopped before a window in which an owl was on display. They immediately began to criticize the way it was mounted. Its eyes were not natural; its wings were not in proportion with its head; its feathers were not neatly arranged; and its feet could certainly be improved. When they finished critiquing the owl, the old owl slowly turned its head . . . and winked at them.

Ross agreed with the elder Pliny's reported dictum that there is no book (or sermon, he would add) so bad that some good cannot be got out of it. Martin E. Marty would agree with this principle: "Review as you would be reviewed." He writes, "Be gentle with one another's efforts. Be kind and considerate with your criticism. Always remember that it's just as hard to write a bad book as it is to write a good book."[20] Why add to the supply of misery and pain in the world when passing through this life?

Ross learned the authentic voice of the "Protestant"—Protestants protest something. The first "Protestants" (the word was born at the Diet of Spener in 1529) protested against Rome. Subsequent "Protestants" have been involved in a plethora of protest movements, and Ross's ministry had its share of "anti-" thrusts, anti-racism, anti-militarism, anti-this, anti-that, all entered into, like his involvement in the Ambridge, Pennsylvania, "protest" seminary, with the best of motives to fight some obvious evil.

Like most of us, Ross took more seriously those books that other segments in the culture were protesting or attempting to ban. It is said that discerning Catholics, in those days when the Vatican issued a periodical *Index of Prohibited Books*, made such an index their library list. But Ross also believed that protest ought to begin at home. The household of God comes under the judgment of God first. What seemed to others as an unduly critical attitude toward his own church was actually Ross's insistence that the Episcopal Church deal with itself internally before unleashing its protest on the outside world.

The larger issue, however, was Ross's conviction that *protest* movements ought to be generated out of and grounded in a *professing* spirit. Movements tend to take on the spirit of the things they oppose. Hatred breeds hatred. Resentment creates resentment. Skepticism engenders skepticism. Protests tend to produce more protests, a state of "always learning, but never coming to a knowledge of the truth." Movements born in a protesting rather than a professing spirit tend to become mirror images of the things they oppose.

The same with theologies. To begin theology in a spirit of methodological atheism is to prejudice its outcome. The importance of skepticism in the scientific method would be hard to overemphasize. The systematic doubting of all received opinion was the major weapon of criticism contributed by Renaissance humanism in the sixteenth and seventeenth centuries. Every tradition must be tested and proved.[21] Actually, this was the heart of the dispute between Luther and Erasmus. Erasmus had a skeptical spirit: suspicious, critical, negative. Luther said, nonsense: "The Holy Spirit is no skeptic." Sadly, Ross believed, Erasmus has won the hearts of large numbers of the Christian church, not to speak of the culture.[22] The human race is not "neatly divided as between those who have faith in God and those who do not," as Ross put it.

There is a precarious balance in every heart between belief and unbelief. Is there any believer who has never at any time been driven to doubt the existence of a benevolent God when crushed by some fearful, meaningless disaster, when the lights go out and yet the world goes on its unheeding way? By the same reasoning, is there any unbeliever who has never experienced a tug from the world unseen and begun to be skeptical about his skepticism?[23]

Postmodern biblical scholar Stephen D. Moore recently made the case for "a criticism that would be graphic, pictorial, and visual." The gospels are "nocturnal writings," Moore contends, more like "dreams" than "dissertations," and "abstract expression is alien both to the gospel and to the dream." The problem is that "biblical scholars and theologians are, for the most part, neither dreamers nor cartoonists, preferring to take a pneumatic drill or jackhammer to the concrete language of the Gospels, to replace graphic images with abstract categories."[24] Higher criticism was a vital means toward the end of higher celebration and higher imagination, Ross insisted. He believed that this "higher" form of exegesis was needed for the Scriptures to be unwrapped, like Lazarus, and come forth with new life and relevance to our day. When you demystify something, you denature it. "Expanded explanation tends to spoil the lion's leap," Marianne Moore contends. "We must be as clear as our natural reticence allows us to be."[25]

In 1914, one of Ross's intellectual gurus, Randolph Bourne, compared American and French universities. If made today, the comparison would be very different since the French tradition of "public intellectuals" who are truly *professorial* has fallen by the critical wayside.

Our Universities still tend to produce as professors the hardworking patient mediocre scholar, or the clear-sighted skeptical critic, rather than the intellectual leader. . . . Our "intellectuals" will have to go sharpen up their knowledge, and stiffen their fibre a good deal, it seems to me, before they can take the commanding place of leadership which they fill in France.[26]

Pros at criticism, amateurs at praise, we moderns are not so much "learning disabled" as "teaching disabled." Our teaching has been deficient in creating a professing tradition, a positive tradition, an Amen tradition of celebration and strategic optimism.

For Ross, this professing tradition branched in all directions, including one's relationship with one's country. Ross was proud to be a patriot. Although he yielded to no one in demanding accountability from national leaders and legislation, he deplored the rhetoric of hate and disrespect that emanated from both the left and right. Too much of the criticism he read seemed to him a cheap shot. "Criticism is a study by which men grow important and formidable at very small expense," Samuel Johnson ventured.[27] The greatest weapon of the Christian in spiritual warfare is not intellectual negation or political bashing or spiritual sabre-slashing, but affirmation.

As much as Ross loved a good debate (he was a star player on his high school and college debate teams), he despised conflict. He could think of few things more sapping of one's mental and physical health than a "cry-baby" spirit. He could not imagine a job he would rather do less than spend each day handling complaints, and felt deeply for Moses and the whining and complaining he had to endure (see Numbers 11:4–6). Ross believed the times required a style of ministry and scholarship that was more "professorial" (that professes something) and celebrative rather than conflictual and critical; a holistic rather than a disciplinary model of inquiry that recognizes we need each other to do our own work, for no one person can know enough or do enough to go it alone. Any glance at the mushrooming number of multiple authorships of articles in refereed journals testifies to the growing complexity of our world and our interdependence on one another.

Perhaps Ross's key bone of contention with the Episcopal Church, a bone he gnawed on with increasing tenaciousness as the decades wore on, was its lack of intellectual vigor. He believed that the Episcopal Church was becoming intellectually and emotionally undemanding to the point of theological toothlessness, gumming and humming its way through life's hardest issues. As one who yearned for the bravery of a conclusion, Ross would have loved the title of Ysenda Maxtone Graham's book describing her year-long sojourn amidst the Church of England: *The Church Hesitant.*[28]

A spirit of affirmation does not mean that questions are unimportant. But there is such a thing as a good question, just as there is such a thing as a good answer. The good question is not the carping question, or the complaining question, or the "narcissism-of-small-differences" (Freud's phrase) question, but the constructive critical question, the creative question, the question that pushes the conversation forward. Not all questions are productive, just as not all criticism is productive. The old adage "There's no such thing as a stupid question" is, to use one of Ross's favorite words, "absurd."

To be a Christian is to say "Yes" to life, to one's self, to one's country (Ross felt good about being known as a "patriot"), to the world, and to God, as God has said "Yes" to us. One of Ross's favorite texts from Matthew—"Let your speech be yes and no. Whatsoever is more than that comes from evil" (5:17–37)—afforded him an opportunity to define what it means ("when all is said and done") to be a Christian:

There are moments in our lives when we are paralyzed and helpless, when we can neither speak nor hear, when we see nothing and feel barely alive. Though we do not see Him, it is then that He comes and puts His well-remembered hand in ours. To all our doubts and to all our questions, He very simply answers: *"Yes,* I have made you; *yes,* I have saved you; *yes,* I do love you; and *yes,* you will be mine forever; and . . . *yes,* I am with you now.[29]

Every "Yes" implies a "No"—a no to sin, to death, to all that binds the confined. Jesus said "No!" to a lot, but he said "No!" because he had already said "Yes!" to God. Ross taught his parishioners to say no to a lot of things. But they could say no because their loyalty to Christ, which is absolute, makes relative all other loyalties.[30] We must never speak a No without first grounding it in a Yes. A No is never enough, as George Bernard Shaw poignantly confessed toward the end of his life:

I am by nature a preacher, but I have no Bible, no creed. The war has shot both out of my hands. And with what result? Just this: that we seem to have outgrown our religion, outgrown our political system, outgrown our strength of mind and character. The fatal word "not" has been inscribed into all our creeds. What next? Is "no" enough, I ask? For a boy, yes; for a man, never. . . . I must have some affirmations to preach . . . oh, if only I could find some.[31]

In breaking free of the critical straightjacket, Ross did not throw away his critical faculties. Ross understood the fundamental spiritual value of the critical method—what Wayne C. Booth calls "relishing the fun of slicing through thickets of nonsense with the sword of skepticism: 'What's your evidence?'"[32] Ross was optimistic. But so too was General Custer. It is not enough simply to be optimistic. One must question the evidence of one's optimism. One must test the spirits to see if they be of God.

In Søren Kierkegaard's penetrating phrase summarizing the biblical story that ended with "the rising sun and the limping man," the biblical witness keeps "the wound of the negative open."[33] Thomas Kuhn's *Structure of Scientific Revolution,* which influenced Ross's thinking as much as it has everyone else's, warns scientists and scholars of the dangers of closing the wound and "uncritically" accepting "paradigms" that guide their thinking and research. The German philosopher Hegel urged the church to criticize the postulates upon which every culture is based: "While the Gates of Hell were never able to prevail against the Christian church, the Gates of Reason have." By throwing aside that which could not be validated by reason or regarded as truths of reason, the church capitulated to the modern culture of reason. Without critical scrutiny, one ends up reflecting rather than attending and transcending the conundrums of the dominant culture. The alternative to critical scrutiny is to surrender to the culture, thereby enriching the myth-kitty of the marketing industry or the coffers of the rich. The incarnation is more than about affirmation. It is about transformation. Jesus didn't just celebrate what he saw in the culture of his day. He transformed it.

But the open "wound of the negative" has become infected with a critical spirit that is unhealthy and may even be rendering the church ineffective in the world today. Our scoffing, skeptical spirit is like wax in the ear. Until we get it removed, we can't hear God speaking clearly. Indeed, the more negatives we allow into our consciousness, the more negative become our experiences of life and each other. America's greatest theologian, Jonathan Edwards, argued this case a quarter of a millennium ago: "It is a most evil and pernicious practice in meditating on our affliction, to ruminate on the aggravations of the afflictions, and reckon up the evil circumstances thereof, dwelling long on the dark side; it doubles and trebles the affliction."[34] Physicians are increasingly telling us how right Edwards actually was. The more negative spirits we allow into our healing treatments, the less positive the outcomes. That is because, in the words of an old Indian saying, *Sarvam-annam*: "All is food." The "all" refers to everything we eat, breathe, and take into our being through our physical and spiritual senses. Spiritual pollution is as dangerous as physical pollution. Destructive, negative consumption will have destructive, negative consequences: Garbage In, Garbage Out.

Ross knew the lurking madness underneath the suburban calm almost as well as film-maker David Lynch (*Blue Velvet*). Week after week Ross looked out at his parishioners and diagnosed their fundamental ailment: soul sickness. People are desperate for affirmations. He was right. *Newsweek* did a feature story on the second biggest publishing market in the country, second only to the Bible: "bedside bucker-uppers" it called these "affirmation books" ("Affies" for short).[35]

The most fundamental need of the church is not for more "Rules of Order," or for more "Rules of Trust," or even for rules of any kind. The fundamental need of the church is for a "right spirit." "Create in me a clean heart and renew a right spirit within me," the Psalmist prays (Psalm 51:10 KJV). The law of spiritual economics says bad spirits drive out good spirits. In other words, the church needs an attitude adjustment, a "right spirit" of thumbs-up thinking and living that would make it into a "So-Be-It" and "So-Do-It" community.

In calling for spirit to come first, Ross adumbrated a whole movement in the corporate world away from "job descriptions" and toward "spirit descriptions." SouthWest Airlines, in announcing the abolishment of line management models and chain-of-command patterns of authority, introduced in place of "job descriptions" something they now call "Attitude Descriptions," the chief of which is "Do you have a sense of humor?" Although Ross's ironizing intellect played to the discriminating smile rather than to the belly-laugh (humor is a sweet wine, wit a dry, implies Ambrose Bierce[36]), virtually every sermon had some form of humor in it. By encouraging his parishioners to laugh at themselves and at life, Ross opened a positive channel through which healing energies could flow and flood one's soul.

Kellogg has introduced into the market a new kind of baseball card, one that features the athlete's values and attitudes about life more than the athlete's statistics. One of the hottest management consultations in USAmerica today is how to get rid of employees, not for bad performance records, but for bad attitudes. The American Society for Quality Control has ranked the following reasons why companies lose customers: death (1 percent of respondents to a survey), moved away (3 percen), influenced by friends (5 percent), lured away by the competition (9 percent), dissatisfied with product (14 percent), and turned off and turned away by a bad attitude on part of company employee (68 percent!). This employee pledge, required by Wal-mart Discount Stores, says it all: "I solemnly promise and declare that for every customer that comes within ten feet of me, I will smile, look them in the eye, and greet them, so help me Sam."

A Christian with a "right-spirited" faith has an oxymoronic mix of confidence and humility. The Apostle Paul brought these two together in his famous statement, "I can do all things.[that's the confidence] through Christ, who strengthens me [that's the humility]" (Philippians 4:13 NKJV).

A right spirit is a humble spirit. A bent and broken spirit is the thread that ties the community of faith together. For Ross, this meant a number of things. Most of all, it meant you shall judge yourself before judging others. Freely translated, Proverbs 23:12 reads, "Don't forget to accept criticism; get all the help you can." In other words, hear what your critics are saying. I call this the Michael Corleone Principle. In *The Godfather, Part II*, Michael Corleone travels to his boyhood home in upstate New York and confesses to a friend: "Pop taught me many lessons in this house . . . one of them was to keep your friends close, and keep your enemies closer." Powerful information is wrapped up in criticism, a source of truth some people never tap.

The French composer Erik Satie died with all the letters he had received unopened. Rainer Maria Rilke, the greatest German lyric poet of this century, confessed that he never read a review of his writings: "I feel that criticism is a letter to the public which the author, since it is not directed to him, does not have to open and read."[37] The contents, however, could be of great value. Some have suggested that Beethoven was as great a composer as he was partly because he was deaf and didn't have to listen to the bad reviews of his work and the bad music of his period. Proust, for want of being deaf himself, made his room deaf by lining it with cork. Though these artists may have profited aesthetically from their retreat into a world impervious to criticism, most of us find such self-imposed defenses a hindrance to spiritual advances. In the words of another of Ross's "spiritual guides," Teilhard de Chardin: "Let us take care not to reject the least ray of light from any side. Faith has need of all the truth."[38]

In fact, we usually learn less from our friends than from our enemies, who give us valuable tips, either about us or (if the critique is off-base) about those who criticize us. Either way, the information can be priceless. Martin Luther once suggested that a good preacher, in order to overcome personal deficiencies, "should be willing to let everyone vex and hack away at him." But one can "hack away" without employing a meathook method of criticism that is brusque, brutal, and leaves the subject hanging like some bloodied, skinned carcass. Ross had less problem with those who criticized him to his face than with those who would say nothing to him but go elsewhere and say everything.

It is possible to be criticized but not take others' negative comments to heart. A wonderful story involving Grant Teaff, the head football coach at Baylor University, nicely illustrates this point. Every summer Teaff conducts a football camp for young boys interested in the game. One summer, after the boys finished their last workout for the day, Coach Teaff gave them a special instruction: "All day tomorrow I want you to consciously try to eliminate negative thoughts from your mind. And then when we get together tomorrow evening, we'll see how we did."

Well, the next day, at the end of the workout, Teaff got the kids together. "How many of you had ten or less negative thoughts during the day?" he asked. A large number of hands went up in the air. He then looked at the guys and asked a second question. "How many of you had five or less negative thoughts during the day?" And only three little hands went up. Then Coach Teaff asked, "And now let me see if anyone went through the entire day and didn't even have one negative thought." To his amazement, a lone hand shot straight up in the air. It was the hand of a little nine-year-old boy by the name of J.J.

"You went through the whole day without one negative

thought, J.J.?" asked Teaff. And the little fellow said, "Yes, sir, I did, Coach." So Teaff told him how proud he was of him, and then the coach had all the boys stand up to applaud J.J.

When the meeting was over and the others had left, Grant Teaff felt someone tugging at his belt. He looked down and, lo and behold, it was J.J. He had a puzzled look on his face. "Coach," he said, "I'm confused. What is a negative thought anyway?"[39]

A person who has a "right spirit" also has the disposition to commend rather than condemn. Business studies have revealed that the ratio of pokes to strokes in the workplace is about 4 to 1. Developing business strategies to invert that ratio has itself become big business. Harvard's Rosabeth Moss Kanter has suggested ten rules for stifling initiative. For example, rule three reads, "Ask departments or individuals to challenge and criticize each other's proposals," and rule four makes this demand: "Express your criticisms freely, and withhold your praise."[40] Even those, like Hendrie Weisinger, who view criticism as a managerial skill, argue that criticism should include more encouragement than anything else.[41]

Ross was more concerned, however, about the implications of a "right spirit" for the church, where clergy find themselves more prone to rag than brag on a colleague. Crucifixion is not just an historical event. It is something Christians do to each other daily. We crucify one another when we "cut her down to size," or when we "drag him down into the mud with the rest of them."

Sally Dyck conducted a study on clergy morale for the Cleveland (Ohio) District Committee on Ministry. One of the "situational causes" of low clergy morale named in this study was the spiritual wounds of those in ministry:

"Who can you trust any more?" is the cry of those who look to the covenant community for support and comfort in times of low morale. Fear, suspicion, and mistrust keep colleagues from truly sharing their hurts and hopes in ministry.[42]

We judge habitats and civilizations by their tolerance of eccentrics. We judge each other in ministry by severe codes of conformity and bureaucratic compliance.

The clerical grapevine is one of the wonders of the modern world. Information passes among clergy at speeds that defy Einstein's long-held maxim that no communication can travel faster than the speed of light. Every community has its information specialists, its news carriers, those who keep the communication flowing and fluid. We in the church have information specialists to put the corporate world to shame. Our sense of humor is much less highly developed than our sense of rumor.

One of the due-process reforms of the 1960s was the Miranda Rule. The reading of Miranda rights is required for every person arrested. The Miranda warnings inform suspects of their right to remain silent (or have a lawyer present), for what they say can and will be used against them. Ross lamented the church's Mirandized ministry—whatever clergy say to one another can, and often will, be used against each other.

I shall never forget a conversation with a denominational official from another state. He started telling me things that I was not comfortable being told. "Are you sure I ought to know this?" I asked. He replied: "Well, the person told me not to tell anyone, that it was between us." "Then why are you telling me this?" He replied: "Come on, Len. Whenever anyone comes to you and says—'This is between us. Don't tell anyone'—they really are asking you to tell people. Don't you know that by now?"

Ross did not believe any of us should know that by now. A great career can be compromised or ruined by a single slur, a lone slander, an idle gossip. Robert Burns once said, "I've never confided anything to any one without having regretted it ever afterward." Those who confide in ministers should not say the same. One of the best definitions of "minister" is someone who knows how to keep other people's secrets, including enemies' secrets. There is enough hearsay, whimsy, and audible gabble of gossip going on behind our backs without colleagues in ministry adding to the pile. Referring to the clergy, Harold St. John once said, "Should a man not lay his hand upon his mouth before he criticizes his brethren?" Or as an old Arab proverb would put it, the words of the tongue should pass through three gateways: 1) Is it true? 2) Is it kind? 3) Is it necessary? In the Islamic tradition, one of the worst things anyone can do in life is to cause disorder or dissension within the community, something called *fitnah*, which brings with it some of the most severe punishments in the Islamic faith (as Salman Rushdie is finding out).

Cyril Connolly says W. H. Auden declared a moratorium on publicly criticizing colleagues.[43] Although Ross never came to this point, he did try not to speak ill of colleagues, living or dead, to anyone but his closest associates. Whenever he could, Ross gave the grapevine, not his ears, but his shears. He strived to find the best in people and build on that; he denounced "gossipers" whenever he could find an opening; and he saved his splintered, critical yardsticks for those who he believed were misusing positions of power and authority, or were unduly critical themselves.

The other half of a "right spirit" is confidence: "I can do *all things. . . ."* Ross quoted an anonymous source in declaring that being a priest "requires the self-confidence which only the devils have in hell."[44] James Dobson, the founder and president of Focus on the Family, says that when he thinks of what it means to be a parent today, he thinks of a photograph in his files. It is of an elegantly dressed lady who is holding a cup of coffee. Her little finger is cocked ever so daintily, and her face reveals utter self-assurance. Unfortunately, this woman does not yet know that her slip has collapsed around her feet. The caption reads, "Confidence is what you have before you understand the situation." Confidence is what the Christian has before, during, and after understanding the situation.

The first mark of this confidence is a So-Be-It spirit. A Christian with such a spirit manifests an affirming theology and a professing ministry. In his 1991 convocation address at Wycliffe College, Toronto, Canon Herbert O'Driscoll lamented the absence of those qualities in the church today:

We have lost the capacity to say "yes" as our first word in reply to the question "Do you believe . . . ?" To questions of belief we have learned to reply tentatively and carefully. We employ such phrases as, "Well, it depends on what you mean by . . ." or "Are you asking me if . . ." or

"Perhaps if I can reshape your question . . ." If this is at all true then I suggest that we very badly need to recapture a way of response that expresses what I will call the child of faith in us rather than the adult of ambiguity.

Let me suggest a perfectly viable succession of questions and responses we might consider. Do you believe that Jesus Christ is the son of God? Yes, I do. Do you believe that Jesus Christ rose from the dead? Yes, I do. Do you believe that the blood of Jesus cleanses us from all sin? Yes, I do. Do you believe that the Bible is the word of God? Yes, I do.

If we do indeed believe, then, without haranguing people or invading them, let us quietly communicate the fact that our first word to God is not "maybe," not "perhaps," not "it depends on . . . ," but a simple YES.[45]

Even when we make peace with the thought of being a "Yes-man" or a "Yes-woman," we quickly slide back into being "No-people" or "No-families." Family meals are an example. How quickly they become times of "picking" on deficiencies of family members rather than occasions for celebrating their joys and successes. For pastors, how quickly we find ourselves sitting with people in their troubles and bad times and seldom sitting down with them when they feel grateful about something and want to celebrate.

Being a "Yes-person" meant for Ross being open to the moment God gives each of us, whether we ask for it or not, and letting life have its way with us. A spirit of criticism evidences the addiction of the modern era to mastery and control. The corrective to criticism is story, image, metaphor, and mystery. Or in the formulation of one of the Episcopal Church's greatest nineteenth-century preachers, Phillips Brooks, the "habit of criticism" is the modern tendency to wrestle everything down and pin it to the mat of human control. It is the "habit of criticism" that makes preachers turn the text of life and the Scriptures into illustration. For biblical scholar John Dominic Crossan, the difference between illustration and metaphor is that we use the former while the latter uses us. Metaphor has its way with us and helps us hear the music that is in our hearts.

Ross's much-loved travel narratives included this one that

stands as his personal version of the "singing-in-the-rain" metaphor:

Sometimes I conduct tours for people in Europe and so does a friend of mine, a priest in Indiana. We often compare notes on the sweet and sour of traveling abroad with others. He was telling me not long ago about his frustration on a recent tour. "When we arrived in London," he said, "everybody immediately began reading brochures about Paris. When we got to Paris, they all unpacked their books on Rome; and when we got to Rome, they all took out their airline tickets to study their itinerary back to Indianapolis. Everywhere they were, they were not there." . . . Some of us are always ahead of ourselves. Some of us are locked into our own artificial world. "Ephaphta!" "Open up!" Thomas Merton, one of my guides, put it this way: "A man will know that he has come to some measure of spiritual success when he can say, 'I was there when it rained on me.'" Be open to life as it happens, as it flows daily from God, like the manna, from heaven.[46]

To read into this statement some semblance of a nineteen-six-tyish "go-with-the-flow" theology, or the moony introspections of the nineteen-eightyish New Age movement, would be unfair. An affirmative theology for Ross meant that the real *profess-ional* concern of ministry was opening people to receive the wisdom and wonder that are all around them. He conveyed this better in a little parable that illustrated his belief that wisdom and wonder were the essential earmarks of a well-educated person. This parable also demonstrates his confidence in being able to turn the most quotidian event, even a bird sitting on a wire, into something interesting and arresting:

The other day my attention was drawn to a little bird with a noisy, terrible, two-note song: "Twit, twat; twit twat." It went on and on, it seemed to me, for an eternity at five in the morning. Nature gives most birds a special song that they are supposed to sing all the time. This one came up with his own invention—and it was no improvement! It is not nice to fool Mother Nature. There he sat on the wire that runs through most of our gardens, the coaxial television cable. "Twit, twat; twit twat," he went on and on. "'Is it a weakness of intellect, Birdie?' I cried, 'or a rather tough worm in your little inside?'" It is rare that I quote Gilbert and Sullivan at five in the morning, but he drew it from me!

"Listen here, Bird," I almost said; "do you realize that just beneath your feet, flowing at the speed of light, there is William Buckley, twitching his nose, both ears and his forehead, all at the same time; and at the same time and in the same wire, there is Dr. Falwell, wagging his finger and shaking his jowls at the world; and at the same time, the Mormon Tabernacle Choir is singing 'The Hallelujah Chorus' like crazy, and Col. North is taking the Fifth Amendment and there is famine in the Sudan and tears are streaming down the face of a young man dying of AIDS in San Francisco, and Miami Vice and the Cleveland Indians trying to play baseball? O you silly bird, you're standing on a miracle, on the amazing, splendid, tragic, crazy, glorious life of the 20th century, and all you have to say about it is, 'Twit, twat.' "

Then, I wondered how different am I, how different are we, from that little bird? We are standing on a marvel to which, by and large, we are completely oblivious.[47]

Ross's So-Be-It spirit went in multiple directions at the same time. He challenged his wealthy congregation to say "Yes!" to the wretched of the earth at the same time he challenged them to say "Yes!" to their riches. This makes Ross very difficult to chart on the traditional ideological spectrum. He would have agreed with former Prime Minister Margaret Thatcher that "no-one would remember the Good Samaritan if he had only had good intentions. He had money as well."[48] A devotee of William F. Buckley, he knew how get-the-rich policies are as damaging as get-rich schemes. You can't soak the rich without getting everyone wet.

Yet he also knew that spirituality is more than a search for one's better self. Spirituality is a life of filling (*plerosis*) through emptying (*kenosis*), of finding oneself by giving oneself away. Ross questioned the church hierarchy's commitment to the poor, the unemployed, the prisoner, the drug-addicted, and AIDS-afflicted. The Platonic philosopher Clesus joked around 180 A.D.—when Christians included the elite, the establishment, the elegant, the well-bred—"if all men wanted to be Christian, Christians would not want them."[49]

In Luke (12:16–21), Jesus condemns a man for storing wealth in bigger barns instead of putting that wealth to work for the poor.

Ross used this story to take on the bigger-barn builders in his own church and in this money-obsessed world. Every church has its share of gold-hoarding dragons, breathing fire at those who threaten their possessions. But Ross's preaching about materialism was more appalled than angry: to my knowledge, he never fingered the hair-trigger text "To hell with you and your money" (Acts 8:20), or encouraged the notion that "every great fortune is a great crime." Not money itself, but lives built on greed, gluttony, selfishness, and arrogance caused the deeper problems in our world. In the words of Paul, "Greed is the same thing as worshipping a false god" (Colossians 3:5). To the bigger-barn builders of the Episcopal Church, Ross reached out in a spirit of tenderness and pity for their poverty of faith, their spiritual backwardness, and theological blight.

What fueled Ross's So-Be-It faith was the Amen-spirit of Christ. In many ways, Jesus displayed a theology of affirmation. First, he affirmed and honored everyone he met. He picked out rather than picked on those most "put down" and "down-and-out." No wonder the spirit of the early church was one of "love one another with brotherly affection; outdo one another in showing honor" (Romans 12:10). Second, Jesus honored people's need. He stopped what he was doing, allowed everyone to waylay and interrupt him, and generally demonstrated that no concern of others was unimportant to him. Third, Jesus affirmed others by acknowledging his need for them in his life (the disciples—Peter, James, and John especially—the Bethany family, and others). We all need to be needed. Fourth, Jesus honored people by his relationship to the powerless who suffer. What was Jesus to do with his powers once he discovered that he had them? By an extreme, extra-human act of identification with the wounded, he chose to give up his powers and die. Finally, Jesus affirmed his Father's will in his life and learned well his mother's words, "Let it be."

In Ross's view, the incarnation was God's absolute affirmation of creation. Jesus came to see the difference, theologian John Haughey writes, "between being a sign and being a spectacle; between pointing to himself and witnessing to the Father"; or in later fashion, Jesus "went from seeing that he was being spoken to, to understanding that he was wholly spoken by the Father."[50] The slave spiritual's contention that "he never said a mumbling word" is not exactly true, but true enough. Ross sought to ground his life in an *imitatio Christi* theology of affirmation.

The confidence that masks a right spirit, Ross believed, not only proclaims "so be it" but also "let's do it." Indecision and in-action are byproducts of a critical spirit. Using the modern scientific method, one can sometimes disprove a hypothesis, but can hardly prove one. No matter how many times the sun rises each morning, there is no way one can prove conclusively that the sun will rise tomorrow. Indeed, one can more effectively prove that there is reason to doubt whether indeed it will rise tomorrow. That is why scientists have such a hard time reaching conclusions on such causal relationships as cancer/smoking; climate changes/acid rain and hfc; greenhouse effect/carbon dioxide. One can always find a "reason" not to say "Yes!"—to some solution, to some strategy, to some action.

Most seriously of all, criticism removes us from reality and makes true understanding and involvement virtually impossible. Media specialist Jeff Jarvis describes the "new cynicism" as "ugly, snide, and overwhelmingly pessimistic." A whole host of television programs carry the same message: "We can't change the world; we can only scoff." Perched in his seat, the scoffer can lament the problems of the world but evade firsthand engagement with them. The danger of criticism, in Wendy Steiner's words, is that "criticism makes nothing happen."[51]

The Russian dramatist Anton Chekov complained about critics in more picturesque terms:

Critics are like horse-flies which prevent the horse from ploughing. The horse works, all its muscles drawn tight like the strings on a double-bass, and a fly settles on his flanks and tickles and buzzes. . . . He has to twitch his skin and swish his tail. And what does the fly buzz about? It scarcely knows itself; simply because it is restless and wants to proclaim: "Look, I too am living on the earth. See, I can buzz, too, buzz about anything."[52]

In a world running out of horses, Ross called for a church that would position itself in a So-Do-It posture toward change in the world and hope in the future:

I remember very well standing one day outside Chartres Cathedral a few years ago. It is impressive from any angle, but one's eye is drawn immediately to the stained glass windows. They are dark, vacant shadows against the stone, almost a disfigurement of the facade, but as you step inside, what appeared to be meaningless and opaque suddenly blazes into a celebration of almost inexpressible joy. . . . A stained glass window means something or nothing to you, depending entirely on where you stand in relation to the light.

So it is with your life and mine. We can be tossed up and down by the stock market or the cost of living index, thrown back and forth by the high tides and low tides of events, alternately happy or sad as we read the daily news. Which is to say: we can *copy* life. Or we can organize it from above, seeing a pattern, a steady continuity, a meaning and purpose which is transparent only as the light of Christ shines through it.[53]

The spiritual attributes of "forgiveness, healing, love" unlock the doors to the future, Ross insisted, just as "anger, guilt, pride, and anxiety" imprison us in the past. Religion can be either imprisonment (what Ross called "a freezing in place") or empowerment ("a venturing forward in journey"). "Every shrine which contains the body of the past hero holds us in the past, but Jesus will not be embalmed in a pyramid on the Mountain of our religious enthusiasm."[54]

Finally, a "right-spirited" faith has a "So-Overcome-It" spirit. An old gospel song entitled "Farther Along" includes the lines "Tempted and tried, we're oft' made to wonder / Why it should be thus all the day long?" Of the 100 billion people who have ever lived on planet Earth, not one of them found a way through life around suffering or heartaches. Every disciple has times when faith becomes broken-backed and paralyzed.

Ross believed that one's spirit can burn the brighter for the dark that surrounds it. His 1987 Christmas Eve sermon illustrates this beautifully. He relates how one winter evening, when the innovative engineer R. Buckminster Fuller was drinking tea by the fire-

place of Professor Hugh Kenner, three-year-old Lisa Kenner pro-
longed her bedtime farewell with the question: "Why is the fire
hot, Bucky?" Kenner describes Buckminster Fuller's response:

He took her on his lap and explained. "You remember, dear, when the
tree was alive, and gathering in the sunlight?" Whenever Bucky talked of
a tree he turned into one. His face sought a phantom sun; his torso
swayed; his hands gathered in light.

"Then men cut the tree down, and sawed it into logs. Some of the logs
came here. And what you are seeing," he gestured toward the fireplace,
"is the sunlight, unwinding from the log."[55]

Ross most often referred to this realization that nothing is outside
God, everything is inside God, as the confidence of hope, as in this
example:

Among the hazards of the ordained ministry, I reckon that there are few
as perilous as the cocktail party. . . . Not very long ago in Cleveland I
went to one of these gatherings. Most of the guests were lively men and
women of the world from the civic, the industrial and the arts community. A rather grim-faced woman approached me as I was standing awk-
wardly balancing my ginger ale and a mysterious canape. I thought to
myself, "Here we go again!" She did, in fact, have a theological question,
which she intended to pose to me. "What is the most important element
in a sermon?" she demanded and ate her olive. It was clear to me that she
had an answer in mind, but I gave a little, pedantic answer of my own.
She listened with vague indifference. Fortunately, I had the presence of
mind to ask her, "Well, what do *you* think is the most important element in a sermon?" "Hope. Hope. Sermons should offer hope," she said
and wandered off. It was an illuminating moment for me, a moment in
which a perfect stranger said something so wonderfully and so powerfully true that it seemed to me that I was hearing it for the very first time.
My interrogator was not talking about cheap hope; she was not talking
about secular optimism or whistle-in-the-dark-positive-thinking. She
was talking about nothing less than a conviction deep in the mind and an
assurance steady in the heart that the outcome of our days will be God's
outcome. That is hope![56]

Ross's life displayed the confidence of hope that kept William
Kennedy "in there" as forty-nine publishers rejected his award-
winning book *Ironweed*; or that kept John Grisham "in there,"

submitting his debut thriller *A Time to Kill* to twenty-five publishers before publisher number 26 deemed it worthy of acceptance. (The movie rights sold in August of 1994 for 6 million dollars.) F. Scott Fitzgerald kept "in there" after the fiasco of *This Side of Paradise* (which Edmund Wilson claimed "has almost every fault and deficiency that a novel can possibly have"). Five years later, Fitzgerald went on to write the classic *The Great Gatsby.* It was Ross's confidence of hope in the strength of weakness that kept him "in there," sometimes on the ropes, sometimes on the run, even when he wanted more than anything to throw in the towel and lie down.

Ross loved to tell the story of a farmer's "Miracle Tree"—an old orange tree that had been badly damaged during a brush fire. Practically all the leaves were burned off and in many places the flames had seared through the bark. The wounded tree had not borne fruit in several years anyway, so the farmer decided to finish it off. He used a tractor with a large scoop to try to push the tree down. Again and again he banged the tree with the scoop, opening up deep gashes in the trunk. But the old orange tree would not budge. Finally, the farmer quit trying, went back to his regular farm chores, and eventually forgot all about the orange tree.

The following spring the farmer was amazed to discover that the tree he had given up on was producing some of the biggest, juiciest oranges he had ever seen, and for many succeeding years the miracle tree continued to bear rich fruit. The farmer explained it this way:

The scoop cut those gashes into the trunk, it forced the energizing sap to begin its natural journey out of the roots and up into the tree. And it just kept on going, right up through the entire tree, giving it new life. The "natural" processes I see and hear on my farm never cease to amaze me. Every day is a miracle, if you are open to what's going on around you. It's *amazing.* The orange tree's recovery seemed like a miracle. Actually what happened was part of a natural, ordinary process that had been retarded by the fire and then shocked back into action by my tractor scoop.[57]

This was the greatest legacy Ross could conceive of leaving his children, the legacy of strength in the broken places: "I sometimes hope that, when they are old and I am gone, my children may remember me kindly as one who liked to help them put the pieces together when it rained."[58]

A few months before his retirement, Ross directed some hard questions to the young people of his congregation: "There will be a Jerusalem in your life. There will be a Holy Week in your life before it is over. You can count on that. In all our lives there are crisis moments when we take personal responsibility or turn aside, when we care for the world or just for ourselves. Certainly there will come a moment when we must suffer because life is tragically imperfect at its best. And, of course, there will come a Friday—or someday—when we must die. Will it be with courage and confident faith, with Jesus, our friend, beside us? Or will it be with fear, self-pity and defeat? These are the issues of faith."[59] Such a Friday came for George Ross a short time later—with courage and confident faith, with Jesus, our friend, beside him.

He closed worship that morning with this prayer:

We come to you today, Lord, as the children came of old to acclaim you. As then, so now our earthly leaders falter, our people drift and die: but we do not ask for you to solve our problems or even that you take away the pain, which we must experience in this imperfect and uncertain life. But this we do pray for today: that you will enter our city and our hearts as One who heals, who loves, who summons us to the greatness that is ours as the children of God. In this most holy week for love that triumphs over loss, we bring our hearts before thy cross to finish thy salvation. Amen.

If our chief end in life, as the Scottish catechism suggests, is to "glorify God and enjoy God forever," George Ross ended his life in the awareness that to glorify is to enjoy, and to enjoy is to glorify.

SERMONS

𝔐𝔚𝔢

Gold in Current Monies

Give the King thy Justice, O God. . . . May he
be like rain that falls on the mown grass, like
showers that water the earth! In his days may
righteousness flourish, and peace abound, till
the moon shall be no more.

Text: Psalm 72:1,6–7

We don't know when those words were written, but we may assume that the time was like our own: a time of unrest and uncer-
tainty. Some people were discouraged for fear of the things that
were coming upon the earth. Other people kept the faith, held
their hope, and looked for better days. The times were like our
own; the people, like us. There were congregations of the discouraged. There were communities of the hopeful.

We have just sung a glorious hymn of the Eastern Liturgy, to a
tune written by William Jones in 1789. The words never fail to
move me. They sum up all we preach in Advent.

Sermon preached at St. Paul's Episcopal Church, Akron, Ohio, on the Second Sunday of Advent, 4 December 1977. George Ross Papers, The University of Akron
Archives.

The King shall come when morning dawns
And light triumphant breaks;
When beauty gilds the eastern hills
And life to joy awakes.

Not, as of old, a little child,
To bear, and fight, and die,
But crowned with glory like the sun
That lights the morning sky.

The King shall come when morning dawns
And earth's dark night is past;
O haste the rising of that morn,
The day that e're shall last;

And let the endless bliss begin,
By weary saints fore-told,
When right shall triumph over wrong,
And truth shall be extolled.

The King shall come when morning dawns
And light and beauty brings:
Hail, Christ the Lord! Thy people pray,
Come quickly, King of kings.[1]

I remember hearing that sung in Greek in the Orthodox Cathedral in Washington, an experience I shall never forget.

"Jesus, the very thought of thee with sweetness fills the breast!"[2] There is the heart of the matter! Christians, like everyone else, are subject to moments of depression. We do not see exactly where the world is going at any given moment, but we know that a "King is coming in glory" and that the future, whatever it is, *is his* future.

Everyone knows this quotation from one of John Donne's sermons: "No man is an island entire of itself. Each man's death diminishes me. Therefore, never send to know for whom the bell tolls; it tolls for thee," but not everyone has read the whole sermon. In it there is another sentence that speaks of our need today: "If a man carry *treasure* in *bullion,* or in a *wedge* of *gold,* and have none coined into current *Monies,* his *treasure* will not defray him as he travells."[3]

"His treasure will not defray him as he travels." That is the way it can be with us and our Creed. It is gold, a Wedge of purest gold, but if we have none of it coined into current monies, it will not defray us as we travel. So it is also with Christian hope. We must mint it in current coinage for our own troublous times.

I remember reading a story about Harry Hopkins's visit to England as World War II began. He arrived at a luncheon party in Scotland, if I remember correctly, and was asked if the United States would cooperate in defeating Mussolini and Hitler. His only reply was a quotation from the Book of Ruth: "Whither thou goest, I will go, and where thou lodgest, I will lodge: thy people shall be my people and thy God my God. Where thou diest, I will die, and there will I be buried: the LORD do so to me and more also, if ought but death part thee and me" [Ruth 1:16-17 KJV].

The joy and hope in the silence that followed were instantaneous and profound. A golden truth was given current coinage.

You may find this story strange, but it has about it a biblical fire that mints a coin for my own travel. I share it with you as an Advent Word about hope. It comes from a favorite book by Loren Eiseley entitled *Night Country*. In it Eiseley tells of being alone at night and inching down a cliff on a narrow ledge. He reached a point where, just a few feet below, there were two great watch dogs, barking and snarling viciously. He let go and this is what happened:

I said something in a voice I tried to keep confident and friendly. I held one arm over my throat and stood stock still. They came up to me warily, but one made a small woofing sound in his throat and I could see the motion of this tail in the dark. Seeing this, I dropped one hand on his head and the other on the other beast, whose jaws had closed with surprising gentleness about my ankle. I stood there for long minutes, talking and side thumping and trying all the dog language I knew. At the end of that time, my foot was reluctantly released and the great hounds, with the total irrationality that prevails over the sheer cliffs of Chaos, leaped and bounded about me, as though I were their returning master.

Each must find personal coinage for the wedge of gold. Something in me resonates, remembers, rises up in recollection of my own conversion, when one man writes of a night experience on this wise: "My foot was released and the great hounds, with the total irrationality that prevails over the sheer cliffs of chaos, leaped and bounded about me as though I were their returning master!"[4]

A great Advent hymn asks the oldest question of the human heart: "Watchman, tell us of the night, what its signs of promise are."[5] The Talmud tells the story of a traveler at night. Looking into the dark horizon, he saw a strange object, shaped like a monster it seemed, coming toward him through the gathering gloom. Summoning all his courage, he walked toward it and discovered that it was a man, which caused some, but not all, of his fear to vanish. Venturing closer still, he found that it was not only a human being like himself, but his own brother.

Jesus, our brother, is coming through our own dark moments! At the end we will meet him face to face and "not as a stranger." That is what the future holds: Whither we go, he will go. Where we lodge, he will lodge. Our people shall be his people. When we die, he will die with us, to lead us through to the other side. This is what the future holds! At the foot of whatever sheer cliff of chaos we creep down, God is there and he is friendly! We will not be destroyed. That is what the future holds! As we venture through the darkness, it may seem sometimes that monsters approach through gathering gloom, but no—the form is human! It is Jesus our dearest friend! That is what the future holds!

You must mint your own coins of hope from the gold of your faith for the needs of your life. Let me share with you a poem which I have read for fifteen years on the Second Sunday of Advent (not always in the pulpit, but always in my private devotions). It is coin of the realm for me. It is an invitation to Christmas. It is a little verse by Edwin Markham:

> Keep heart, O Comrade;
> God may be delayed by evil
> But He suffers no defeat.
> Even as a chance rock in an upland brook
> May change a river's course,

> But no rock, no, nor the baffling mountains of the world,
> Can hold it from its destiny, the sea,
> God is not foiled;
> The drift of the world will is stronger than all wrong;
> Earth and her years,
> Down joy's bright road or sorrow's longer path,
> Are moving toward the purpose of the skies.[6]

That is the Holy Fire of Advent, Advent—to mint coins of gold for daily living until he comes again!

> The king shall come when morning dawns
> And light triumphant breaks;
> Hail, Christ, the Lord! Thy people pray,
> Come quickly, King of kings. Amen.

What God Can Do, What We Must Do: The Feeding of the 5,000

Text: John 6:1–14

I have rather a bold plan for my sermon this morning. In the space of a few moments I propose to answer for you the only two questions which ought to be asked in the Christian church, or for that matter in all of human experience. The two questions are the following: What can *God* do, and what must *we* do? It would be folly for any preacher to claim personal wisdom sufficient to such a sermon; but mercifully, God gives us the answer to both of these questions in a story which even a little child can understand.

WHAT GOD CAN DO

One day our Lord preached to a large congregation. The service concluded. The organ played the postlude. The ushers opened the door. The acolytes put out the candles; and one of the assisting clergy said, "All right, folks, that is it; the service is over." But no one left; they all stayed where they were. They were waiting for something. I think that many a service of preaching ends this way. Something in the eyes tells you that something more is still needed. The Word without the Sacrament is not enough. Jesus understood this. Turning to his disciples, he said, "These people are hungry. Tell me; where may we buy bread that these may eat?" Five thousand people, thereupon, fell silent, strained forward and

Sermon preached at St. Paul's Episcopal Church, Akron, Ohio, on the Fourth Sunday in Lent, 17 March 1985. George Ross Papers, The University of Akron Archives.

waited for the church's answer. Reach deep within yourself and you can feel the discouragement which swept through all five thousand hearts when the church replied, "We have insufficient money to feed them. Two hundred denarii, which is all we have, is not enough." Reach into your memory and feel again what it is like to look for love and find it not, to ask for help and get it not, to pray to God and hear only your own words echoing back to you from the void. Even such a personal memory is insufficient to comprehend the social melancholy which overwhelmed the five thousand when the church turned its back and said, "We cannot help." In our day a hungering humanity is asking its technology, science, politics and industry, the university and the United Nations and every other institution, "Feed us, feed us! We are hungry; we are starving for a purpose big enough to nourish our souls and make us strong. We have heard all of your words and still we wait. We have watched all of your modern miracles, and here we linger. We are hungry deep within us. O, give us something to eat in this wilderness, for we stand here on the razor's edge between despair and riot." And back comes the answer from all these institutions: "We have not enough for such a magnitude of hunger that everyone might eat a little."

How far should a sermon go, I wonder, to stir the heart or stimulate the mind to an awareness that only God can fill the spiritual void of humankind? The church's dawning intuition is also its final wisdom: that our human resources are not and cannot be enough. The hunger of the multitudes in the wilderness is a hunger for reality, for eternity, for final assurance that life is going somewhere and that death is not the ultimate absurdity it appears to be.

What can God do? God can feed us. Through the valley *he* can lead us; to the still waters *he* can bring us. It is *his* table that he spreads, *his* chalice that runneth over. The whole Bible and the whole story of humankind is summarized in this little story and its radical meaning. Only God can feed us. The church was wise to confess that; for without its own humiliation first, the miracle cannot happen. Apply this to yourself today. I take it as indisputable that each one of us here is facing problems far greater than apparently available resources. Life twists itself into a tangle that we cannot untie. The hunger pains become intense when the normal protections of good health or job success or marriage happiness crumble and we find ourselves hungering in the wilderness. Then Christ comes to us and precisely then, when we are at the end of our resources and find them to be woefully inadequate, precisely then, Jesus comes to tell us what to do.

WHAT WE MUST DO

And that is the second question: What can we do, if anything? Jesus gives us three utterly simple instructions. This is what you can do when your problems are too big for your powers. First, sit down; second share what you are given; finally, gather up the fragments that nothing be lost.

The first instruction is simple: sit down. "Make the people sit down," said Christ. And so they made the people sit down, in number about five thousand, in groups of one hundred each. The first thing that we can and must do is reduce the big problem to a small one. Look at five thousand and you are paralyzed. Work with one hundred and you are energized. That is the simplest thing in the world, and Jesus knew it perfectly. Look out over the next three hundred and sixty-five days and you will be paralyzed. But live this day with God and you can do what you must do. "Sufficient for the day" is a precept that makes the five thousand sit down. Or ordain a man to the priesthood of the church and tell him that he must preach twenty-six hundred sermons in his pulpit and he will faint dead away. Ask him to preach one sermon about his life with Christ this Sunday, and he will be anxious, but not devastated. The enormous problem is too much for us; but reduce it to manageable size and we begin to function. If you called Thomas Edison into your candle factory and told him to illuminate the planet earth with electricity tomorrow, he would be prostrate; but give him a little room and a small glass bulb and some filaments to play with, and the man becomes a whirlwind of ima-

ginative and persevering activity. Sufficient for today's need is today's grace. Do not globalize your troubles. Take them one at a
time and let God help you with them, and you will be helped.

The second instruction is equally simple: share. We learn also
that God's grace comes to us when we gather in communities in
which people can talk to each other. Five thousand is too many.
Break that down, said Christ, into smaller groups where people
can visit with each other. This, surely, is the challenge of the
church today, when the anonymity and the loneliness of modern
life make our hunger for love driven and compulsive. Sit down
with a few people, says Christ. There may be someone here who
came to hear just this Word from God this morning. You may be a
person facing enormous difficulties and you wonder whether you
can manage them. The answer is very simply: No, you cannot.
No, you cannot; do not even try. But you can do something. You
can sit down with a few others and, together with them, receive
the grace and guidance which you need from God. Do not mill
about in the anonymous crowd complaining about your many
problems and your tremendous hunger. Sit down with a few people and open yourself with them to what God can do for you in
this hour of need. That advice is sound, not only for the crisis moments in life; it pertains to all of our experiences, both good and
bad alike. And so we are faithful to God and obedient to Christ
this morning as we gather to receive his bread in a community of
caring and loving persons—the church. Every church is the anonymous mob sitting down in a community of life to be fed by grace.
If you want to know why you ought to belong to a church, that is
why. Sit down and share. The miracles of grace come flooding in
and not only are we fed, we are abundantly fed.

The third instruction is also extremely simple: gather. Gather
up the fragments that nothing be lost. And so they gathered up
twelve baskets over and above the bread that was eaten. Everyone's life consists of fragments, fragments of grace. Listen to
Christ as if he were speaking directly to you: gather up your fragments that nothing be lost. God's grace must not be wasted. You
will need every fragment of God's grace by and by. I could preach a

sermon entitled "The Grace of Fragments and the Fragments of Grace." They are the same. The fragments that need to be gathered are the happy experiences of living—the laughter of a child, the kiss of a woman, the caress of a man, the blue light of dusk, the orange glow of dawn, the sound of girls' voices singing a festival in the church, a race won, an hour of strength, the empty tomb, Pentecost. Gather such fragments that nothing be lost. Your life consists of such fragments. Other fragments there are which also must be gathered in our little baskets—the broken home, the unhappy family, the starless night, the sound of silence, the race lost, the hour of weakness, the Gethsemane, the Golgotha. Fragments of grace, every single one of them. Gather them all up in your little basket that nothing be lost. Do not throw away anything in your experience. You will need all the fragments of your life when the jigsaw puzzle is fitted together one day.

Is this sermon too daring? Perhaps. But God's word to us in the Scripture is an audacious message, and it must be audaciously preached and heard. Human resources are *not* enough. Our powers are insufficient to our problems, but God can help us when we cannot help ourselves. That is the humility of faith which must be confessed before the miracle can happen. And yet Christianity is not passively standing about in tearful longing or mournful hunger. There is much that we can and must do. We can sit down with others to be fed, and so we do in this hour of grace. We can share with others the love of God, and so we do both now at the altar of Christ and as we go forth into the world in the power of the Spirit. We can gather up the fragments of life that nothing be lost and that is what we must do at home and at work and upon the road and in the hour of death.

What can *God* do? He can feed you. What must *we* do? Sit down; share, gather up; rise up and go our way into the world rejoicing. In a word: Eucharist. That happened once when the hungry met with Christ. And it can happen even now. Thank God!

꧁꧂

Pyramid or Pilgrimage
(On the Transfiguration)

And lo, they saw the Lord in raiment white
and glistening and with him stood Moses and
Elijah. Peter said, "Lord, here let us stay, and
I will build three tabernacles: one for you, one
for Moses and one for Elijah," not knowing
what he said for he was afraid. And a voice
from heaven said, "This is my Son; listen to
him." The cloud went away, and they went
down the mountain.

Text: Mark 9:3–7

This is the story the church always tells just before Lent. The Transfiguration story summarizes and concludes one half of the story of Jesus Christ and introduces us to the second half. Surely, it is clear in the New Testament that the Transfiguration moment was the turning point in the career of Christ. Until then our Lord had been climbing steadily upward, welcomed by the crowds, surrounded by their applause. Fevers left at his touch; demons fled at his command; storm-tossed seas were calmed by his voice; and men left all to follow him. Multitudes were fed; water turned to wine. In other words, *until* then he had been climbing upward,

Sermon preached at St. Paul's Episcopal Church, Akron, Ohio, on the Last Sunday of Epiphany, 17 February 1985. George Ross Papers, The University of Akron Archives.

and *from* then he was to journey down the mountain and to the cross. This crisis in his life is prosaically summarized in the words of Scripture: "Thereafter he set his face steadfastly toward Jerusalem" (cf. Luke 9:51). In liturgy, therefore, we turn today from Christmas and Epiphany to Lent, Holy Week and Good Friday; and this is the story we tell.

What interests us, or what ought to intrigue us, in this story, among other things, is how St. Peter, the average man, instinctively resisted going down the mountain with the Lord. "*Here* let us *stay*," he pleaded. "Here, let us build tabernacles and stay." I wouldn't speak for you; but, for me, I know exactly why Peter said this. "Old roads never seem as dusty as after some great stirring of the heart" (Morrison). When you have a truly wonderful moment, what is more natural than to wish to hold onto it?

I. HOLDING ONTO THE HIGH

Let this be our first observation: Not only Simon Peter but all of us hope to hold onto the high. Life is, for most of us, a fabric of difficulty interwoven with patterns of transient happiness. Up on the mountain, in the white and glistening moment of eternity, there was for Simon Peter, at last, some kind of peace. Down in the valley there is conflict. People do not understand us down there. Love is tough down there; but here, lifted up above it all, it is quite wonderful. That, I take it, is the siren call of alcohol for some of us, of compulsive sexuality for others, of emotional withdrawal and control for countless more. Only the willfully ignorant or the spiritually barren can fail to appreciate exactly how Simon Peter felt as he tried to hold onto the high. What husband, in the raptures of his honeymoon, has not whispered to his wife, "Darling, I wish, oh how I wish, this could go on forever!" What mother, holding her baby and knowing full well that life must unfold with all its uncertain destiny of sickness, sorrow and separation, does not hold her little one, nevertheless, a little closer to her breast and pray, "Oh God, let this last! Like this: perpetual madonna and everlasting child!" Who has not lingered on some mountain top, reluctant to turn back again to crowded streets and quarreling families and difficult work and painful life? Given the frailty of things and the transitoriness of time, who can fail to feel what Peter felt when, groping for words, he stammered his plaintive, yet passionate prayer and turned to Christ and said, "Please, Lord, here let us stay!"

> A thousand ages in thy sight are like an evening gone;
> Short as the watch that ends the night before the rising sun.
> Time, like an ever-rolling stream, bears all our years away;
> They fly, forgotten, as a dream dies at the opening day.[7]

If you don't feel the existential shudder in that, you are not paying attention to your own life. "Please let us stay here, O King, in your beauty. Oh God of the mountain top, let me stay here, a holy refugee from history." We all have prayed this.

II. STOPPING THE CLOCK

If the folly and the frenzy of youth is the frantic effort to hold on to the high, no doubt the besetting frailty of age is the vain endeavor to stop the clock; or, if we are middle-aged, to turn it back. "Here let us stay," say the young. "Let us build tabernacles," say the old. "Let us control and hold tight," say the middle-aged. I never walk through the Egyptian galleries of a museum that I do not feel in my heart the melancholy which can nearly overwhelm those of us who, through many follies and failures, have come to understand that the pyramid approach to life is doomed to disaster. Every pyramid was someone's prayerful effort to stop the clock; so, in a sense, is every photograph we paste into the family album. So is every shrine in which we reverently inter the mummified remains of yesterday's saint, calling it a church. Peter said, "Let us build shrines, tabernacles, for the eternal on the everlasting mountain top. Let's box up this precious thing called 'life' and hope that somehow the rude assaults of time, the crucifix of this world's sin, will never, never touch this beauty," completely forgetting that it was the pyramid builders whose compulsion to stop the clock enslaved the pilgrim people of God.

The perpetuation of the ecstatic moment, holding onto the high, and the anxiety which compels us to try and stop the clock account for a great deal of contemporary religion. Bishop Kenneth Kirk once wrote of mountain top religion these words, which I believe have special relevance to us when the lure of religious ecstacy and sectarian certainty attracts our compulsion-driven souls:

The systematic quest of ecstacy, or any other form of "experience," merely for the gratification which will be received therefrom is [essentially] irreligious. Such a quest . . . turns the seeker's mind back upon himself and his own states of consciousness, and so induces once again just that self-centredness which it is the whole purpose of [true] religion to annihilate.[8]

Holding onto the high is more a function of anxiety than of faith. Building tabernacles around an inerrant Bible or an infallible pope or a charismatic experience, the enshrining instinct turns gracious ministries into hardened institutions and the living Word into an aggressive agency of vicious egoism. No wonder robust secular men and women in this age, observing Peter or his latter-day successors hunkering down in their expensive tabernacles, want nothing to do with such a pathological response to life.

III. LISTENING TO THE LORD

Let us now turn from St. Peter to attend to the Voice from the cloud. Peter (which is to say all of us) wants to hold onto the high, to stop the clock, to preserve the precious moment on the mountain, but from the cloud there comes an alternative proposal. The Voice says, "This is my Son. Listen to him." Now, if we listen to him and attend carefully to what he says and what he does, will we not soon see that every place he touches is a transfigured place? Karl Barth's words rob every pyramid of its fatal fascination: "The mystery reveals to us that for God it is just as natural to be lowly as it is to be high, to be near as it is to be far, to be little as it is to be great, to be abroad as it is to be at home."[9] God is not, in other words, found on mountain tops any more than in valleys, in churches any more than in factories, in so-called religious moments any more than in so-called mundane moments. He is equidistant from every moment; and therefore we can let go of what we have already mastered to receive what he wants to give us next, where he wants to give it next. Not a costly pyramid but a courageous pilgrimage is the plan of God for you and for me; and to yield to that plan with trust is faith. St. Paul became so excited by this new way of seeing things and this new way of living life that his words tumbled over themselves in joy when he wrote: "We all, with unveiled face, beholding the glory of the Lord, are being changed into his likeness from one degree of glory to another; for this comes from the Lord who is the Spirit" (2 Corinthians 3:18 RSV).

Think of all that St. Peter would have missed if God had granted his prayer to stay there! He would never have seen the healing of the man at the foot of the mountain, never watched Zacchaeus come down from the tree in Jericho, never heard the children cry hosanna on Palm Sunday, never witnessed the cleansing of the Temple, never felt the hands of Jesus bathing his tired feet, never taken the cup of trembling in his hands, never held the broken bread, never slept through Gethsemane nor flinched in the High Priest's courtyard, nor heard the cock crow twice, and, in spite of all that, never seen the risen Lord, never felt the flame and wind of Pentecost, never preached a single sermon, never healed a single sick person, never met St. Paul, never dreamed of God's great grace for all, never gone to Rome—never, in summary, been remembered for anything except that he was pathetically one among the many who having had a high tried to hold onto it and to stop the clock.

Don't you see that there are two ways of living your life? Imagine a great river flowing by and you in the middle of it. Out there in the middle of this river, one of two choices must be made. Do we decide to face downstream in this river, so that our present tense is flowing from behind us, with all the drift, debris and garbage of our past floating by and our life floating downstream with it? This is one way. Or do we, one day, decide to face upstream so that now our now is coming to meet us? If the present is coming toward me out of the future, then I must struggle forward over the contradiction between what is and what can be. That will be my spirituality. But, if the present is something given entirely by the past, then I am condemned by the contradiction between what is and what might have been or what used to be and I see only an everlasting stream bearing all its sons, including me, away; and I am filled with dreadful fear. The present, as Christians experience it, is not arriving from our past but from God's future. This is what our Lord meant when he preached about the great and coming day and the coming Kingdom of God. Once you begin to think of your life now as flowing in from Christ's future, not just out of your past, wonderful insights can animate your life. You begin to see, in the transfiguration moment of that reversal, that faith and forgiveness, hope and love and prayer open you to the future just as surely as guilt and anger and resentment, pride, self-pity, and fear drain you to the past. Everything depends on which way you decide to face as you stand in the river of life.

"Listen to him!" Jesus came down from heaven into the life of the world, and so the church must go down from the Transfiguration experiences of prayer and communion into the life of ministry and mission. As Bonhoeffer says somewhere, "We shall never know what we do not do." Life is not something you can hold on to; it is something that grows in you as you give it away. Life is not something you can preserve in a tabernacle or embalm in a pyramid; it is something you discover on a pilgrimage. God is not something you enshrine in charismatic ecstacy or in inerrant books or in infallible ideas. He is Someone you meet on a cross of compassionate love where cross the crowded ways of life. Peter is the symbol of the church, not because he got all this right from the beginning, but because, in spite of his many failures, mistakes and fears, he stayed with Jesus and dared to listen to him. May that be said, or something like that be said, of us when someday we wade all the way upstream to find the mountain source from which the waters of life flow toward us from eternity.

LET US PRAY:

Lord, the night is dark, the day is fleeting and our brief moments of beauty and love and joy are tremendously important to us. Help us not to cling to them too tightly. Help us never to stop growing. Protect us from our own compulsive need to preserve the holy times of life and give us courage to find life's challenges and difficulties a means of grace. We want to listen to you, Lord, and we ask that you accept and reckon this desire to know you as faith. Lord, help us to let go of self that we may go with you down any mountain, through any valley, till we come at last through life to Life. *Amen.*

Let Your Light Shine

Jesus said: "You are the light of the world. Let your light shine."

Text: Matthew 5:13–20

I was a sophomore in college. The year was 1953, and I was a delegate to the National Student Christian Federation Conference, held that year in Athens, Ohio. The speaker was a little known minister from Alabama. It is safe to say that none of us at that conference could have imagined at that time that one day he would change the course of American history. I regret that I do not remember more of what he said, but I do remember one thing. Martin Luther King, Jr., said: "Young ladies and gentlemen, the Lord does not ask you to solve the great problems of the world. He does not ask you to unravel the enigmatic mysteries of life." Then I remember how he paused and gathered that passion which would one day propel him to the forefront of the world's life. He said: "Brothers and sisters, this is all you have to do. You have to let *your* light shine. Don't be a part of the darkness. Let your light *shine*."

Not much later I found myself working as a summer counselor in Akron, at a Rotary Club camp for crippled children. (That was my first introduction to Akron, and I did not return until twenty years later when I came to this parish.) One night as we sat around

Sermon preached at St. Paul's Episcopal Church, Akron, Ohio, on the Fifth Sunday after Epiphany, 8 February 1987. George Ross Papers, The University of Akron Archives.

234

a campfire, the YMCA leader handed out candles; and as we sang a certain song, we lighted the candles, one by one, until for a moment the darkness was somewhat diminished. I remember the words of the song. If you have ever gone to summer camp, you've sung it too: "This little light of mine, / I'm gonna let it shine. / This little light of mine, / I'm gonna let it shine." So we sang, five college students and twenty-two children in wheelchairs; and an idea imprinted itself in my mind: namely, that to light a candle and not to curse the darkness is the way of courage and the walk of grace. "This little light of mine, I'm gonna let it shine!" Thirty-five years, several universities and a small library of books later, I find it impossible to improve upon those words as a summary of all that Jesus said in the Sermon on the Mount.

In the prologue of the fourth Gospel, St. John wrote: "He is the true light which is in everyone who comes into the world. This light shines in the darkness, and the darkness will never put it out" (cf. John 1:4–5). Jesus Christ, I believe, is the light of the world. That is half the message; and the other half is this: that light which is in Jesus Christ is a light which is also in all of us. He said, "Let it shine."

Do you remember how, in the old mythology, Prometheus climbs Mt. Olympus, steals fire from the gods, returns to earth and gives it to humanity, and, as a result, is punished by the gods through all eternity? It is sad, but true to say, that many people think that that is the way it still is. They think that they must climb a mountain. They suppose that they must sneak up on the fire of life and steal it from a reluctant custodian. The result is that they are condemned to long seasons of unhappiness, not because they fail, but precisely because they may succeed in their Promethean endeavor. The old myth is right, at least about this one thing: namely, that if we organize our lives around what we lack, we will be miserable. Simone Weil said it well when she wrote that every sin is merely the endeavor to fill a void. May God give us wisdom when we confess our sins to grasp the melancholy truth of that!

Jesus breathed his spirit into the disciples. He said, "My spirit is in you now. Let it flow." He said, "The light of God is in you now. You lack nothing. Let it glow! You have within you the light of God. Let it shine!" Here, we are very close to the central truth of our religion. The joy of the Christian faith arises from a spiritual awakening, an awakening to the awareness that there is a life in you, a gift from God in you that is yours by right and by creation. You did not earn it. You certainly do not need to steal it. God put an inner light in every human life, and the task now is not to achieve something that we lack or to fill a void that we have come to despise. "The only task in life," said Jesus Christ, "is to let your God-given inner light out into the world."

Many people miss the point of the Christian faith altogether by making it either too hard to grasp or too hard to do. A woman once confessed to Will Rogers, "My sin is pride. Every day I get up and look in the mirror and say, 'You are the most beautiful woman in the world.'" Will Rogers cleared his throat and said, "Oh, Lady, that ain't pride; that's jest ignorance!" Many people miss the point of the Christian faith, not because of pride, but because of ignorance about what Jesus actually said. What did he say? He said that all God wants from you is your consent, your permission, to let your own light shine. "Your life can be wonderful if you will let your light shine," he said. "I have given you permission; I have given you consent; I've given you the authority and I give you the enabling power. Let it shine!"

Mark Twain, by all accounts, was not a very devout Christian. He presented an habitually cynical face to the world, but I think we may touch upon a deeper feeling in a little known book of his entitled *The Diaries of Adam, Eve and Satan*, a book which he wrote just after his wife's death. In it Adam cynically questioned God's ways. When he ate the apple, he said that it was not because he was disobedient, but simply because he was hungry. He fussed with Eve because she talked too much and thanked God when the snake came along, so that she could talk to it and leave him alone. Typical Mark Twain, you say. And then one day Eve died and the diary ended; but we are allowed to hear the last words of Adam, spoken at Eve's grave. Overcome with grief, he said, "Where she was, there was Eden."[10] It is an old, old story, is it not? Maybe the first one we ever told. A woman's love had shined upon a man; and that, he thought, was the whole story of his life. There had been a lot of trouble in their lives together. They had lost a lot of things. They had lost their innocence. They had lost their home. They had lost a child. Finally, one of them had been lost; but the light of their love shined on, even at the grave. That is what Jesus is talking about. He is asking us to let the light shine, to permit our love to get out. Let your love out. Let it shine.

You can give your own illustrations for this sermon. I found one the other day in the biography of Bonnee Hoy, the gifted North Carolina composer who died recently in the prime of life. At her memorial service a friend said that Bonnee Hoy had a kind of radiance about her. He remembered how a mockingbird used to sing under Bonnee's window on summer nights. She would stand at her bedroom window peering into the darkness, listening, marveling at the songs the mockingbird sang. Then one night, musician that she was, she decided to sing back; so she whistled the first four notes of Beethoven's *Fifth Symphony*. Lo and behold, the bird learned the song and sang it back to her in perfect pitch. Then the bird went away for a while. Toward the end of her life, when she was terribly sick, the bird returned and sat on a tree outside Bonnee's window. Several times, amongst its other songs, it sang the first four notes of Beethoven's *Fifth Symphony*. Her friend, with tears in his eyes, concluded the eulogy with these worlds: "It's awfully good to know, it's really good for me to know, that out there in the world somewhere there is a mockingbird who sings Beethoven because of Bonnee."[11] When the shadows gather and the night falls on you, wouldn't it be grand, wouldn't it be rather grand, if you could go down to your grave and up to God with joy because someone wanted to say something like that about you?

Let your light so shine that the Father may be glorified by those who counted it a privilege to have known you. Upon the mountain, Jesus affectionately looked upon his disciples, and, with the radiance of divine love sparkling in his eyes, he said to them: "You are the light of the world. Let it shine!"

LET US PRAY:

Heavenly Father, at the dawn of time this was your command: "Let there be light!" And behold there was light and all things began and it was very good. In your Son Jesus Christ you spoke again into the darkness. Once again you commanded: "Let there be light!" And there was light and all things began anew and it was very good. You have said through your Son to each of us: "Let there be light! May your love for us so open our eyes that we may at last see one another only in the radiant light of his grace; through the same, Jesus Christ, our Lord. *Amen.*

"I Thank God on Every
Remembrance of You"

As you may imagine, I have chosen my text for this final sermon to you as your Rector with care. From the Letter of St. Paul to the Philippians, chapter one, verses two through twelve:

Grace to you and peace from God our Father and the Lord Jesus Christ. I thank my God upon every remembrance of you, always in every prayer of mine for you all making my prayer with joy, thankful for your partnership in the Gospel from the [very] first day until now. And I am sure that he who began a good work in you will bring it to completion at the day of Jesus Christ. It is right for me to feel thus about you all, because I hold you [with love] in my heart. . . . It is my prayer that your love may abound more and more, with knowledge and all discernment, so that you may approve what is excellent and may be pure and blameless for the day of Christ, filled with the fruits of righteousness which come through Jesus Christ to the glory and love of God.

As it has so often been, that is my twofold theme today: thankful remembrance and confident expectancy.

I. THANKFUL REMEMBRANCE

"I thank my God on every remembrance of you. . . ." As I look back over our eighteen years together, my heart is filled with gratitude upon every remembrance of you. I think gratefully of our splendid staff and our partnership in the Gospel; and of the five young men who were ordained to the priesthood during my tenure

Sermon preached at St. Paul's Episcopal Church, Akron, Ohio, on the Fifteenth Sunday after Pentecost, 16 September 1990. George Ross Papers, The University of Akron Archives.

as your Rector; of the literally hundreds I have baptized and married and presented for confirmation. In the last several weeks I have, of course, received a number of letters. I thank you for them all, and I cherish them all. But one is especially dear to me. In her letter, this friend speaks of the funerals of her grandson and of her mother and of some other troubled times that we have lived through together in her life; and then she reminded me of the time when I baptized six of her grandchildren in the chapel. And she goes on to speak of our partnership in ministry, especially among the poor and the disenfranchised and the suffering of our community. I read this letter, I think, not less than six times. Such is the warp and woof of the seamless fabric of a pastor and his parish, and I am grateful for it beyond words to express.

What a flood of memories rush in on me this morning. I think of so many of you with whom I have shared happy moments of ministry to the children of St. Paul's Church. As I saw the teachers climbing the stairs this morning, my mind raced back through all these years. Hundreds of teachers returned to me through the haze of memory. What happy, happy times we have had—some of them quite hilarious. I remember, for example, the morning when I was called upon to speak at the Sunday school chapel service because the person in charge had the flu. The topic that morning was the Holy Ghost. I tried to explain to the boys and girls that the Holy Ghost is God inside us. I told one little boy by the name of David to put his hand inside his shirt, which he obediently did. Reminding him that God was inside, I asked, "Now, David, what does God feel like?" He furrowed his forehead in thought and then answered soberly, "Damp. It feels damp." Well, the chapel service ended abruptly—with gales of holy laughter.

And I remember, also, the tears, the many tears throughout the years. I think of all the dear friends who meant so much to me, but who have passed over to the other side and who dwell now upon another shore and in a kindlier light. I am so grateful, for example, for my remembrance of dear Ralph who struggled through a long and painful illness. I think of the final prayers which we offered together toward the end. I said, "Ralph, may God bless you forever" and in his weak but still resonant voice, Ralph answered,

"And may God have mercy also on you, dear George." I multiply moments of mutual blessings like that with grateful remembrance.

I thank God for the magnificent ministry of music in this congregation; for the inspiration of our liturgy; and especially for the great privilege which has been mine to preach the Gospel of Jesus Christ, his death for our redemption, his resurrection for our justification, and his never-failing strength and love wherever two or three gather together in his name. I thank God for every remembrance of those who in the Spirit of Jesus have caught a vision of the ministry of this parish church to the poor and needy and the frail, the imprisoned and the sick of this community. I thank God for every remembrance of those who have given selflessly of themselves, their treasure, their talent and their time and their unfailing good will to build up the congregation of St. Paul's Church. I thank God for each of you, who in your prayers and patience, in your love and faith, have embraced me and my family through all these eighteen years together. Both this morning and through all that lies ahead, we thank God upon every remembrance of you.

II. CONFIDENT EXPECTANCY

This is a day for looking back in grateful remembrance; but it is also, and perhaps even more importantly, a day for us to look forward with confident expectancy. This morning we turn a new page in the history of St. Paul's Church. Let us do so with confident expectancy for his grace in times to come. As it has always been, the future is both bright with promise and dark with foreboding. The future is bright with promise if we keep the faith and are kindly affectioned, one for another and remain loyal to Jesus Christ and to the everlasting Gospel of God's grace. But the future is dark with foreboding if, in willful self-centeredness or ungodly self-assertion, we forget the high calling angels cannot claim, if we forget our membership in charity, one with another, in the Body of Christ.

Forgetting what lies behind, let us press on confidently, expectantly, to claim the goal of maturity in Christ Jesus, our Lord. This morning as we let go of the past with gratitude, let us lay hold of the future with enthusiasm. We pray for the right choice of the next rector; and, even now, let us, before a choice is made, pledge to him or to her our loyalty and our undivided support. Of all the light bulb jokes, the one I like best is this one: How many Episcopalians does it take to change a light bulb? Answer: Four, one to change the light bulb, and three to discuss how wonderful the old light bulbs were under the previous rectors! Let there be none of that! Keep the Vestry in your prayers as they seek God's guidance in selecting a new rector; and when he or she comes, let us embrace him or her with our love and our support, even as you have so embraced me from the first day until now.

III. WHETHER TOGETHER OR ALONE, WE ARE TOGETHER

We come now to a fork in the road. I take the path that will lead me to a new ministry in the church. You take your path, together, into the future of St. Paul's Church. Often I turn to the writings of Robert Frost for inspiration. Yesterday I thumbed through the well-worn pages and found something which speaks to me of one of God's greatest blessings in life—of the discovery of dear friends and soul mates who share with us along the way their love and their vision of the fair beauty of life. This is the way Robert Frost speaks of the inestimable benediction:

> I went to turn the grass once after one
> Who mowed it in the dew before the sun.
>
> The dew was gone that made his blade so keen
> Before I came to view the levelled scene.
>
> . . . .
>
> But he had gone his way, the grass all mown,
> And I must be, as he had been—alone,
>
> "As all must be," I said within my heart,
> "Whether they work together or apart."
>
> But as I said it, swift there passed me by
> On noiseless wing a bewildered butterfly,

Seeking with memories grown dim o'er night
Some resting flower of yesterday's delight.
. . . .

And then he flew as far as eye could see,
And then on tremulous wing came back to me.

I thought of questions that have no reply,
And would have turned to toss the grass to dry;

But he turned first, and led my eye to look
At a tall tuft of flowers beside a brook,

A leaping tongue of bloom the scythe had spared
. . . .

The mower in the dew had loved them thus,
Leaving them to flourish, not for us,

Nor yet to draw one thought of ours to him,
But from sheer morning gladness at the brim.

The butterfly and I had lit upon,
Nevertheless, a message from the dawn,

That made me . . . .
. . . feel a spirit kindred to my own;
So that henceforth I worked no more alone;

But glad with him, I worked as with his aid,
And weary, sought at noon with him the shade;

And dreaming, as it were, held brotherly speech
With one whose thought I had not hoped to reach.

"[We] work together." I told him from the heart,
"Whether [we] work together or apart."[12]

As we part our way today as Rector and parish, let us thank God that we are forever together in Christ, that we work together whether we work together or apart. Truly, that is a message from the dawn and morning gladness at the brim.

I want to make some words of the Apostle Paul's my final words to you. They exactly express the feelings in my heart this morning. From the second chapter of the First Letter to the Thessalonians:

Just as we were entrusted by God with the Gospel, so we have spoken, not to please men, but to please God who tests the heart. For we never used words of flattery with you, as you know, . . . nor did we seek glory from any person, whether from you or from anyone else, . . . but we were gentle among you. . . . So, being filled with affection for you, we were ready to share with you, not only the Gospel of God but also our own selves, because you had become so very, very dear to us. (cf. 1 Thessalonians 2:4-8)

You are very, very dear to me, my precious friends. Wherever we may go, we are one in the Spirit; and from this day henceforth, whether we work together or alone, we work together in Christ. "I thank God upon every remembrance of you always in every prayer for you—thankful for your friendship and for our partnership in the gospel from the first day until now."

LET US PRAY:

Most merciful Father who hast called us to thy service in the fellowship of the Gospel, we beseech thee to bless and to prosper thy work in this parish church. Unite us, one with another in love; teach us to worship thee in spirit and in truth. Be pleased to use our endeavors to extend thy Kingdom in the hearts and homes of all our people. Thou knowest the needs of thy church in every place. Look graciously at this time upon the people of this parish and give to them a faithful pastor who may serve before thee in all diligence and lowliness of heart; and by thy blessing bring many souls to the joys of thy Kingdom; through Jesus Christ, our Lord. *Amen.*

CONCLUSION

Broken Things

[God] giveth more grace when the burdens grow greater,

He sendeth more strength when the labors increase,

To added affliction He addeth His mercy,

To multiplied trials His multiplied peace.

His love has no limit, His grace has no measure,

His power has no boundary known unto men;

For out of His infinite riches in Jesus,

[God] giveth, and giveth and giveth again!

—*Annie Johnson Flint*[1]

THORNTON WILDER'S three-minute drama, "The Angel that Troubled the Waters," is based on the story in the Gospel of John of the pool of Bethesda (John 5). The chief character is a doctor, sick with a wound that will not heal. He waits with others at the pool for the moving of the waters and the healing that comes with dipping in the pool.

An angel suddenly cries out: "Draw back, physician . . . healing is not for you. Without your wound, where would your power be? It is your very remorse that makes your low voice tremble into the hearts of men. The very angels themselves cannot persuade the wretched and blundering children on earth as can one human being broken on the wheels of living. In love's service, only the wounded can serve."

As the doctor turns away in disappointment, a patient comes running to him, pleading with him to help and heal his sick son and daughter.[2] Only you who are wounded can heal.

In the French language, *blesser* means "to wound." That is precisely the double meaning of Jacob's words to the angel he wrestled all night: "I will not let you go unless you bless me" (Genesis 32:26). As we have seen throughout this book, woundedness and blessedness go together in mysterious and strange ways beyond human comprehension. Could that be why "helping professions" like ministry, psychotherapy, and social work seem to attract more than their share of the physically, emotionally, and spiritually deformed, a phenomenon Henri Nouwen calls "wounded healers"?[3] Indeed, being wounded is being blessed from a biblical perspective in which God strengthens weaknesses.

In the words of Hebrews 13:3—"Visit those in prison as if in prison with them. Care for the sick because you are still in the body." Ministry is not a matter of the well helping the sick, but the sick helping the sick. We are all on the same road: growth toward wholeness and wellness. We are not whole yet. In the words of the Reformer Martin Luther, whom Ross loved to quote:

This life is not righteous, but growth in righteousness; is not health, but healing; not being, but becoming; not rest, but exercise; we are not yet what we shall be, but we are growing toward it; the process is not yet finished, but it is going on; this is not the end, but it is the road; all does not yet gleam in glory, but all is being purified.[4]

"I am like a broken vessel," the Psalmist confesses (Psalm 31). A handful of common clay come to consciousness, that is what we are.

I. BROKEN VESSELS

In a multitude of ways and through a mosaic of voices throughout this book, the choice of every human being is twofold. We can either tumble into and fall through the cracks of our lives, or we can shine through life's cracks. Indeed, one might say of George Ross's ministry what Dame Edith Sitwell reportedly said of William Blake: that he was cracked, but that's where the light shined through.

For Ross, the tidal pull of the eucharistic vocabulary of brokenness structured the Lord's Supper's double furniture of altar and table. In the sacred circle of sacrifice and communion, offering and reception, it is the body *broken* that makes us strong; it is the blood *poured out* that replenishes us. The most dramatic moment in the Eucharist is not the eating and drinking, but the breaking and pouring: This is the way life is . . . broken. This is the way life is . . . poured out. British sociologist David Martin has joined forces with British theologian P.T. Forsythe on this point: "The act of breakage is the point of communion. The fracture of the body is the healing of the body, and the body of Christ is brought together by being torn apart. Life is poured out and therefore remains unexhausted and inexhaustible."[5]

Ross's best friend in the early years of his life and ministry was theologian and priest Joseph Goetz. Goetz has written that each of these human gestures—"pouring out, handing over, breaking, sharing"—finds its ritual form and fulfillment in small objects that contain infinite possibilities: "the blood of a lamb and its roasted flesh, a jug of cleansing water, a loaf of bread, a cup of wine."

Take, for example, the gesture of pouring. The most profound thing any of us can say about God in his relation to us is that he has poured existence into his world, into us—those in whom he is imaged. As water is poured from a jug on dusty feet, so has he poured out his own being upon us, bits of clay and sinew. He has also handed himself over, as food is handed round. He has broken open the gift of life even as bread is broken for the sharing. He has given us to drink deep of his Spirit in the same way one drains a cup of wine for refreshment.[6]

Only a broken Christ can heal a broken world. An uncrucified Christ, a Christ who did not give his own life, an abstract Christ, is impotent to build a new creature or a new creation. Only a poured-out Christ, the Crucified One, can fill the emptiness within and without. The curse of the cross became the blessing of salvation for the world. An eighteenth-century physician and theologian named Sir Thomas Browne put the mystery of Good Friday like this: "Ice splits starwise."[7] He noted how a single tap of an ice pick at the right point on the block of ice will send fissures shooting out in all directions, and the solid block of ice will split in two at the star. The promise of the cross is that life can split starwise.

That is why the wounds of brokenness, which Jesus took with him into eternity, stayed with Ross as a talismanic medal of faithfulness and honor all his life. In a story circulated from Alan Paton's writings, a character speaking of heaven allegedly says, "When I go up there, which is my intention, the Big Judge will say to me, 'Where are your wounds?' And if I say, 'I haven't any,' he will say, 'Was there nothing to fight for?' I couldn't face that question."[8]

As much as Ross loved that story, he insisted that for wounds to become badges of truth and healing, the pride of self-ownership must be broken first. We are not our own. We are bought with a price. By *his* stripes we are healed. We cannot ourselves transform our curses into blessings. For Ross, the resurrection was not something that took place two thousand years ago, or will take place two thousand years hence. The resurrection is an event that is still happening today. Don't look back at resurrection. Don't look forward to resurrection. Look around. Carl Jung loved to quote a long poem in which the seventeenth-century mystical poet Angelus Silesius makes this precise point:

> God make me pregnant, and his Spirit shadow me,
> That God may rise up in my soul and shatter me.
> What good does Gabriel's, "Ave, Mary" do
> Unless he give me that same greeting too?[9]

II. EARTHEN VESSELS

We end where we began in this theological reverie on the life of George Ross: We all hold these truths in earthen vessels. We are all broken vessels. We are all chips off the original block. Three pottery stories, one from the British Isles, another from the American Southwest, the last from the Asian East, illuminate these words from the Apostle Paul to the church at Corinth: "We hold these truths in earthen vessels. . . . We are afflicted in every way, but not crushed; perplexed but not driven to despair; persecuted, but not forsaken; struck down, but not destroyed" (2 Corinthians 4:7–9).

Ross told the first pottery story after he returned from a four-week trip with his daughters and some members of his congregation to the great cathedrals of Italy, France, and England.

I asked one of our traveling companions to identify the church which moved her most deeply. She answered without hesitation, "The first church we saw: Winchester Cathedral." I asked, "Why *that* church? Of all the churches we have seen, why did that church touch you?" And again without hesitation, she said, "The window. The marvelous window." And then I understood.

The window she remembers *is*, indeed, extraordinary. It consists of medieval glass of high quality and great beauty; but that is not what one notices. . . . The window at Winchester tells no Biblical story; it refracts no mystical light, but rather radiates a kaleidoscope of brilliant colors.

The Winchester window was not always as we see it now. One day in the 17th century armed troops, soldiers of Cromwell's army, with sticks and iron bars destroyed the ancient windows of Winchester Cathedral along with all the medieval statuary. Outside the cathedral on that dark day, the lawn was strewn with tiny fragments of glass, irrevocably shattered. As the soldiers left, the people came out to look at the ruins. A man stepped forward and began to collect the shattered fragments. Soon the whole community joined him until many bushels were collected and hidden away until the troubled season passed. When the glass was later unearthed, it was evident that a reconstruction of the original work would be impossible. But a cathedral glass worker said, "Let me have the pieces and I'll see what I can do." So step by step, inch by inch, high on a scaffold above the cathedral nave, the workman put the little pieces into an intricate abstraction. Nothing like it has ever been seen before in Europe. Some of the more traditional laity and clergy, no doubt, shook their heads and grumbled at the novelty. Finally, however, the great window was finished; all the motley little pieces were fitted together in an array of jewels. Those who visit that cathedral today stand in a light that ra-diates through broken glass, and some thank God that, with the shat-tered, broken fragments of life, Christian people can create inexpressible beauty.[10]

The second story comes from the pueblos of the Southwest, where the Navahos and the Hopis throw sturdy pottery with wide mouths and thick sides. It is not made for luxury, but to fulfill the everyday tasks that are necessary for survival. After they have fin-ished a piece, they let it harden in the sun, but the sun-hardened pottery is still fragile. To achieve a durability that will match its utilitarian purpose, the pottery is fired. But since the pueblos have no kilns, the potters go about the firing in an unorthodox way.

To begin, they stack firewood on the ground in the shape of a large square. They cover the wood with a metal grate and careful-ly place the hardened pottery on the grate. Then they take dung that has been collected from the pueblo's animals and pack it care-fully around and between the pots. As the pots are covered, inside and out, a mountain of dung is created around the whole batch. The outside of this dung heap is then covered with scrap metal that has been collected. Old hub caps go on. TV dinner trays. Any-thing that will reflect the heat of the fire that is about to begin. A match is then set to the wood at the bottom and the whole mound is allowed to burn down an entire day. In the end, there is only a low stack of ashes, scattered with blackened scrap metal.

The potters pick through the ashes. One by one, they find their pieces. But the pots are no longer fragile. They have achieved a rock-hard consistency that protects them from chips and break-age. In the process of the firing, the pots also receive a new beauty that reflects the elements that were used to make them.

The third story comes from a Chinese village, known for sever-al centuries, down through many dynasties, for its exquisite and fragile porcelain. Especially striking were its urns. High as tables, wide as chairs, they were admired around the globe for their strong form and delicate beauty. Legend has it that when each urn was finished, there was one final step: a shattering moment. The artist *broke* it—and then put it back together with gold filigree.

An ordinary urn was thus transformed into a priceless work of art. What seemed finished wasn't . . . until it was broken.

At every Eucharist George Ross asked, in one way or another: Is your heart breaking? Then let it break here. Is your body broken? Then bring its broken parts here. Does your mind sometimes break down in hidden anguish so deep you didn't even know it was there? Then bring its broken fragments here. Then and only then can we say with Julian of Norwich, "All our wounds are seen before God not as wounds but as worships."[11]

Ross let the fragments of his broken life testify to a worshipping vessel—a vessel daily dedicated on the altar and table for God to make whole, a vessel now in God's hands, a vessel at last *free*. *Free* is the last word of Shakespeare's last play, *The Tempest*, which I believe Ross loved more than any other of Shakespeare's works, a play that begins with a shipwreck and ends with an old magician working a "prayer / which pierces so that it assaults / Mercy itself, and frees all faults."[12]

Like George Ross, earthen vessels we may be. But also like George Ross, we hold so great a treasure.

NOTES

𝔰𝔴𝔢

GRACE

1. David Hockney as quoted in Jon Winokar, *Friendly Advice* (New York: Dutton, 1990), 44.

FOREWORD

1. As quoted in Tim Stafford, "The Hidden Gospel of the 12 Steps," *Christianity Today*, 22 July 1991, 14.

2. Thanks to the ministry of Sam Shoemaker in a small Episcopal Church in New York City, a man known as Bill W. became sober enough to hold a job. His first weekend in Akron, Ohio, where he had landed a temporary consulting job, found him wandering into the hotel bar. Just before he went in, he caught himself and turned his back on the bar. There he saw in front of him a church directory where St. Paul's was listed. He called the church, where a layperson put him in touch with Dr. Bob. This was the beginning of the development of the Twelve Steps of Alcoholics Anonymous.

3. As quoted in George Ross, "Annual Address," 19 January 1986. George Ross Papers, The University of Akron Archives.

4. In *Alchemical Studies*, vol. 13 of *The Collected Works of C. G. Jung* (Princeton, N.J.: Princeton University Press, 1967), 37, Jung states: "The gods have become diseases."

5. Thomas Moore, *Care of the Soul: A Guide for Cultivating Depth and Sacredness in Everyday Life* (New York: HarperCollins, 1992), 168.

6. Philip Holtrop, *The Bolsec Controversy on Predestination, from 1551 to 1555: The Statements of Jerome Bolsec, and the Responses of John Calvin, Theodore Beza, and Other Reformed Theologians* (Lewiston, N.Y.: Edwin Mellen Press, 1993). Also see Timothy H. Wadkins, "A Recipe for Tolerance: A Study of the Reasons Behind John Calvin's Approval of Punishment for Heresy." *Journal of the Evangelical Theological Society* 26 (December 1983): 431–41.

7. See Tom Shone's review, "Suspiciously Wholesome," *TLS: Times Literary Supplement*, 8 October 1993, 26.

8. G. K. Chesterton, *The Everlasting Man* (Garden City, N.Y.: Image Books, 1955), 171.

INTRODUCTION

1. John Mortimer, *Clinging to the Wreckage: A Part of Life* (New Haven: Ticknor and Fields, 1982), 1.

2. Edith Wharton, *The Reef* (New York: Appleton, 1912), 315.

3. Some of the most original writing today on the spirituality of illness is by AIDS patients. See, for example, the work of Mark Matousek, whose concept of "savage grace" is introduced in "Savage Grace," *Common Boundary: Between Spirituality and Psychotherapy*, May/June 1993, 22–31. See also Kat Duff's response to chronic fatigue syndrome in *The Alchemy of Illness* (New York: Pantheon Books, 1993) as excerpted in *Common Boundary*, May/June 1993, 38–45.

4. George Everett Ross, "Let Us Live Before We Die," 10 September 1989.

5. Ross, "The Puzzle," 6 October 1985.

6. Colin Morris, *Wrestling With An Angel* (London: Collins, 1990), 158.

7. Frederick Buechner, *Telling Secrets: A Memoir* (San Francisco: HarperSanFrancisco, 1991), 3.

8. See Matthew 1:1–16.

9. As quoted in Alastair Duke, *Reformation and Revolt in the Low Countries* (London: Hambledon Press, 1990), 45. For this utterance the locksmith had his tongue pierced.

10. Robert Wuthnow, *Christianity in the Twenty-first Century: Reflections on the Challenges Ahead* (New York: Oxford University Press, 1993), 72.

11. R. S. Thomas, "Pardon," *Experimenting with an Amen* (London: Macmillan, 1986), 29.

12. George F. Kennan, *Around the Cragged Hill: A Personal and Political Philosophy* (New York: W. W. Norton, 1993).

13. Henry Fielding, *Tom Jones: An Authoritative Text, Contemporary Reactions, Criticism*, ed. Sheridan Baker (New York: Norton, 1973), 81.

14. Quoted in James Madison Stifler, *The Religion of Benjamin Franklin* (New York: D. Appleton, 1925), 40.

15. Alec R. Vidler, *Christian Belief* (London: SCM Press, 1950), 92.

16. The French philosopher Bertrand Very isolates two phases in this process: first, the injection of meaning into an everyday event or commonplace fact; second, the injection of emotion into the turbocharged fact until it becomes "entangled—as in a musical score—with other motives, its meaning gains more weight and it leads the situation towards a certain outcome." See his article "Milan Kundera or The Hazards of Subjectivity," *Review of Contemporary Fiction* 9 (Summer 1989): 81.

17. W. H. Auden, "The Witness," *The Collected Poetry of W. H. Auden* (New York: Random House, 1945), 185.

18. Aleksandr I. Solzhenitsyn, *The Gulag Archipelago 1918–1956: An Experiment in Literary Investigation, I–II* (New York: Harper & Row, 1973), 168.

19. *Facing Evil*, with Bill Moyers (New York: Public Affairs Television, PBS Video [distributor], 1987).

20. Ross, "Plain Speaking," 28 February 1988.

21. "A Portrait of the Artist as a Creep," in Martin E. Marty's *Context*, 15 September 1989, 4.

22. Ross, "Ennobling Influence of Jesus Christ," 4 October 1987.

23. Mark Twain, *Following the Equator: A Journey Around the World* (New York: Harper, 1897), 2:350.

24. Edward Schillebeeckx insists "we are not redeemed *thanks to* the death of Jesus but *despite it.*" As quoted in William B. Frazier, "The Incredible Christian Capacity for Missing the Christian Point," *America*, 21 November 1992, 399.

25. As quoted by Frazier, "The Incredible Christian Capacity," 398.

26. Ibid., 400.

27. John Bowring, "In the Cross of Christ I Glory," words from *The Hymnal 1982: According to the Use of the Episcopal Church* (New York: Church Hymnal Corp., 1982), 441.

28. Cornel West, "Critique and Mercy in the Cross of Christ," *The Other Side*, July–August 1993, 8, 9.

29. Ernest Hemingway, *A Farewell to Arms* (New York: Charles Scribner's Sons, 1929), 249.

30. *The Vance Havner Quotebook: Sparkling Gems from the Most Quoted Preacher in America*, comp. Dennis J. Hester (Grand Rapids, Mich.: Baker Book House, 1986), 20.

31. Eberhard Bethge, *Dietrich Bonhoeffer: Man of Vision, Man of Courage* (New York: Harper & Row, 1970), 829.

32. Ross, "Ordination Sermon," 16 April 1988.

33. See Edith Sitwell, "Holiday," *The Collected Poems of Edith Sitwell* (New York: Vanguard Press, 1954), 302; Elizabeth Jennings, *Times and Seasons* (Manchester: Carcanet, 1992), 44.

34. C. S. Lewis, "Love's as Warm as Tears," *Poems*, ed. Walter Hooper (New York: Harcourt, Brace and World, 1965), 124. Reprinted by permission.

35. Thomas Parnell, "On Divine Love by Meditation on the Wounds of Christ," *Collected Poems of Thomas Parnell*, ed. Claude Rawson and E. P. Lock, (Newark: University of Delaware Press, 1989), 287–88.

36. Richard Selzer, *Down from Troy: A Doctor Comes of Age* (New York: William Morrow, 1992), 253. See also his quote: "The best part of a wound is that it offers you a chance to heal it" (164).

37. See Leonard I. Sweet, *Health and Medicine in the Evangelical Tradition* (New York: Trinity Press International, 1994).

38. Quoted in Kenneth Leech, *True God: An Exploration in Spiritual Theology* (London: Sheldon 1985), 317.

39. The quote is from the Catholic author Angelus Silesius (a.k.a., Johann

Scheffler), as cited in Herbert Moller, "Affective Mysticism in Western Civilization," *Psychoanalytic Review* 52 (Summer 1965): 123.

40. As quoted in Moller, "Affective Mysticism," 123.

41. This statement is attributed to J. S. Whale but could not be verified.

42. Andrew Breeze, "The Number of Christ's Wounds," *Bulletin of the Board of Celtic Studies* 32 (1985): 84–91. The number 5 has become as symbolic of the wounds of Christ as the number 1 has become the symbol of unity, the number 2 the two natures of Christ, and the number 3 the Trinity. But there is much disagreement over how many specific wounds Jesus bore on his body. Most commonly the number of wounds classified within the "five wounds" was the equivalent of fifteen paternosters said each day for a year— 5475; the second most common number was 6666.

43. See Martin Hengel, *Crucifixion in the Ancient World and the Folly of the Message of the Cross* (Philadelphia: Fortress, 1977).

44. See the critique of N. Haas's work in Joe Zias and James H. Charlesworth, "Crucifixion: Archaeology, Jesus, and the Dead Sea Scrolls," in James H. Charlesworth, *Jesus and the Dead Sea Scrolls* (New York: Doubleday, 1992), 273–89.

45. William D. Edwards, Wesley J. Gabel, Floyd E. Hosmer, "On the Physical Death of Jesus Christ," *Journal of the American Medical Association* 25 (25 March 1986): 1455–63. Howard A. Matzke, "An Anatomist Looks at the Physical Sufferings of Our Lord," *Lutheran Witness* 80 (21 February 1961): 6–7.

46. See Lionello Puppi, *Torment in Art: Pain, Violence, and Martyrdom* (New York: Rizzoli, 1991) and Erich H. Kiehl, *The Passion of Our Lord* (Grand Rapids, Mich.: Baker Book House, 1990).

47. John Wilkinson, "The Physical Cause of the Death of Christ," *Expository Times* 83 (1971–72): 104–7. See Vincent Taylor, *The Gospel According to Mark* (New York: Macmillan, 1957), 596; Pierre Barbet, *A Doctor at Calvary* (New York: Image Books, 1963); John Cameron, "How Our Lord Died," paper presented to the Third International Congress of Catholic Doctors, Lisbon, June 1947; and William Stroud, *The Physical Cause of the Death of Christ, and Its Relation to the Principles of Christianity* (New York: Appleton, 1871).

48. Ernest F. Scott, *The First Age of Christianity* (New York: Macmillan, 1926), 84.

49. As quoted in Nicholas Dawidoff, "One for the Wolves," *Audubon* 94 (July–August 1992): 43.

50. Chad Walsh, *God at Large* (New York: Seabury Press, 1971), 118.

51. Helen Smith Shoemaker, *I Stand by the Door: The Life of Sam Shoemaker* (New York: Harper & Row, 1967), 190.

52. Eugene O'Neill, *The Great God Brown*, in *The Great God Brown, The Fountain, The Moon of the Caribbees, and Other Plays* (New York: Horace Liveright, 1926), 39.

53. Hans Küng, *On Being a Christian* (Garden City, N.Y.: Doubleday, 1976), 436.

54. *A Rumor of Angels,* ed. Gail Perry and Jill Perry (New York: Ballantine Books, 1989), 101.

55. Ross, "The Gospel in Samaria," 18 March 1990.

56. Ross, "Make Straight His Way," 10 December 1989.

57. Ross, "Help From the Hills," 12 June 1988 and Ross, "Ordination Sermon," 16 April 1988.

58. Ross, "Newness of Life," 10 June 1989.

59. Ibid.

60. A. N. Wilson, *C. S. Lewis: A Biography* (New York: Norton, 1990), 107.

61. Ross, "Witness," 14 January 1990.

CHAPTER I: WOUNDED HANDS AND FEET

1. Walter Russell Bowie, "Lord, Christ, When First Thou Cam'st." From *The Book of Hymns.* Copyright © 1964, 1966 by Board of Publication of the Methodist Church, Inc. Words used by permission of Abingdon Press.

2. J. Barrie Shepherd, *Praying the Psalms: Daily Meditations on Cherished Psalms* (Philadelphia: Westminster Press, 1987), 39.

3. George Everett Ross, "Christmas Hope," 24 December 1987.

4. Clovis Chappell, "Facing the Future," in *Sermons from the Psalms* (Nashville: Cokesbury Press, 1931), 27.

5. For more homiletical elaboration of the *though* and *through* scene, see Karen Elizabeth Rennie and Leonard I. Sweet, "The Six Longest Short Verses in the Bible," *Homiletics* 7 (April–June 1995), 23–26.

6. Peter Barnes, *The Spirit of Man and More Barnes' People: Seven Monologues* (London: Methuen Drama, 1990), 28.

7. Judith Z. Abrams, "Was Isaac Disabled?" *Reconstructionist* 66 (Autumn 1990): 20–21.

8. Ross, "A Religion for the Foothills," 26 October 1975.

9. See Charles J. Sykes, *A Nation of Victims: The Decay of the American Character* (New York: St. Martin's Press, 1992).

10. As quoted in Martin Marty's *Context,* 15 January 1994, 4.

11. George Will, "1993: Natures Hysterics and More," *Newsweek,* 27 December 1993, 58.

12. Ross, "Refreshments and Responsibilities," 4 May 1986.

13. James Michener, *Chesapeake* (New York: Random House, 1978).

14. As quoted in "A Credible Witness," *Context,* 15 November 1992, 3.

15. Ross found these words and the story in Bryant M. Kirkland's undated sermon manuscript, "Marks of Maturity," Fifth Avenue Presbyterian Church, New York City.

16. Kenneth Caraway, "Boxed In But Not Out," *Alive Now* 4 (March/April 1974), 15. Reprinted by permission.

17. Ross, "Easter: the Event, the Effect," 30 March 1986.

18. Quoted in Andre Dubus, *Broken Vessels* (Boston: David R. Godine, 1991), 167.

19. Ross, "The Transfiguration," 7 August 1977.
20. Phone interview with Almus M. Thorp, 1 June 1992.
21. Ibid.
22. Roland H. Bainton, *Pilgrim Parson: The Life of James Herbert Bainton 1867–1942* (New York: Nelson, 1958), 1–2.
23. Ross, "The Grace of Gratitude," 12 October 1986.
24. Ross, "The Longest Distance: From Zero to One," 15 October 1985.
25. Ross, "Witness," 14 January 1990.
26. Ross, "The Power of the Spirit," 3 June 1990.
27. Mother Goose, *Oxford Nursery Rhyme Book,* comp. Iona Opie and Peter Opie (London: Oxford University Press, 1955), 23.
28. Ibid., 35.
29. Ross, "Our Questions and God's," 24 November 1985. Ross is quoting from T. S. Eliot, *Four Quartets,* "The Dry Salvages," in *The Complete Poems and Plays, 1909–1950* (New York: Harcourt, Brace, 1952), 133. See also these lines from Elliot's "East Coker,"

> The wounded surgeon plies the steel
> That questions the distempered part;
> Beneath the bleeding hands we feel
> The sharp compassion of the healer's art
> Resolving the enigma of the fever chart.
>
> Our only health is the disease
> If we obey the dying nurse
> Whose constant care is not to please
> But to remind of our, and Adam's curse,
> And that, to be restored, our sickness must grow worse.

Eliot, *Four Quartets,* 127. Thanks to Elton Glaser for directing me to this poem.
30. Ross, "I Will Die in My Nest," 5 October 1975.
31. Ibid.
32. Ross, "Living with the Unsolved," 8 October 1989.
33. Ibid.
34. Ibid.
35. Ibid.
36. John Masefield, *The Widow in the Bye Street,* in *The Everlasting Mercy and the Widow in the Bye Street* (New York: Macmillan, 1916), 221.

CHAPTER 1: SERMONS

1. Last line of the chorus of Fanny J. Crosby, "My Saviour First of All," with words from *Down Memory's Lane: Old–Time Evangelistic Choruses,* comp. E. B. Harris (Millersburg, Penn.: Locker, n.d.), 64.
2. Helen Keller, *The Story of My Life* (New York: Grosset & Dunlap, 1904), 30–31.

3. Ibid., 31.

4. Attributed to Benjamin Franklin, *Poor Richard's Almanack: Being the Choicest Morsels of Wisdom, Written During the Years of the Almanack's Publication* (Mount Vernon, N.Y: Peter Pauper Press, n.d.), 51, where it reads: "For want of a Nail the Shoe is lost; for want of a Shoe the Horse is lost; for want of a Horse the Rider is lost."

5. William Shakespeare, *The Tragedy of Hamlet, Prince of Denmark*, in *The Riverside Shakespeare*, ed. G. Blakemore Evans (Boston: Houghton Mifflin, 1974), 2:1159.

6. William Shakespeare, *The Third Part of King Henry the Sixth*, in *The Riverside Shakespeare*, 1:704.

7. Martin Luther, "A Mighty Fortress Is Our God," stanza 2, *The Hymnal 1982 According to the Use of the Episcopal Church* (New York: Church Hymnal Corp., 1985), 687.

8. Mother Goose, *Oxford Nursery Rhyme Book*, comp. Iona Opie and Peter Opie (London: Oxford University Press, 1955), 23.

9. Ibid., 35.

10. William Shakespeare, *The Tragedy of Julius Caesar*, in *The Riverside Shakespeare*, 2:1127.

11. G. K. Chesterton, *Charles Dickens: The Last of the Great Men* (New York: Press of the Reader's Club, 1942).

12. J. R. R. Tolkien, *The Lord of the Rings* (New York: Houghton, 1954–1955).

13. The editor has been unable to identify this title.

14. Albert Schweitzer, *The Quest for the Historical Jesus: A Critical Study of Its Progress from Reimarus to Wrede* (London: A. & C. Black, 1922), 401.

CHAPTER 2: WOUNDED SIDE

1. Herman Melville, *Moby-Dick, or The White Whale* (New York: Dodd, Mead, 1942), 271–72, 270.

2. Aristophanes says that Zeus "split our original whole selves in two, like hard-boiled eggs with a wire." Then "the halves go looking for each other."

3. Catherine Keller, "Scoop Up the Water and the Moon Is in Your Hands: On Feminist Theology and Dynamic Self-Emptying," in *The Emptying God*, ed. John B. Cobb, Jr. and Christopher Ives (Maryknoll, N.Y.: Orbis Books, 1990), 110.

4. *Ruth*, trans. L. Rabinowitz, vol. 8 of *Midrash Rabbah*, ed. H. Freedman and M. Simon (London: Soncino, 1939), 87.

5. This is the argument of Kenneth Grayston, *Dying, We Live: A New Enquiry into the Death of Christ in the New Testament* (New York: Oxford University Press, 1990).

6. Stanza 4 of Matthew Bridges and Godfrey Thring's hymn, "Crown Him with Many Crowns," with words from *The United Methodist Hymnal* (Nashville: United Methodist Publishing House, 1989), 327.

7. A. F. Sava, "The Wound in the Side of Christ," *Catholic Biblical Quarterly* 19 (1957): 343–46.

8. See Donald M. Joy, "On Splitting the Adam!" chapter 2 of his *Bonding: Relationships in the Image of God* (Waco, Tex.: Word Books, 1985), 14–32.

9. Raymond d'Aguilers, *Historia Francorum qui Ceperunt Iherusalem,* trans. John Hugh Hill and Laurita L. Hill (Philadelphia: American Philosophical Society, 1968), 127–28.

10. Milenko Matanovic, *Meandering Rivers and Square Tomatoes* (Issaquah, Wash.: Morningtown, 1988), 32.

11. Jack and Carole Mayhall, *Marriage Takes More Than Love* (Colorado Springs: Navigator Press, 1978), 21.

12. Luciano De Crescenzo, *Thus Spake Bellavista: Naples, Love, and Liberty* (New York: Grove Press, 1988), 149.

13. For Miguel de Unamuno's belief that "all living beings are united by suffering," see *The Tragic Sense of Life in Men and Nations* (Princeton, N.J.: Princeton University Press, 1972), 224.

In *The Agony of Christianity* (New York: Payson & Clarke, 1928), he writes that "what binds men most to each other is their discords. And what unites a man most with himself, what makes the intimate unity of our lives, is our inner discords, the innate contradictions of our discords" (23). This theme of what unites and what divides was a persistent one in de Unamuno's writings. See, for example, "Solitude unites us . . . just as much as society separates us." "Solitude," *Essays and Soliloquies* (New York: Alfred A. Knopf, 1925), 166.

14. Abraham Cowley, "The Wish," in *The Complete Works in Verse and Prose of Abraham Cowley,* ed. Alexander B. Grosart (Edinburgh: Edinburgh University Press, 1881; reprint New York: AMS Press, 1967), 1:110.

15. Letter to Gay Jennings, 15 January 1990.

16. George Everett Ross, "I Thank God on Every Remembrance of You," 16 September 1990.

17. As quoted in Jonathan Green, *The Cynic's Lexicon* (New York: St. Martin's Press, 1984), 203.

18. Ross, "Witness to the Light," 13 December 1987.

19. D. W. Winnicott, *Human Nature* (New York: Schocken Books, 1988), 80. "The greatest suffering in the human world is the suffering of normal or healthy or mature persons."

20. Antonio Porchia, *Voices: Aphorisms,* sel. and trans. W. S. Merwin (New York: Alfred A. Knopf, 1988), 31.

21. Ibid., 27.

22. Frederick Buechner, *The Sacred Journey* (San Francisco: Harper & Row, 1982), 46.

23. Ross, "The Son of Encouragement," 11 June 1989.

24. Ross, "White–knuckled Love," 18 October 1987.

25. Interview with Bill Moyers, as quoted in Cornish R. Rogers, "The Goggles of Easter," in *Preaching Through the Apocalypse,* ed. Cornish R. Rogers and Joseph R. Jeter, Jr. (St. Louis: Chalice Press, 1992), 64.

26. James A. Michener, *The World Is My Home, A Memoir* (New York: Random House, 1992), 485–86.

27. Truman Capote, *Music for Chameleons* (New York: Random House, 1980), 261–62. Ross found this quote in Sam A. Portaro, "Lillian Hellman and Truman Capote: An Appreciation," *Christian Century*, 15 May 1985, 497.

CHAPTER 2: SERMONS

1. K. Moore, "Dormant No More: Duncan Macdonald Is Erupting," *Sports Illustrated*, 14 February 1977, 34–37.

2. C. S. Lewis, *The Great Divorce* (New York: Macmillan, 1963), 83.

3. John Greenleaf Whittier, "Forgiveness," in *Treasury of Christian Poetry*, comp. Lorraine Eitel (Old Tappan, N.J.: Fleming H. Revell, 1982), 174.

4. Carl Rogers, *Freedom to Learn* (Columbus, Ohio: Charles E. Merrill, 1969), 236.

5. Mary Ann Bird, *The Whisper Test*. The editor can find no record of this book.

6. M. Scott Peck, *The Road Less Traveled: A New Psychology of Love, Traditional Values and Spiritual Growth* (New York: Simon and Schuster, 1978), 15.

7. The actual quote is: "It is only with the heart that one can see rightly; what is essential is invisible to the eye." Antoine de Saint-Exupéry, *The Little Prince* (New York: Harcourt, Brace & World, 1943), 70.

8. Belden Lane, "Fierce Landscapes and the Indifference of God," *Christian Century*, 11 October 1989, 907–10.

9. As related by Lane, "Fierce Landscapes," 908.

10. *Sayings of the Jewish Fathers, comprising Pirqe Aboth in Hebrew and English*, ed. for the Syndics of the Cambridge University Press by Charles Taylor (Cambridge: University Press, 1897), 23.

CHAPTER 3: WOUNDED HEAD

1. George Everett Ross, "The Shepherd in the Shadow," 19 June 1988. Ross is quoting from Gerard Manley Hopkins's sonnet, "No worst, there is none. Pitched past pitch of grief," *The Poems of Gerard Manley Hopkins*, 4th ed., ed. W. H. Gardner and N. H. Mackenzie (New York: Oxford University Press, 1967), 100.

2. Ross, "His Eye Is on the Sparrow," 21 June 1987.

3. David James Randolph, *The Power that Heals: Love, Healing and The Trinity* (Nashville: Abingdon, 1994), 125.

4. Ernest Hemingway, *Death in the Afternoon* (New York: Charles Scribner's Sons, 1932).

5. Ross, "The Solemn Reserve of the Healing Christ," 4 September 1988.

6. Arthur Miller, *After the Fall* (New York: Viking Press, 1964), 22.

7. Ross, "The Shepherd in the Shadow."

8. Thomas Aquinas, *Summa* I, Q.43, Art. 5.

9. St. Augustine, *De Trin.* ix,10.

10. Bill McKibben, *The Age of Missing Information* (New York: Random House, 1992).

11. Abraham Heschel, *Between God and Man* (New York: Harper, 1959), 41.

12. Benjamin Franklin's notes listing questions to be asked includes this one that defines in good Enlightenment fashion wisdom as the self's knowledge of itself: "Q. What is Wisdom? A. The knowledge of what will be best for us on all Occasions and the best Ways of attaining it." See *The Papers of Benjamin Franklin,* ed. Leonard W. Larabee et al. (New Haven: Yale University Press, 1959), 1:262–63.

13. Quoted in David Marr, *Patrick White: A Life* (New York: Knopf, 1991), 481.

14. Camille Paglia, *Sex, Art, and American Culture: Essays* (New York: Vintage Books, 1992), 34.

15. John Cheever, as quoted in Rust Hills, "How Writers Live Today," *Esquire,* August 1984, 37.

16. Robert Frost, "The Figure a Poem Makes," in *Complete Poems of Robert Frost* (New York: Henry Holt, 1949), vi.

17. See William Hasker, *God, Time and Knowledge* (Ithaca, N.Y.: Cornell University Press, 1989).

18. W. H. Auden, "Psychology and Art Today," in *Arts To-day,* ed. Geoffrey Grigson (London: John Lane, 1935), 21; repr. in *The English Auden: Poems, Essays, and Dramatic Writings, 1927–1939,* ed. Edward Mendelson (New York: Random House, 1977), 341–42.

19. Richard Rogers, as quoted in *The Columbia Dictionary of Quotations,* ed. Robert Andrews (New York: Columbia University Press, 1993), 20.

20. Ross, "Come and See," 18 January 1987.

21. René Descartes, "Meditations on the First Philosophy in which the Existence of God and the Distinction Between Mind and Body are Demonstrated," in *The Philosophical Works of Descartes,* trans. Elizabeth S. Haldane and G. R. T. Ross (Cambridge: University Press, 1967), 1:168.

22. Robert Lowell used these terms to distinguish between two types of poets. For example, Allen Ginsberg is raw, Richard Wilbur is cooked.

23. Catherine Cameron, "God, Who Stretched the Spangled Heavens," *The Hymnal According to the Use of the Episcopal Church* (New York: The Church Hymnal Corp., 1982), 580. The words were written by Catherine Cameron in 1967, but the tune is from an early nineteenth-century shaped–notes songster. Copyright © 1967. Hope Publishing Co., IL 60188. All rights reserved. Used by permission.

24. As told in *Hungry Mind Review,* Summer 1992, C–12.

25. From a quote attributed to chemist R. Garth Kidd, as quoted in Walter Brueggemann, *Israel's Praise: Doxology Against Idolatry and Ideology* (Philadelphia: Fortress Press, 1988), 12.

26. M. Enid Watson, as quoted in *Touch Holiness: Resources for Worship,* ed. Ruth D. Duck and Maren C. Tirabassi (New York: Pilgrim Press, 1990), 176.

27. David Jones, "Art and Sacrament," *Epoch and Artist* (London: Faber, 1959), 156.

28. Camille Paglia, *Sexual Personae: Art and Decadence from Nefertiti to Emily Dickinson* (New Haven: Yale University Press, 1990), 105.

29. Cynthia Serjak, *Music and the Cosmic Dance* (Washington, D.C.: The Pastoral Press, 1987), 15.

30. This story is told in *The Body on the Cross,* by Gérard Régnier et al. (Montreal: Montreal Museum of Fine Arts, 1992), 59.

31. Creation–as–combination is not the whole story, however, as Margaret A. Boden makes clear in her book *The Creative Mind: Myths and Mechanisms* (New York: Basic Books, 1990), 23. This is taken from Arthur Koestler, *The Act of Creation* (New York: Macmillan, 1964), 123, where he writes: "The basic, bisociative pattern of the creative synthesis: The sudden interlocking of two previously unrelated skills, or matrices of thought."

32. Philip Toynbee, *End of the Journey: An Autobiographical Journal, 1979–81* (London: Bloomsbury, 1988), 119, 129.

33. John Calvin, *Institutes of the Christian Religion,* I.xi.12.

34. Richard Dinwiddie, "Songs to a Higher Power," *Christianity Today,* 25 November 1991, 64.

CHAPTER 3: SERMONS

1. The editor has been unable to identify this title.

2. Dorothy Parker, "The Veteran," in *Collected Poems: Not So Deep as a Well* (New York: Viking Press, 1937), 52.

3. Phillips Brooks, *The Duty of the Christian Business Man* (New York: H. M. Caldwell, n.d.), 75.

4. Peter de Vries, *Witch's Milk* in *The Cat's Pajamas and Witch's Milk* (Boston: Little, Brown, 1968), 291.

5. G. K. Chesterton, *Orthodoxy* (Garden City, N.Y.: Image Books, 1959), 94.

6. T. S. Eliot, "Little Gidding," *Four Quartets,* in Eliot, *The Complete Poems and Plays, 1909–1950* (New York: Harcourt, Brace, 1952), 145.

7. William Wordsworth, "Lines Composed a Few Miles Above Tintern Abbey," *The Complete Works of William Wordsworth* (London: Macmillan, 1921), 94.

8. The editor has been unable to verify this quote. Although Ross attributes it to Dietrich Bonhoeffer, two Bonhoeffer scholars, Dr. F. Burton Nelson and Dr. Geffrey B. Kelly, concur that the attribution is erroneous. The language is not that of Bonhoeffer nor was he ever in the Lehrter Street Prison.

9. John V. Taylor, *The Go–between God: The Holy Spirit and the Christian Mission* (Philadelphia: Fortress Press, 1973), 243.

10. Ibid.

11. John Milton, *The Areopagitica,* in *The Harvard Classics,* ed. Charles W. Eliot (New York: P. F. Collier, 1909) 3:239.

12. Richard Hooker, *The Works of . . . Richard Hooker, with an Account of His Life and Death,* by Isaac Walton (Oxford: University Press, 1841), 2:233.

13. T. S. Eliot, "What the Thunder Said," *The Complete Poems and Plays,* 48.

14. The editor has been unable to find the source of this quote by G. K. Chesterton.

15. *Rubáiyát of Omar Khayyam,* trans. Edward Fitzgerald (Garden City, N.Y.: Doubleday, 1952), 77.

16. William Walsham How, "For All the Saints," stanza 5, *The Hymnal 1982 According to the Use of The Episcopal Church* (New York: Church Hymnal Corp., 1985), 287.

CHAPTER 4: WOUNDED BACK

1. F. Scott Fitzgerald, *Tender is the Night* (New York: Macmillan, 1962), 168.

2. Mary McGarry Morris, *Vanished* (New York: Viking, 1988), 86.

3. Feodor Dostoyevsky, *The Brothers Karamazov,* trans. David McDuff (London: Penguin, 1993), 369–71.

4. George Everett Ross, "Wondrous Grace, Awful Judgment," 16 October 1988.

5. I am heavily dependent here on Erich H. Kiehl, *The Passion of Our Lord* (Grand Rapids, Mich.: Baker Book House, 1990), 129.

6. As quoted in Will Campbell, *Brother to a Dragon Fly* (New York: Seabury Press, 1977), 179.

7. Ross, "Beauty and Duty," 14 February 1988.

8. Thornton Wilder, *The Skin of Our Teeth,* in *Three Plays by Thorton Wilder* (New York: Harper & Row, 1957), 200–201.

9. Ross, "Life Is Too Short to be Little," Pentecost, 1989.

10. Ibid.

11. Ross, "The Only Test of True Religion," 14 December 1986.

12. Thomas Paine, *Common Sense and Other Political Writings* (Indianapolis: Bobbs–Merrill, 1953), 51.

13. Ross, "Ennobling Influence of Jesus Christ," 4 October 1987.

14. Ross, "Great Expectations," 30 November 1986.

15. Undated newspaper clipping, George Ross Papers, The University of Akron Archives, Box F.

16. Frank Church to St. Paul's Church, 21 November 1983, George Ross Papers, The University of Akron Archives, Box 4, File 2.

17. Ross, "The Solemn and Awful Courage," 19 November 1989.

18. *Cleveland Plain Dealer,* April 8, 1976.

19. See Beebe Folder, Box #1, George Ross Papers, The University of Akron Archives.

20. Pauline Webb, *She Flies Beyond* (Geneva, Switz.: WCC Publications, 1993), xi.

21. *Congressional Record—Senate*, 3 June 1971, 8117.

22. Ross, "Through the Season of the Shadow," 8 June 1986.

23. Quoted in John Ellis, *On the Front Lines: The Experience of War Through the Eyes of the Allied Soldiers in World War II* (New York: John Wiley, 1990), 332.

24. Ross, "The Good Shepherd," 17 September 1989.

25. Peter Dunwiddie, "The Study of Useless Things," *Sanctuary: The Journal of the Massachusetts Audubon Society*, January 1990, 26.

26. Arthur Binstead, *Pitcher's Proverbs* (London: Everett, 1909).

27. See William Bradford, *Bradford's History of the Plymouth Plantation, 1606–1646*, ed. William T. Davis (New York: Charles Scribner's Sons, 1908), 96.

28. Ross, "Rogation Sunday, 1987," 24 May 1987.

29. "The land is mine; with me you are but aliens and tenants. Throughout the land that you hold, you shall provide for the redemption of the land" (Leviticus 25:23–24 NRSV).

30. Joseph Mary Plunkett, "I See His Blood Upon the Rose," in *Masterpieces of Religious Verse*, ed. James Dalton Morrison (New York: Harper, 1948), 201. Reprinted by permission.

31. Barry Lopez, *Arctic Dreams: Imagination and Desire in a Northern Landscape* (New York: Charles Scribner's Sons, 1986), 112.

32. Cambium is a delicate tissue that originates all secondary growth in plants by producing new inner bark on the outside and new wood on the inside of stems, roots, etc.

33. Origen, *Leviticum Homiliae*.

34. As quoted by David Martin, *Divinity in a Grain of Bread* (Cambridge: Lutterworth Press, 1989), 10–11.

35. Henry Vaughan, "Rules *and* Lessons," *The Complete Poetry of Henry Vaughan*, ed. French Fogle (New York: Norton, 1969), 192.

36. Vaughan, "The Morning–Watch," *Complete Poetry*, 176–77.

37. Undated clipping of a newspaper article by Joan Rice entitled "A Reporter Goes to Church," George Ross Papers, The University of Akron Archives.

38. Ibid.

39. Ibid.

CHAPTER 4: SERMONS

1. Eliza Scudder, "Thou Life Within My Life," *Masterpieces of Religious Verse*," ed. James Dalton Morrison (New York: Harper, 1948), 32.

2. The editor has been unable to identify this verse.

3. David Elkind, *The Hurried Child: Growing Up Too Fast Too Soon* (Reading, Mass.: Addison–Wesley Publishing Co., 1981).

4. William Wordsworth, "A Poet's Epitaph," in his *Lyrical Ballads and*

Other Poems, 1797–1800, ed. James Butler and Karen Green (Ithaca, N.Y.: Cornell University Press, 1992), 237.

5. Harry Emerson Fosdick, "Six Ways in Which a Modern Man May Pray," in his *Successful Christian Living: Sermons on Christianity Today* (Garden City, N.Y.: Garden City Books, 1937), 14.

6. Dietrich Bonhoeffer, *Temptation* (New York: Macmillan, 1955), 14.

7. R. S. Thomas, "A Peasant," *Song at the Year's Turning* (London: Rupert Hart–Davis, 1963), 21.

8. Walker Percy, *The Second Coming* (New York: Farrar, Straus, Giroux, 1980), 124, 19.

9. Vincent Van Gogh, *Dear Theo: The Autobiography of Vincent Van Gogh,* ed. Irving Stone (Garden City, N.Y.: Doubleday, 1937), 454.

CHAPTER 5: WOUNDED HEART

1. I owe this observation to Donald E. Demaray, *Laughter, Joy and Healing* (Grand Rapids, Mich.: Baker Book House, 1986), 37.

2. Nikos Kazantzakis, *Zorba the Greek* (New York: Simon and Schuster, 1953), 278.

3. Maxwell Maltz, *Psycho–Cybernetics* (New York: Essandess Special Edition, 1960), 7–8.

4. Andre Dubus, *Broken Vessels* (Boston: David R. Godine, 1991), 194: "My physical mobility and my little girls have been taken from me; but I remain. So my crippling is a daily and living sculpture of certain truths: we receive and we lose, and we must try to achieve gratitude; and with that gratitude to embrace with whole hearts whatever of life that remains after the losses."

5. Ibid., xviii–xix.

6. H. Richard Niebuhr, *Faith on Earth: An Inquiry into the Structure of Human Faith,* ed. Richard R. Niebuhr (New Haven: Yale University Press, 1989), 63–82.

7. Ross did not elevate to sainthood his "spiritual guides" like C. S. Lewis, Thomas Merton, and others. Indeed, Ross would have agreed with Tolkein that C. S. Lewis's prejudices and preconceptions were "impenetrable even by information."

8. C. S. Lewis, *Reflections on the Psalms* (New York: Harcourt, Brace, 1958), 90–98, 94.

9. Walter Brueggemann, *Israel's Praise: Doxology Against Idolatry and Ideology* (Philadelphia: Fortress Press, 1988), 27.

10. Abraham Heschel, *Man's Quest for God: Studies in Prayer and Symbolism* (New York: Charles Scribner's Sons, 1954), 82.

11. Abraham Heschel, "On Prayer," *Conservative Judaism* 25 (Fall 1970): 7.

12. Marianne Moore, *Complete Poems* (New York: Macmillan, 1967), 174.

13. Roger Scruton, *The Philosopher on Dover Beach* (New York: St. Martin's Press, 1991). Scruton makes this devastating observation: "A work [of

art] can now perform its economic function without being loved or admired; nobody need be enchanted by it or moved by its deeper meaning. The money pours through it unrestricted, like sewerage through a drain, and the civilizing function of art . . . has been finally set aside" (161).

14. Sigmund Freud, *Civilization and Its Discontent*, vol. 21 of *The Standard Edition of the Complete Psychological Works of Sigmund Freud* (London: Hogarth Press, 1961).

15. *Horse Feathers* (Hollywood: Paramount Publix Corp., 1932). MCA Home Video in University City, California, made a reprint in 1990.

16. This quote from "The Death of the Author" originally appeared in *Manteia* in 1968. The quote also is found in Roland Barthes, *The Rustle of Language*, trans. Richard Howard (New York: Hill and Wang, 1986), 49.

17. G. K. Chesterton, *Charles Dickens: The Last of the Great Men* (New York: Press of the Reader's Club, 1942), 173.

18. See Norman Hampson's review of Lionel Gossman, *Between History and Literature* (Cambridge, Mass.: Harvard University Press, 1990), *TLS: Times Literary Supplement*, 4 January 1991, 5.

19. Mary Midgley, *Wisdom, Information, and Wonder: What Is Knowledge For?* (New York: Routledge, 1989), 252, 253.

20. Malcom Cowley, as quoted in Martin E. Marty's, *Context*, 1 March 1991, 6.

21. See Anthony Grafton, *Defenders of the Text: The Tradition of Scholarship in an Age of Science, 1450–1800* (Cambridge, Mass.: Harvard University Press, 1991).

22. See, for example, "If eternal vigilance is the price of freedom then unswerving skepticism is the price of scientific truth." Michael Disney, Welch observational astronomer and space shuttle scientist, in *The Hidden Universe* (New York: Macmillan, 1984), 223.

23. George Everett Ross, "The Good Man: Joseph," 3 January 1988.

24. Stephen D. Moore, *Mark and Luke in Poststructuralist Perspectives* (New Haven: Yale University Press, 1992), 129, 71.

25. Marianne Moore, *Predilections* (New York: Viking, 1955), 3.

26. Bourne to Prudence Winterrowd, 11 March 1914, in *The Letters of Randolph Bourne: A Comprehensive Edition*, ed. Eric J. Sandeed (Troy, N.Y.: Whitson Publishing Company, 1981), 228.

27. Samuel Johnson, *The Idler*, in *Essays from the Rambler, Adventurer, and Idler*, ed. W. J. Bate (New Haven: Yale University Press, 1968), 328.

28. Ysenda Maxtone Graham, *The Church Hesitant: A Portrait of the Church of England Today* (London: Hodder and Stoughton, 1993).

29. Ross, "A Simple Yes and No Will Do," 15 February 1987.

30. Eberhard Jüngel explains how the church had to say "No!" to Nazism, but only because it had already said "Yes!" to Christ. See Jüngel, *Christ, Justice and Peace: Toward a Theology of the State* (Edinburgh: T. & T. Clark, 1992).

31. The editor has been unable to locate the source of this quotation by George Bernard Shaw.

32. Wayne C. Booth, "'What's Your Evidence?' 'Why Do You Ask?' 'Or: The Teacher as Learner,'" *The University of Chicago Record*, 26 (21 November 1991): 9.

33. As quoted in Gabriel Josipovici, *The Book of God: A Response to the Bible* (New Haven: Yale University Press, 1988), 309.

34. Jonathan Edwards, "Extracts from His Private Writings" (Thursday, November 26, 1723), in *The Works of President Edwards* (London: 1817; reprint, New York: Burt Franklin, 1968), 1:24.

35. "A Pocketful of Miracles," *Newsweek*, 23 September 1991, 58–59.

36. Ambrose Bierce speaks of "enlightened souls who prefer dry wines to sweet, sense to sentiment, wit to humor." See *The Devil's Dictionary*, vol. 7 of *The Collected Works of Ambrose Bierce* (New York: Gordian Press, 1966), 10.

37. Robert Hendrickson, *World Literary Anecdotes* (New York: Facts on File, 1990), 204.

38. Pierre Teilhard de Chardin, "Fossil Man," in his *The Appearance of Man* (New York: Harper and Row, 1956), 32.

39. A special thanks to Barry P. Boulware for this story. (He was told the story by H. Eugene Cragg.)

40. Rosabeth Moss Kanter, *The Change Masters* (New York: Simon and Schuster, 1993), 110.

41. One should criticize the work, never the worker, Hendrie Weisinger insists. Further, good criticism involves empathy (putting oneself in the criticized's place) and listening (criticism is a dialogue more than a monologue). It always is done privately, never in public, and it shows management's belief that the person can do better. The one making the criticism should plan for follow–up ways to help the criticized person do better. Little wonder Weisinger estimates that only two in ten have critiquing abilities. See Weisinger, *The Critical Edge: How to Criticize Up and Down Your Organization, and Make It Pay Off* (Boston: Little, Brown, 1989).

42. Sally Dyck in an unpublished report on the Cleveland District of the United Methodist Church.

43. See Galen Strawson's review of Nicholson Baker, *U and I: A True Story* (London: Grants in Association with Penguin, 1991) in *TLS*, 19 April 1991, 21. While Baker criticizes Updike for fictional or "critical cruelty," Auden is quoted as saying: "You should not speak ill of any writer, living or dead, to anyone but your closest friends, and absolutely not in print. Simply don't talk about, don't give space to, things you don't like."

44. Ross is quoting an unnamed source in his sermon "Tough Love," 11 December 1988.

45. As quoted in Donald C. Posterski and Irwin Barker, *Where's a Good Church?* (Winfield, B.C.: Wook Lake Books, 1993), 25.

46. Ross, "Ephaphta," 8 September 1985.

47. Ross, "The Breath of Life," 7 June 1987.

48. Quoted in Jonathan Green, *The Cynic's Lexicon* (New York: St. Martin's Press, 1984), 189.

49. Quoted in Pierre Chuvin, *A Chronicle of the Last Pagans* (Cambridge, Mass.: Harvard University Press, 1990), 16.

50. John Haughey, *The Conspiracy of God* (Garden City, N.Y.: Doubleday, 1973), 36, 21.

51. See Wendy Steiner's review of the "Monumental Histories" issue of *Representations*, *TLS*, 15 November 1991, 29.

52. Quoted in *TLS*, 18 May 91, 14.

53. Ross, "Faith in Troubled Times," 13 October 1974.

54. George Ross in 3" by 5" card entitled "Status Quo."

55. Hugh Kenner, "Why a Fire Is Hot," in "Personal Glimpses of Bucky Fuller," by Robert D. Kahn, Studs Terkel, Martin Meyerson, Edward P. Morgan, Claiborne Pell, Henry J. Heimlich, Peter H. Wagschal, Hugh Kenner, Medard Gabel, Sam Maitin, Samuel Rosenberg, O.B. Hardison, Jr., J. Baldwin, and James D. Sanders, *The Futurist*, October 1983, 24–25.

56. Ross, "Christmas: Hope," 24 December 1987.

57. Ross, "The Puzzle," 6 October 1985.

58. Ibid.

59. Ross, "Palm Sunday, 1990," 8 April 1990.

CHAPTER 5: SERMONS

1. John Brownlie, tr., "The King Shall Come When Morning Dawns," words from *The Hymnal 1982 According to the Use of The Episcopal Church* (New York: Church Hymnal Corp., 1985), 73.

2. From the twelfth–century Latin hymn "Jesus the Very Thought of Thee," trans. Edward Caswall, with words from *The Hymnal 1982*.

3. John Donne, *Devotions Upon Emergent Occasions*, ed. Anthony Paspa (New York: Oxford University Press, 1987), 86–87. "No Man is an *Island*, intire of it selfe; every man is a piece of the *Continent*, a part of the maine .... Any mans *death* diminishes *me*, because I am involved in *Mankinde*; and therefore never send to know for whom the *bell* tolls; it tolls for *thee*."

4. Loren Eiseley, *The Night Country* (New York: Charles Scribner's Sons, 1971), 42–43.

5. John Bowring, "Watchman, Tell Us of the Night," with words from *The Hymnal 1982*, 640.

6. Edwin Markham, "Keep Heart, O Comrade." The editor has been unable to find this poem in a published collection.

7. Isaac Watts, "O God, Our Help in Ages Past," stanzas 5 and 6, with words from *The Hymnal 1982*, 680.

8. Kenneth E. Kirk, *The Vision of God: The Christian Doctrine of the Summum Bonum* (New York: Longmans, Green, 1934), 90.

9. The editor has been unable to locate this passage in Karl Barth's writings.

10. Mark Twain, *The Diaries of Adam and Eve* (Lawrence, Kan.: Coronado Press, 1971), 28, 31, 91.

11. The editor has been unable to find a biography of Bonnee Hoy.

12. Robert Frost, "The Tuft of Flowers," *Complete Poems of Robert Frost* (New York: Henry Holt, 1949), 31–32.

CONCLUSION

1. Annie Johnson Flint,"He Giveth More Grace," words from *The Singing Church* (Carol Stream, Ill.: Hope Publishing Co., 1985), 291.

2. Thornton Wilder, *The Angel that Troubled the Waters and Other Plays* (New York: Coward–McCann, 1928), 147–49.

3. Thomas Maeder, "Wounded Healers," *Atlantic Monthly*, January 1989, 37–47. For a positive rationale for the phenomenon, see Henri Nouwen, *The Wounded Healer: Ministry in Contemporary Society* (Garden City, N.Y.: Doubleday, 1972).

4. This is a paraphrased summary from a variety of Martin Luther's writings, including: "For the condition of this life is not that of having but of seeking God" (*Lectures on Romans*, vol. 25 of *Luther's Works*, ed. Hilton C. Oswald [Saint Louis: Concordia Publishing House, 1972], 225); "Our life is one of beginning and growth, not one of consummation" (Preface, Psalms 1 and 2, from *Works on the First Twenty–two Psalms, 1519–1521*, vol. 14 or *Luther's Works*, 285); "The virtue of Christians grows when it is reproached and when it suffers" (*Lectures on Romans*, 178); and "All righteous works which are done in grace are only preparatory for the growth of righteousness which follows" (*Lectures on Romans*, 246).

5. David Martin, *The Breaking of the Image: A Sociology of Christian Theory and Practice* (New York: St. Martin's Press, 1979), 76.

6. Joseph Goetz, *Mirrors of God* (Cincinnati: St. Anthony Messenger Press, 1983), 87–88.

7 . Thanks to James A. Harnish of Tampa, Florida, for pointing me to this illustration.

8. The editor has been unable to locate this quote in Alan Paton's writings.

9. Angelus Silesius, *Cherubinischer Wandersmann*, 2:103–104, as quoted in *The Collected Works of C. G. Jung* (New York: Pantheon Books, 1963), 14:319.

10. George Everett Ross, "Light Through Broken Glass," 30 August 1987.

11. "Thouz he be heled, his wonndes er sene before god nowht as wonndes bot as wyrschippes," *The Book of Showings to the Anchoress Julian of Norwich*, ed. Edmund College and James Walsh (Toronto: Pontifical Institute of Mediaevel Studies, 1978), 1:256.

12. William Shakespeare, *The Tempest*, Epilogue. *Shakespeare: The Complete Works*, ed. G. B. Harrison (New York: Harcourt, Brace, and World, Inc., 1952), 1501.

ABOUT THE AUTHOR

Leonard I. Sweet is Dean of the Theological School at Drew University in Madison, NJ, and President of SpiritVenture Ministries, a nonprofit orginization. A Master of Divinity and a Ph.D. in American history, he is both minister and scholar, combining these pursuits as editor of *Homiletics*, writer of *Soul Cafe*, and associate editor of the *Journal of the American Academy of Religion.* Author of more than 120 articles, Dr. Sweet has also published nine books, from *Black Images of America* in 1976 to the recent best-seller, *FaithQuakes.*

ABOUT THE BOOK

Strong in the Broken Places was designed and typeset on a Macintosh in Quark XPress in 10.5/14 Trump Mediaeval by Kachergis Book Design of Pittsboro, North Carolina.

Strong in the Broken Places was printed on sixty-pound Glatfelter Supple Opaque Recycled and bound by Thomson-Shore, Inc., Dexter, Michigan.